Earth Bible Commentary

Series Editor
Norman C. Habel

COLOSSIANS

An Eco-Stoic Reading

Vicky Balabanski

LONDON • NEW YORK • OXFORD • NEW DELHI • SYDNEY

T&T CLARK
Bloomsbury Publishing Plc
50 Bedford Square, London, WC1B 3DP, UK
1385 Broadway, New York, NY 10018, USA
29 Earlsfort Terrace, DUblin 2, Ireland

BLOOMSBURY, T&T CLARK and the T&T Clark logo are trademarks of Bloomsbury
Publishing Plc

First published in Great Britain 2020
This paperback edition published in 2021

Cover design: Eleanor Rose
Cover image © Vince Cavataio/Getty Images

A catalogue record for this book is available from the British Library.

A catalog record for this book is available from the Library of Congress.

ISBN: HB: 978-0-5676-7439-5
PB: 978-0-5677-0214-2
ePDF: 978-0-5676-7440-1
eBook: 978-0-5676-9301-3

Typeset by Deanta Global Publishing Services, Chennai, India

To find out more about our authors and books visit www.bloomsbury.com
and sign up for our newsletters.

To Peter
Partner in this journey of life

CONTENTS

ILLUSTRATIONS

Figures

Tables

PREFACE

A biblical scholar walks into a room filled with experts in the field of ancient philosophy, particularly that of the Hellenistic and Roman periods, and challenges the room with the following words:

'Stoic philosophy was the most influential philosophy in the first century of the common era in Asia Minor!'

A few heads turn to see who is bothering their conversations with a truism that is hardly controversial, but no one stands up to disagree. Someone calls out, 'Don't forget the Epicureans!' There is a murmur of appreciation for the repartee, then all reach for their wine glasses and hors d'oeuvres.

The same biblical scholar goes next door into a parallel room filled with New Testament experts, and calls out again:

'Stoic philosophy was the most influential philosophy in the first century of the common era in Asia Minor!'

Lots of heads turn this time, with eyebrows raised. Various scholars spring to their feet. Someone calls out, 'What does Athens have to do with Jerusalem?'[1] Several raise their glasses to this, and agree that Greek philosophers were the source of all heresy.[2] Others admit that Justin Martyr had an ongoing interest in philosophy, but point out that his most prized philosophy was Platonism – certainly not Stoic philosophy.[3] 'Yes', a particularly erudite voice calls out, 'the European philosophical tradition consists of a series of footnotes to Plato!'[4] Applause.

As the scholars return to their previous conversations, various murmurs can be heard expressing doubt that philosophy was at all influential on the writings of the New Testament. Once the conviviality has been restored, someone sidles over to chat about the depiction of philosophy in Acts 17, and offers the crestfallen scholar a *petit four*. Then a handful of scholars join the conversation, and as the *petit fours*

---

1. Tertullian, *Prescription against Heresies* 7, available online: http://www.newadvent.org/fathers/0311.htm (accessed 26 May 2019).

2. Andrew Davison, *The Love of Wisdom: An Introduction to Philosophy for Theologians* (London: SCM Press, 2013), 74.

3. Vicky Balabanski, 'Stoic Echoes in non-Stoic Sources: Exploring Stoic Influence in the First and Second Centuries CE', in *Living in a Cultural Wilderness, Journal of Modern Greek Studies (Australia and New Zealand) – Special Issue*, ed. George Couvalis, Michael Tsianikas and Maria Palaktsoglou, *Modern Greek Studies (Australia and New Zealand)* Supplementary Volume, 2017 (Adelaide, 2017), 1–26, at 18–19.

4. Alfred North Whitehead, *Process and Reality* (New York: Free Press, 1979), 39.

disappear, it turns out that there is a quiet groundswell of research into Stoicism and early Christianity, though it goes largely unnoticed by the academy.

What is an Eco-Stoic reading of the Letter to the Colossians?

An Eco-Stoic reading is built on three premises. The first is that Stoic philosophy was the most influential philosophy in the first century CE in Asia Minor, even though this influence is less apparent to biblical scholars than to philosophers.[5] This means that Stoic ideas formed an important context and dialogue partner with the Gospel as it spread across the Roman Empire. The second is that Stoic influence can be seen in Colossians, and so an understanding of Stoic thought can aid our interpretation of this intriguing Letter. The third, and most important for an *Eco*-Stoic reading, is that Stoic ideas, including Stoic cosmology and Stoic ethics, are first and foremost about living in agreement with nature, and so lend themselves to ecological reflection.

In the face of the most intractable and urgent issues of our time – human-induced climate damage and the destruction of Earth's biodiversity – an ecologically attuned framework can enable us to read Colossians in ways that are both relevant for today and true to the original nuances of the Letter.

An Eco-Stoic reading of Colossians differs from a conventional commentary in that it is explicitly selective about the issues raised. Bringing a neglected background (Stoicism) and a vital foreground (ecological crisis) into sharper relief means that some passages are treated in greater detail than others. These are often passages which have received less scholarly attention. Rather than seeking to be comprehensive, an Eco-Stoic reading seeks to be attentive to the wisdom that this movement between text and contexts can offer.

---

5. I offer several reasons for this in Balabanski, 'Stoic Echoes in Non-Stoic Sources', 13–16.

ACKNOWLEDGEMENTS

I acknowledge with thanks my colleagues at the three academic institutions within which I work: Flinders University of South Australia, the Adelaide College of Divinity and the Uniting College for Leadership and Theology. Particular thanks are due to the board of Uniting College for funding the study leave in semester one, 2018, during which much of this work was written. Thanks to the staff of the Adelaide College of Divinity Library for their support. Within Flinders University, thank you also to my colleagues in Modern Greek, who host the LOGOS Australian Centre for Hellenic Language and Culture, whose international conferences gave me opportunity to present at various times on Stoic philosophy, and interact with eminent scholars on Stoicism such as Professors Dirk Baltzly and Johannes Baltussen.

I am grateful to all at Tyndale House, Cambridge, UK, for the wonderful working environment that they provide. Also in Cambridge, I am grateful to Professor David Sedley, who generously met with me to talk about Stoic concepts. Many of the translations used in this book are the work of Professors Long and Sedley, and I acknowledge with thanks their permission to use them.

Thank you to Professor Norman Habel, whose insightful comments and questions have shaped this book for the better. More broadly, my gratitude is due to the various Earth Bible colleagues who have helped to sharpen my skills in reading the Bible in solidarity with Earth, and to Earth itself for sustaining us all. I would like to acknowledge by name one fellow traveller, Professor Denis Edwards, who was an inspiration to me, and to many.

Thank you to Rev. Mark Hewitt, who brings art and Christian ministry together in remarkable ways, and who drew the diagram of the interconnected domains of the Body of Christ (Figure 7.1).

My thanks are due to the staff of Bloomsbury T & T Clark, particularly Sarah Blake and Domic Mattos, for their expertise and their patience.

Warm thanks are due to our daughters Anna, Laura and Shekayla, whose giftedness amazes me. Profound thanks go to my husband Peter Balabanski, whose encouragement, support and eagle eye have been crucial at every step. Finally, thanks be to God, the Father of our Lord Jesus Christ, who embodies and reveals Godself in and through the natural world.

ABBREVIATIONS

AB	Anchor Bible
AJP	*American Journal of Philology*
AnBib	Analecta biblica
BCE	Before the Common Era – equivalent to 'BC'
BJS	Brown Judaic Studies
BNTC	Black's New Testament Commentaries
BZNW	Beihefte zur *ZNW*
CBQ	*Catholic Biblical Quarterly*
CE	Common Era – equivalent to 'AD'
CurBR	*Currents in Biblical Research*
ECL	Early Christianity and its Literature
HNT	Handbuch zum Neuen Testament
IPBES	United Nations' Intergovernmental Science-Policy Platform on Biodiversity and Ecosystem Services
JBL	*Journal of Biblical Literature*
JSNTSup	*Journal for the Study of the New Testament, Supplement Series*
L&S	A. A. Long and D. N. Sedley. *The Hellenistic Philosophers. Vol. 1: Translations of the principal sources with philosophical commentary.* Quotations of translated texts from L&S will be acknowledged in parentheses in the text, or if too long, in a footnote, giving the classical writer's name (if known), the title of the work cited, standard reference numbers, page number(s) from L&S, and where appropriate, the reference in *Stoicorum Veterum Fragmenta (SVF)*.
L&S vol. 2	A.A. Long and D.N. Sedley. *The Hellenistic Philosophers. Vol. 2: Greek and Latin texts with notes and bibliography.* Quotations as for L&S vol. 1.
LCL	Loeb Classical Library. Quotations from the LCL will be acknowledged in parentheses in the text, or if too long, in a footnote, giving the classical writer's name (if known), the title of the work cited, standard reference numbers and the LCL volume and page numbers.
LSJ	H.G. Liddell, Robert Scott and H. Stuart Jones, *Greek–English Lexicon* (Oxford: Clarendon Press, 9th edn, 1968)
LXX	Septuagint – the Greek Old Testament
NCCS	New Covenant Commentary Series
NICNT	New International Commentary on the New Testament
NovT	*Novum Testamentum*
NTD	Das Neue Testament Deutsch
NTOA	Novum Testamentum et orbis antiquus
NTS	*New Testament Studies*

NTTSD	New Testament Tools, Studies and Documents
PhA	Philosophia Antiqua
RBL	*Review of Biblical Literature*
SBFA	Studium Biblicum Franciscanum Analecta
SBL	Society of Biblical Literature
SBT	Studies in Biblical Theology
SHBC	Smyth and Helwys Bible Commentary
SNTSMS	Society for New Testament Studies Monograph Series
SPhiloA	Studia Philonica Annual
SUNT	Studien zur Umwelt des Neuen Testaments
SVF	Hans von Arnim. *Stoicorum Veterum Fragmenta*. Where Long and Sedley or others give a citation from this collection, the reference is included to give the reader access to the original texts in their fullest available context.
TynBul	*Tyndale Bulletin*
WBC	Word Biblical Commentary
WUNT	Wissenschaftliche Untersuchungen zum Neuen Testament
YCS	Yale Classical Studies
ZBK	Zürcher Bibelkommentare
ZNW	*Zeitschrift für die neutestamentliche Wissenschaft*

Translations of passages from the Letter to the Colossians will be my own unless otherwise specified. However in Chapter 1, which introduces Stoic philosophy, translations of passages from Colossians will be taken from the New Revised Standard Version (NRSV), unless otherwise specified.

Translations from other books of the Bible will be taken from NRSV unless otherwise specified.

Where translations of ancient texts have been modified to make them more gender-inclusive, this is indicated by (modified).

INTRODUCTION

The earth shall soon dissolve like snow,
The sun forbear to shine;
But God, who called me here below,
Will be forever mine.

('Amazing Grace', verse 6, John Newton, pub.1779)

There are few songs that have shaped Christian expressions of faith so profoundly – and positively – as John Newton's 'Amazing Grace'. Yet this verse – originally the final verse – expresses a view that is problematic for all of us who understand ourselves as part of creation. This famous verse depicts the earth as transitory and expendable, soon to be thrown away like some disposable packaging. It celebrates the permanence of our relationship with God, but does so by severing our connection with the rest of creation. This may represent one understanding of the future and fate of all things, but there are other biblical affirmations that tell a different story, namely that all things cohere and are sustained by God.[1]

The Letter to the Colossians documents a different attitude to the natural world from the one expressed in Newton's final verse. Colossians states that in Christ, all things hold together and all things are reconciled (Col. 1.17, 20). The Letter affirms that the presence of Christ permeates all things, and in Christ they cohere and are sustained (Col. 2.9). It also proclaims that Christ is the icon or image of God, making God's presence visible and tangible (Col. 1.15). All this means that the material world is of abiding value to God – the oceans, the soil, the air and all creatures that are sustained and nurtured by the mutually dependent web of life. This commentary places these convictions at the centre of how we interpret all aspects of this remarkable Letter.

---

1. John Newton's final verse is not often sung today, and was soon supplemented by another final verse that moved away from seeing an imminent end of creation as core to God's future:

When we've been there ten thousand years,
Bright shining as the sun,
We've no less days to sing God's praise
Than when we'd first begun.

This anonymous final verse was published in 1829, and reflects a different attitude to eschatology.

Given the abiding value of the natural world – 'all things' – to God, the contention of this commentary is that an Eco-Stoic reading of the Letter to the Colossians can make a difference in shaping attitudes to the most pressing issue of our times: the ecological crisis. This crisis is multifaceted, but at the heart of it for humanity is an inability to embrace our interconnection with the natural world and make the attitudinal and structural changes necessary to allow all creation to flourish. There is urgent need to reflect on our own decisions, values and priorities in the Anthropocene era,[2] recognizing that we are complicit in many acts that are changing the world, and at the same time, breaking down the resilience of the natural world to adapt to the changes we have introduced. The more we can reflect as individuals and communities in company with foundational sources of wisdom, the more we can shape our common life towards the common good, understood as the community of all things, not just humans.

Every day brings new reports of the ecological crisis – heat waves and fire, droughts and floods and the extinction of species at rates never previously seen. As I write these words, news of the death of the world's last male northern white rhinoceros in Africa has just come through, marking the nearly certain extinction of another subspecies. Every day there seems to be a shared inertia at all levels of human community in recognizing these signs for what they are. For those aware of these things, hope is in short supply. Hope is a theme that this Letter addresses, seeing it as something stored up in the divine realm, yet also something proclaimed to 'every creature under heaven' (Col. 1.23). Hope for us is also hope for the creation and for every creature.

In 2015, *Laudato Si': On Care for Our Common Home* – Pope Francis' Encyclical Letter[3] – brought both hope and challenge to Catholics and Protestants alike. It addresses 'every person living on this planet' (#3) to value and care for our Common Home, and challenges all Christians to 'ecological conversion' (#217). It is a profoundly wise, urgent and challenging call to shape our world differently. To that end it looks to 'ecological education' (#213 and #214).

This Eco-Stoic reading of the Letter to the Colossians can be viewed as one such contribution to recognizing and valuing our Common Home.

An Eco-Stoic reading of Colossians

The Earth Bible series is known for the ways in which it takes up a hermeneutic of suspicion, identification and retrieval; each volume does so in ways that are

---

2. This term refers to the era in which humans have profoundly altered the earth, including the atmosphere, the climate, the oceans and the biodiversity of the land and even human evolution itself, leading to an accelerated rate of species extinction and increasing instability in all the earth's systems. At the time of the writing of this commentary, the term is widely accepted, but there is no consensus as to when the Anthropocene began.

3. Francis, *Encyclical letter Laudato si' of the Holy Father Francis on Care for Our Common Home* (Vatican City: Libreria Editrice Vaticana, 2015).

appropriate to the text and to the interpreter.[4] In the case of this reading of Colossians, the foundational 'suspicion' – or one might say conviction – is that interpreters have assumed the original audience tended to hear this Letter from a dualistic perspective, shaped by a Platonic cosmology, with God at a great remove from the material world, and the believers' ultimate destination: a 'spiritual'– disembodied – heaven.[5] In doing so they have overlooked or suppressed the indications in the text that the divine presence permeates reality – an insight central to Stoic thought – and the way in which this changes humanity's relationship with the material world and with the God who permeates (but is not confined to) the material world.

The *hermeneutical basis* of this reading is thus to be found in this movement from suspicion, through identification towards retrieval: suspicion that we have overlooked the significance of Stoic thought mirrored in this Letter; identification of ourselves as part of the Earth community, and identification of God's profound and ongoing presence in creation; and retrieval of insights into the nature of reality, of God and of ourselves that were more available to the original readers than they have been to us.[6]

However, the *hermeneutical approach* of this reading is more dialogical than one which confines itself to suspicion, identification and retrieval.[7] This commentary seeks to bring three 'worlds' into dialogue: first, the 'world' behind this Letter to the Colossians, with particular emphasis on Stoic philosophy; second, the 'world' of the Letter to the Colossians, with its distinctive cosmology and Christology; and third, the 'world' in front of the text, which is our own world of contemporary ecological thought and theology.

Each exegetical chapter (Chapters 2–9) begins with a Stoic reading context, selected to shed light on the passage from Colossians that follows. This 'world behind the text' helps to introduce the sorts of ideas and concepts that the original recipients of Colossians brought to their hearing of this Letter, and enables us – who are a great distance from those original recipients – to notice different aspects of the text. The 'world of the text' includes translations which emphasize aspects of the language that resonate with Stoic thought. Where there is a clear poetic or prose structure in the text, the translations are laid out to indicate this visually. This 'world' also includes an exegetical commentary on each passage of Colossians. These

---

4. The Earth Bible Commentary Series is introduced by the General Editor, Norman C. Habel, in his volume *Finding Wisdom in Nature: An Eco-Wisdom Reading of the Book of Job* (Sheffield: Sheffield Phoenix Press, 2014), 1–9.

5. For a critique of this eschatology, see J. Richard Middleton's *A New Heaven and a New Earth: Reclaiming Biblical Eschatology* (Grand Rapids, MI: Baker Academic, 2014).

6. In Earth Bible scholarship, when Earth is capitalized, it refers to the interconnected web of life in all its aspects.

7. Suspicion and retrieval have been critiqued with some justification as undermining the trust necessary to allowing Scripture to form and transform us. See Richard B. Hays, 'A Hermeneutic of Trust', in his book *The Conversion of the Imagination: Paul as Interpreter of Israel's Scripture* (Grand Rapids, MI: Eerdmans, 2005), 190–201.

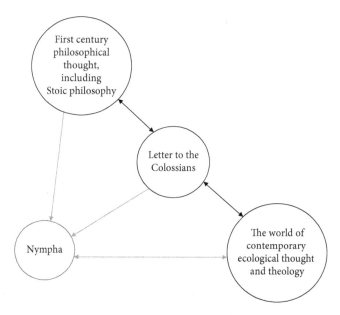

Figure 0.1 An Eco-Stoic reading of Colossians.

are shaped by the interests and emphases already identified in the Stoic Reading Contexts. The Letter will at times confirm what the original recipients might have comprehended about their faith in Christ in keeping with Stoic ideas, and at times it will correct and challenge them to rethink these ideas in the light of the Gospel of Christ. Next, we turn to the 'world' in front of the text – our own world – with the ecological and ethical questions that we bring to the text. In some chapters, this hermeneutical aspect is in a separate section ('Hermeneutical reflections'), and in others, these ecological reflections are interwoven into the commentary.

Each chapter concludes with a brief imaginative section from the perspective of Nympha, who is greeted by name in Col. 4.15 and identified as the head of the church in her house. She is imagined as a woman with a Stoic heritage, and because of Stoicism's high valuing of the natural world, as having an affinity with Earth. So Nympha receives this Letter and articulates her thoughts in response. As a figure drawn from the world behind the text who is engaging with the world of the text, her insights and responses can help us – the people in front of the text – both to identify with and to retrieve certain insights (Figure 0.1).

As in any dialogue or conversation, there is in this reading both a linear development, represented by stepping through the worlds of the text, and an implicit circularity, as different contexts and perspectives make space for one another. This reading makes no claim to being a comprehensive commentary on every aspect of the text. Rather, the reader is invited to notice aspects of the text afresh. As we bring ancient wisdom and contemporary concerns into dialogue with the Letter to the Colossians, we are making room for the Letter to form and transform us.

Why bring these particular three 'worlds' into dialogue?

What does Stoic thought, refracted and at times critiqued by the Letter to the Colossians, have to do with our contemporary world and with ecological concerns in particular? In earlier studies[8] I have argued the case that Colossians gives us a vision of all reality being not only created in and through Christ but also permeated by Christ and presently sustained in Christ:

> He himself is before all things, and in him all things hold together. (Col. 1.17)

This distinctive vision of Christ's cosmic presence in the world makes best sense against a Stoic cosmology, as we will see in Chapter 1. Stoics saw the divine presence permeating reality, and doing so in an embodied way, whereas Platonic cosmology, by contrast, saw God at a great distance from the creation, mediated through lesser beings. In Colossians, the cosmic presence of Christ is also seen in bodily terms, not just referring to the incarnation, Jesus' earthly life, but his present bodily reality:

> For in Him the whole fullness of deity dwells bodily. (Col. 2.9)

'Dwells', present tense, shows that this is an ongoing reality being described. 'Bodily', a hallmark of Stoic cosmology, is in an emphatic position in the sentence. It is very striking that 'the whole fullness of deity', or divinity, is bodily present in Christ. For the original recipients of the Letter, who had heard and received the Gospel as pagans, this connected with a distinctively Stoic concept of the spiritual yet bodily presence of deity. More will be said about this in Chapter 7, but we can see from just these two verses that Colossians invites reflection on the cosmic significance of Christ, and does so in Stoic terms.

The ecological significance of Colossians seen in this framework becomes readily apparent. If Christ is not only the One through whom all things were made (Col. 1.16) but also the One in whom they are presently sustained (Col. 1.17), then Christ is not simply Saviour but also Source and Sustainer of non-human creation ('all things') too. This presses us beyond our human-centred categories to seeing Christ as the Christ for all things, all parts of the web of life,

---

8. Vicky Balabanski, 'Critiquing Anthropocentric Cosmology: Retrieving a Stoic "Permeation Cosmology" in Colossians 1:15–20', in *Ecological Hermeneutics*, ed. Norman C. Habel and Peter Trudinger, SBL Symposium Series 46 (Atlanta, GA: SBL, 2008), 151–9; Vicky Balabanski, 'Hellenistic Cosmology and the Letter to the Colossians: Towards an Ecological Hermeneutic', in *Ecological Hermeneutics: Biblical, Historical and Theological Perspectives*, ed. David G. Horrell, Cherryl Hunt, Christopher Southgate and Francesca Stavrakopoulou (London & New York: T & T Clark / Continuum, 2010), 94–107; Vicky Balabanski, 'The Holy Spirit and the Cosmic Christ: A Comparison of Their Roles in Colossians and Ephesians, or, Where Has the Holy Spirit gone?' *Colloquium* 42/2 (2010): 173–87.

not just humanity. The invitation and imperative is there to recognize ourselves as divinely connected with other species, not simply because they feed, clothe, entertain and interest us but because we humans are part of 'all things', and hence they are part of us.

Similarly, if we reflect deeply on the mystery that 'in Him the whole fullness of deity dwells bodily' (Col. 2.9), then bodiliness and divinity, God's presence, are not opposites. In fact, we need to look afresh at corporeal reality and expect to see there something of Christ's bodily presence. As Christians we have practised this kind of seeing in the context of the sacraments, and in particular, in the Eucharist or Holy Communion. We have also known, though more intermittently, that Christ is visibly present to us in the face of another person, the poor, the hungry, the sick. But in our present time, we need to extend that sacramental way of seeing Christ's bodily presence to other creatures, to the world around us; not just the beautiful mountain tops and rainforests, but the broken and bleeding places of this world too. We need to be able to glimpse Christ in places of brokenness and suffering and find compassion and common ground with other creatures through Christian spiritual practices.

Both cosmology and ethics are part of the bridge between these worlds. A cosmology of divine permeation links the Letter to the Colossians with Stoic ideas, and invites us to rethink how we view the world around us and ourselves in the web of life. Ethics is also part of the framework that connects Colossians with Stoic ideas. The Letter's ethical teachings, grounded in the life of Christ and the community of believers that is formed in him, have many parallels with Stoic ethics, which are grounded in the Logos and the ensuing life of wisdom. These are themes that this commentary pursues.

When discussing the Hebrew Scriptures and writings which engage primarily with them, Wisdom – not Logos – is the key term. It not only denotes a specific collection of writings but also has various specific domains: cosmological, innate (biological), ethical, spiritual, proverbial and intellectual.[9] Against a Stoic background, Logos occupies a similar range. While both backgrounds are arguably important for understanding the Letter, the neglected Stoic background is given greater attention in this book.

This Eco-Stoic reading seeks to demonstrate that the 'worlds' of ancient Stoic philosophy and contemporary ecological concerns can be legitimately and fruitfully connected in and through a study of the ancient piece of Scripture known to us as the Letter to the Colossians. Stoic philosophy lends itself to ecological reflection by virtue of the fact that it rejects dualistic thought and sees the Logos/the divine presence permeating and sustaining all reality. Stoic thought also lends itself to eco-friendly practices by validating the concept and choice of self-restraint. Colossians, read 'stoically', reveals Stoic philosophy as influencing the thought world of the Letter. The Christology of this Letter can be perceived more clearly with this lens, not only in its original context but also in our contemporary context.

---

9. Habel, *Finding Wisdom in Nature*, 10–15.

Authorship and dating of the Letter to the Colossians

The opening claim of the Letter is that it is authored by Paul and Timothy. Since at least the late eighteenth century, scholars have questioned whether Paul could have been the author, given the distinctive features of the Letter[10] and the difficulty of fitting it into Pauline chronology.[11] The position of this commentary is that Timothy is the primary composer of the Letter, but that Paul's presence and co-authorship is real rather than fictional.[12] One could describe this position either as 'co-authorship', or as 'partial pseudepigraphy'. Paul and Timothy's long-standing partnership in the Gospel, pre-dating the earliest Pauline letter we have (1 Thess. 1.1), means that their collaboration in the letter writing, though not seamless,[13] is natural.

Several other scholars have come to similar conclusions about the authorship of Colossians, including Eduard Schweizer, James Dunn, Ulrich Luz and Carl R. Holladay,[14] and other scholars are also emphasizing a more collaborative model of Pauline writing.[15]

---

10. These include stylistic features, such as the fact that Colossians as a whole has substantially fewer conjunctions than Paul's undisputed letters, and instead uses relative clauses and relative pronouns more frequently. Alongside these features, there are distinctive theological and rhetorical nuances. The most detailed study of the stylistic distinctives of Colossians is Walter Bujard's *Stilanalytische Untersuchungen zum Kolosserbrief*, SUNT 11 (Göttingen: Vandenhoeck & Ruprecht, 1973). Bujard's study does not distinguish between different sections of Colossians.

11. Paul Foster, *Colossians*, BNTC (London: Bloomsbury/T & T Clark, 2016), 73–9.

12. I discuss this claim in more detail in Chapter 9.

13. Despite the stylistic differences between much of Colossians and the rest of the Pauline corpus that Bujard has documented, the opening and closing of Colossians (1.1-14 and 4.2-18) cannot be distinguished stylistically from Paul's other writings. The frequent plerophoric use of *pas* ('every/all'), conveying full conviction and certainty, is prominent in Col. 1.1-11 (seven times) but also in Phil. 1.1-11, where it is used eight times.

14. Eduard Schweizer, *The Letter to the Colossians: A Commentary* (London: SPCK, 1982), 23; James Dunn, *The Epistles to the Colossians and Philemon: A Commentary on the Greek Text* (Carlisle: Paternoster, 1996), 38; Ulrich Luz, 'Der Brief an die Kolosser', in *Die Briefe an die Galater, Epheser und Kolosser*, translation and commentary by Jürgen Becker and Ulrich Luz, NTD 8:1 (Göttingen: Vandenhoeck & Ruprecht, 1998), 185; Carl R. Holladay, *A Critical Introduction to the New Testament: Interpreting the Message and Meaning of Jesus Christ* (Abingdon: Abingdon Press, 2005), 557.

15. Michael F. Bird, *Colossians and Philemon: A New Covenant Commentary*, NCCS 12 (Eugene, OR: Cascade, 2009), 5–9; John Paul Heil, *Colossians: Encouragement to Walk in All Wisdom as Holy Ones in Christ*, ECL 4 (Atlanta, GA: SBL, 2010), 5–7; Derek J. Tidball, *In Christ, in Colossae: Sociological Perspectives on Colossians* (Milton Keynes: Paternoster, 2011), 10–11; Nijay K. Gupta, *Colossians*, SHBC 27c (Macon, GA: Smyth & Helwys, 2013), 3–10. See also Gupta's article, 'What Is in a Name? The Hermeneutics of Authorship Analysis Concerning Colossians', *Currents in Biblical Research* 11/2 (2013): 196–217.

Colossians is a letter written from prison (4.3, 10, 18). There has been no consensus as to which imprisonment is meant; Ephesus, Caesarea and Rome have all been considered. I have strong reasons for holding that Colossians was written during Paul's (and his co-workers') imprisonment in Rome. The key to this position lies in the relationship between the Letter to Philemon and Colossians 4, as these two name many of the same people – no less than nine people, in fact – implying a similar context and time. I have argued in detail elsewhere that both Letters were written during Paul's Roman imprisonment, though *not* at the same time.[16] The Letter to Philemon was written earlier, in about 60 CE, and the Letter to the Colossians somewhat later, in about 62 CE. A clear indication that Philemon was written earlier is the change in status of Onesimus. Paul's Letter to Philemon is focused on exhorting Paul's 'beloved brother and co-worker' Philemon to deal favourably and generously with his slave Onesimus. The fact that Onesimus had absconded from his master and had sought out Paul – through whom he had then come to faith – is a very delicate and live issue in the Letter to Philemon. By contrast, the passing mention of Onesimus in Col. 4.9 as 'the faithful and beloved brother, who is one of you' implies that this issue has been resolved, and that Onesimus has had time to establish himself as a reliable co-worker, ready to be entrusted with the task of accompanying Tychicus to Colossae (Col. 4.7-9).

A further indication that the Letter to Philemon reflects an earlier dating and a different context from Colossians is the role of Aristarchus. In Philemon he is a 'fellow-worker' (Phlm. 24), free to move around, whereas in Colossians he is now a 'fellow-prisoner' (Col. 4.10).

Once it is clear that Philemon is earlier than Colossians, we can avoid the mistake that has so often been made, namely mixing the information gleaned from Philemon and Colossians in such a way as to suggest that Philemon, Apphia and their church community are in Colossae. This is almost universally assumed by scholars, and I have demonstrated in detail why this rests on a mistake in logic. In fact, Philemon, Apphia and their house church are much more likely to have been in or near Rome, perhaps in the Roman port town of Puteoli (Acts 28.13-15), so that when Paul writes to them to prepare a guest room for him (Phlm. 22), he was envisaging a relatively short trip. Colossae, by contrast, is a land and sea journey of over a thousand miles from Rome and its ports. A letter from Rome to Colossae needed major forward planning and entrusting to two named letter bearers (Tychicus and Onesimus).

In the period between the writing of Philemon and Colossians, Archippus, the 'fellow-soldier' who had been with Philemon, Apphia and their house church (in the vicinity of Rome), has been redeployed to the Lycus Valley in Asia Minor. Colossians 4.17 contains a message to him: 'See that you complete the task that you have received in the Lord.' Paul and his team's ministry was far-reaching and strategic – but perhaps not all 'fellow-soldiers' were as reliable as they expected.

---

16. Vicky Balabanski, 'Where Is Philemon? The Case for a Logical Fallacy in the Correlation of the Data in Philemon and Colossians 1.1-2; 4.7-18', *JSNT* 38/2 (2015): 131–50.

They think that enough time has elapsed for Archippus to have completed his assignment by now, and to have made the return trip from the Lycus Valley.

Given the gap in time implied by these various events, particularly Archippus' deployment to the distant Lycus Valley, it is likely that at least two years have passed between the writing of the first prison letter (Philemon), in which Paul confidently expects to be released (Phlm. 22), and Colossians, in which no release is envisaged and in fact more arrests have been made (e.g. Aristarchus, Col. 4.10).

Between these two letters, I consider it likely that the Letter to the Philippians was written, also from Rome. By the time Philippians is written, Paul's imprisonment has been of some duration, as the 'whole imperial guard' has come to know that Paul has been imprisoned for Christ (Phil. 1.13-14). Nevertheless, Paul expresses some hope of release soon (Phil. 2.24). Timothy is prominent in this Letter too, as co-author (Phil. 1.1) and Paul's emissary and as a most valued and trusted co-worker (Phil. 2.19-24). Timothy is 'like a son' to Paul (Phil. 2.22), which can explain why he stands alongside Paul as co-author, despite the presence of other valued co-workers like Epaphroditus (Phil. 2.25-30) or Epaphras (Col. 1.7-8; 4.12-13), who know their respective communities well – or better – than Paul and Timothy do.[17]

The Letter to the Philippians provides an important comparison to Colossians. They are similar in length, and from a similar period. Yet Philippians is vintage Paul in style and theology, and Colossians is not. In Philippians, Paul is striving with the 'circumcision' (Phil. 3.2-3), whereas in Colossians the 'circumcision' includes a few trusted fellow workers, but has otherwise left him alone (Col. 4.11). In both, we find a Christ hymn used prominently as a way of helping the recipients to grasp a central concept (Phil. 2.6-11; Col. 1.15-20). In Philippians, Paul affirms that 'our citizenship is in heaven', whereas in Colossians, our 'hope is laid up … in heaven' (Col. 1.5): similar, but different. In Philippians, the Lord Jesus Christ 'will transform the body of our humiliation that it may be conformed to the body of his glory, by the power that also enables him to make all things subject to himself' (Phil. 3.21). Various themes that become prominent in Colossians are present here (body, glory, power, all things): again, similar, but different. Paul knows the Philippians personally, and exudes warmth towards them (Phil. 1.3-8), whereas he (and Timothy) have not met the believers in Colossae and Laodicea personally. He prays for them (Col. 1.9) and strives for them (Col. 2.1), but Colossians is not personal in quite the same way as Philippians. The difference in personal connection can also make for a difference in style.

The 'Colossian problem'

There is a rich scholarly array of reconstructions as to what may have been troubling the fledgling group of Christ-followers at Colossae – or what Paul and Timothy may

---

17. Epaphras is a shortened form of Epaphroditus, but these two are not the same figure; Col. 4.12 specifies that it is referring to the Colossians' 'own' Epaphras who sends greetings.

have thought was troubling them. The believers had formerly been uncircumcised Gentiles (Col. 1.27, 2.11), and through the work of Epaphras, had come to faith in Christ, and to a different understanding of themselves in relation to God. In a departure from most of the undisputed Pauline letters, we are not told explicitly what has prompted Timothy and Paul to write at this time (compare 1 Thess. 3.6; Gal. 1.6-10; 1 Cor. 1.11; Rom. 15.23-33; Phlm. 10; Phil. 4.10-20). Both Epaphras and the letter writers are concerned about the Colossians and others in the Lycus Valley; Epaphras is 'striving in prayer on [their] behalf' (4.12) and Paul is 'striving for [them]' (2.1). It may be that their morale, their unity (2.2) and their maturity in Christ (4.12) are at a low ebb or in danger. Key to this is the impression that they might be under pressure to supplement their faith in Christ with another type of religious experience or set of practices, so the Letter emphasizes the universal scope of Christ and Christ's work.

The position this commentary takes is that the Letter to the Colossians is primarily a pastoral rather than a polemical letter. The tone of the Letter is gracious and universal. One might expect this, given that it is written to a community that was not founded by the letter writers. This is also true of the Letter to the Romans of course, even though Romans is very different from Colossians in scope and tone. In the case of Romans, a personal visit from Paul is on the horizon, and there is already quite an extensive web of relationships between Paul and Rome.[18]

Colossians also envisages a forthcoming visit, but not by Paul or Timothy; Tychicus and Onesimus are going to visit, bearing the Letter and the news (Col. 4.7-9). Colossians sets out the Gospel too, though in a way that appears very confident that the recipients share the foundational concepts and are firmly established in the faith (Col. 2.5-7). This confidence is linked with the confidence the writers have in Epaphras, who founded the community of believers at Colossae (Col. 1.7), and is now with Paul and Timothy in Rome (Col. 4.12).[19]

What prompted the writing of this Letter? Were the Colossians succumbing to pressures of false teaching and heresy? Morna Hooker has argued persuasively that the evidence points not so much to a specific heresy or group of false teachers as to the sorts of pressures that any fledgling community of believers would experience in leaving behind accepted practices in pagan society and gravitating towards Jewish practices.[20] The teaching about Christ in Col. 1 does not have a polemical

---

18. See Sigve Tonstad, in *The Letter to the Romans: Paul among the Ecologists* (Sheffield: Phoenix Press 2016), 68.

19. Many ancient manuscripts, including Vaticanus and Alexandrinus, include a subscription 'from Rome'. See Bruce Metzger, *A Textual Commentary on the Greek New Testament: A Companion Volume to the United Bible Societies' Greek New Testament (Fourth Edn, Revised)*, 2nd edn (Stuttgart: Deutsche Bibelgesellschaft, 1994), 560.

20. Morna Hooker, 'Were There False Teachers in Colossae?' in *From Adam to Christ: Essays on Paul*, ed. Morna D. Hooker (Cambridge: Cambridge University Press, 1990), 121–36, esp. 123, 129, 136. This view has been supported by some other scholars, including Angela Standhartinger, 'Colossians and the Pauline School', *NTS* 50/4 (2004): 572–93, 588; Peter Müller, 'Gegner im Kolosserbrief: Methodische Überlegungen zu einem schwierigen

tone, but rather emphasizes what has been achieved by God through Christ (1.13, 20, 21-23) with confidence that this Gospel has been proclaimed to every creature under heaven (1.23). The Colossians' hope is laid up for them in heaven (1.5) and has been bearing fruit and growing in the whole world (1.6). The mystery that has been hidden throughout the ages and generations has now been revealed to them, and the glorious riches of this mystery are theirs: 'Christ in you – the hope of glory' (1.26-27). All this has an expansive, confident, reassuring ring to it.

The Letter gives no direct indication that the writers have recent, explicit news about the situation of the Colossians. This gives the Letter something of the feel of a letter written 'on spec', without certain knowledge of what the letter bearers will find when they get there. An array of possible issues is canvassed, without any one of them being unequivocally shown to be a problem in the community: distraction by empty deceitful philosophy (Col. 2.8), attraction to Jewish practices like circumcision (Col. 2.10), certain feasts or Sabbath practices (Col. 2.16), or attraction to ascetic practices modelled on mystery cults (Col. 2.18). The ethical exhortations of Colossians 3 and the Household Code suggest possible intra-community strife. And the final admonition to conduct oneself wisely towards outsiders rounds out the widespread pastoral scope of the Letter.

The Letter appears to be well informed and confident about the foundations of the believing communities in the Lycus Valley, presumably due to Epaphras' report. Given the various issues that are addressed, it is likely that Paul, Timothy and Epaphras are not at all certain about the recent developments over the past months or perhaps even one or two years. Even so, there has been a 'Letter from Laodicea', as mentioned in Col. 4.16, and it is possible that this may have raised issues that find expression in Colossians.[21]

Colossians presents as a 'circular' letter to specified Lycus Valley communities – primarily Colossae and Laodicea (Col. 2.1; 4.13, 15, 16), with Nympha and the church in her house mentioned, and a passing reference to Hierapolis (Col. 4.13). The Letter serves to introduce Tychicus and Onesimus, the letter bearers (Col. 4.7-9), to admonish Archippus by calling his attention to the fact that a certain task is not yet complete (Col. 4.17), to refresh the connection between the Lycus Valley communities and their leader Epaphras (Col. 1.12; 4.12-13) and, finally, to establish more securely the oversight of Paul and Timothy.

A further pressure on the Lycus Valley and its inhabitants should be mentioned. We know that the people of the region were experiencing, or had experienced earthquakes and aftershocks that caused considerable suffering.[22] The concern

Kapitel', in *Beiträge zur urchristlichen Theologiegeschichte*, ed. Wolfgang Kraus and Ulrich Müller, BZNW 163 (Berlin/New York 2009), 365–94, 369.

21. See the discussion in Chapter 9.

22. Alan H. Cadwallader, 'Refuting an Axiom of Scholarship on Colossae: Fresh Insights from New and Old Inscriptions', in *Colossae in Space and Time: Linking to an Ancient City*, ed. Alan H. Cadwallader and Michael Trainor, NTOA – SUNT 94 (Göttingen: Vandenhoeck & Ruprecht, 2011), 151–79.

of Paul and his Rome-based team for the Colossians' and Laodiceans' well-being (2.1) may allude to an awareness that there was turmoil in the region, although no specific knowledge of it is evident. Both the striving/wrestling for the Colossians and Laodiceans (and those in Hierapolis, 4.13) and the vision of confidence that the Letter seeks to convey could reflect awareness, in general terms, of such events. But the Letter states that the Colossians' hope is secure (1.5); God has reached out for the Gentiles, not only warning everyone but also teaching everyone with wisdom (1.28). No recent events could in any way negate their faith, nor could they undermine the spread of the Gospel. The Letter emphasizes that suffering is part of Paul's experience in the Gospel; the emphasis on suffering in the Letter may mirror an awareness of the recipients' suffering, without naming anything explicitly. Participating in Christ's suffering is a cause of rejoicing (1.24).

It used to be widely accepted that Colossae was no longer inhabited after these earthquakes, but this has been proven not to be the case. The resilience and persistence of the inhabitants of this region is shown in the ongoing inscriptions and evidence of rebuilding.[23] The nearest thing we have to explicit concern is expressed in Col. 2.1 ('how greatly I am striving on your behalf') and 4.12 (Epaphras is 'always striving in prayer on your behalf'). These may simply be standard expressions,[24] but alternatively they may actually reflect genuine and deep concern about events, though without any direct recent knowledge of them. Given the confidence that the rest of the Letter expresses with regard to the Colossians' faith, this great and ongoing striving is surprising, and implies something more than the issues referred to in Col. 2.8–3.4 – which, in any case, are not named as their own current experience (2.6-8).

In view of this context in the early 60s, I consider it plausible that the task Archippus is urged to complete (4.17) may have been an extended visit to bring encouragement and possibly financial assistance to the Christ-followers of the region.[25] Paul and Timothy are concerned either by the lack of news, or the length of time that this is taking, or both.

External evidence for the pressure of natural disasters – particularly on Laodicea – comes from Tacitus' *Annals* 14.27.1. Tacitus had described the military march of Nero's general Gnaeus Domitius Corbulo against the Armenian city Tigranocerta in 14.23–6, and then wrote: 'In the same year, Laodicea, one of the famous Asiatic cities, was laid in ruins by an earthquake, but recovered by its own resources, without assistance from ourselves' (LCL 322: 150–1).

Tacitus, writing in the second decade of the second century, had access to the official sources of the Roman state: the *acta senatus* (the minutes of the session of the Senate) and the *acta diurna populi Romani* (a collection of the acts of the government

---

23. Cadwallader, 'Refuting an Axiom of Scholarship on Colossae', 170–5.

24. On the topic of the metaphor of 'AGON' (striving/fighting/wrestling) and its similarity to popular Stoic imagery, see Bernhard Heininger, 'Soziale und politische Metaphorik im Kolosserbrief', in *Kolosser-Studien*, ed. Peter Müller, Biblisch-Theologische Studien 103 (Neukirchen-Vluyn: Neukirchener Verlag, 2009), 70.

25. See the discussion of this possibility in Chapter 9.

and news of the court and capital). But his use of these must be approached with some caution.[26] The date Tacitus refers to may have been 59–60 or 61 CE.[27]

Another ancient source, the Sibylline Books (IV, 107), states: 'Hapless Laodicea, thee shall an earthquake lay low in ruin, but thou shalt stand again.'[28] Laodicea is only about eighteen kilometres from Colossae. It is mentioned in Colossians as the other community for whom the writers are striving (2.1), and is also referred to in Col. 4.15 and 16. The Letter envisages a close connection between these two communities.[29]

One may object that there is no explicit reference to natural disasters of any sort in this Letter. 'Everything' that they are to endure (1.11) is not made explicit. Indeed, as stated above, the circular nature of this Letter means specific references to events or situations are much less prominent than one would expect in a letter written to a community undergoing trauma. It is certainly true that a letter written when the news of disaster first came through could be expected to be more precise. But it seems that any explicit report from the region was now old news, received prior to Archippus' departure, which was many months – possibly even a year or two – earlier, given the travel times involved. The Letter suggests that the writers were concerned not because they had bad news from the region, but because they had no recent news. The warnings reflect what the Rome-based team knew of common dangers besetting the fledgling communities of Christ-followers in various places.

26. G. A. Harrer, 'Senatorial Speeches and Letters in Tacitus' Annals', *Studies in Philology* 15/4 (1918): 333–43, 340; A. W. Mosley, 'Historical Reporting in the Ancient World', *NTS* 12/1 (1965): 10–26; Brian J. Wright, 'Ancient Rome's Daily News with some Likely Implications for Early Christian Studies', *TynBul* 67/1 (2016): 145–60, 149.

27. Tacitus' reference is generally dated to 60 CE, though the events described as falling in the same year may push this date out to 61 CE. See the problem of ascribing everything in chs 23–26 to 60 CE as set out by John Jackson in LCL 322: 149 n. 3. See also T. E. J. Wiedemann, 'Tiberius to Nero', in *The Cambridge Ancient History*, Vol. 10, 2nd edn, ed. A. K. Bowman, E. Champlin and A. Lintott (Cambridge: Cambridge University Press, 1996), 248. Eusebius, in his *Chronicle*, written early in the fourth century CE (*Chron.* 210), and Orosius (7.7.12), writing a century later, dated the earthquake to 64. See the discussion of this in Janice Capel Anderson, *Colossians: An Introduction and Study Guide: Authorship, Rhetoric, and Code*, T & T Clark's Study Guides to the New Testament (London: T & T Clark, 2018), 20. Ben Witherington considers that there may have been two earthquakes in these years. See his *The Letters to Philemon, the Colossians and the Ephesians: A Socio-Rhetorical Commentary on the Captivity Epistles* (Grand Rapids, MI: Eerdmans, 2007), 19, 34. See also James A. Kelhoffer, *Conceptions of 'Gospel' and Legitimacy in Early Christianity*, WUNT 1/324 (Tübingen: Mohr Siebeck, 2014), 235–7.

28. R. H. Charles dates Book IV 'by general consent' to about the year 80 AD, *The Apocrypha and Pseudepigrapha of the Old Testament*, Vol. 2 (Oxford: Clarendon Press 1913), 373. While this reference does not contribute to a reliable dating, it is the probably the earliest extant reference to an earthquake devastating Laodicea.

29. Paul Trebilco 'Christians in the Lycus Valley', in *Colossae in Time and Space: Linking to an Ancient City*, ed. Alan Cadwallader and Michael Trainor (Göttingen: Vandenhoeck & Ruprecht, 2011), 184–5.

Colossians is a letter that downplays imminent eschatology. This is widely recognized as one of its most distinctive features: its eschatology lacks the balance of the 'already' and 'not yet' that we find in the undisputed Pauline letters, and rather foregrounds the 'already' – they have (already) been raised with Christ (3.1). With regard to the coming of Christ, the language used to refer to it is distinctive: 'Christ will be *revealed*' (Col. 3.4). Imminent eschatology is downplayed in favour of seeing the long-term view across the ages and generations (1.26). We have in this Letter a cosmic Christology and an expansive universal picture of the Gospel.[30] If this Letter, drafted by Timothy together with Paul during Paul's imprisonment in Rome, downplays imminent eschatology, it does so to encourage the believers to stay the course, to live as people confident that they are already part of the kingdom of God's beloved Son (1.13-14), in whom 'all things hold together' (1.17).

An Earth Bible reading strategy

The Earth Bible approach is known for using six principles as guides for reading biblical texts:

1. The Principle of Intrinsic Worth:
   The universe, Earth, and all its components have intrinsic worth/value.
2. The Principle of Interconnectedness:
   Earth is a community of interconnected living things that are mutually dependent on each other for life and survival.
3. The Principle of Voice:
   Earth is a living entity capable of raising its voice in celebration and against injustice.
4. The Principle of Purpose:
   The universe, Earth and all its components are a part of a dynamic cosmic design within which each piece has a place in the overall goal of that design.
5. The Principle of Mutual Custodianship:
   Earth is a balanced and diverse domain in which responsible custodians can function as partners, rather than rulers, to sustain a balanced and diverse Earth community.
6. The Principle of Resistance:
   Earth and its components not only suffer from human injustices but actively resist them in the struggle for justice.

---

30. Scholars have tended to see these things as an indication of a post-Pauline pseudepigraphon dating into the 70s or beyond, yet the first Jewish War and its aftermath tended to heighten rather than reduce apocalyptic expectation. See Vicky Balabanski, *Eschatology in the Making: Mark, Matthew, and the Didache*, SNTSMS 97 (Cambridge: Cambridge University Press, 1997), 207.

These principles were framed in discussion with ecologists rather than theologians, and have formed a set of heuristic tools designed to bring biblical texts and ecological concepts into dialogue. The first, second and fourth principles are of particular relevance to an Eco-Stoic reading of Colossians, as they emphasize the permeation of God's presence in the natural world, sustaining and connecting all things, directing the whole towards life. What I am seeking to discover/uncover in this reading of Colossians is how to read Scripture as a citizen not just of heaven but also of Earth. If God is the Creator of 'all things', then 'all things' – not just humans – matter in God's eyes. In order to shift my gaze away from my narrow horizon, and find ways of interpreting the Letter inclusively, each section will include an imaginative reading from the perspective of Nympha (Col. 4.15).[31]

Why Nympha?

Nympha is the only woman named in Colossians. The reference to Nympha and the church in her house (Col. 4.15) is the only unambiguous reference in the Pauline letters to the leadership of a house church by a woman.[32] Many other women are named as leaders in the undisputed letters of Paul: Phoebe, deacon of the church at Cenchreae, patron/benefactor and probably the lector of Romans (Rom. 16.1-2); Prisca, Paul's co-worker, who together with Aquila 'risked her neck' for Paul, who led a church in their house and influenced all the Gentile churches (Rom. 16.3-5); Mary, who 'worked hard among you' (Rom. 16.6); Junia, 'prominent among the apostles', relative of Paul [and Andronicus] (Rom. 16.7); Tryphaena and Tryphosa, 'workers in the Lord', (Rom. 16.12); Rufus' mother – 'a mother also to [Paul]' (Rom 16.13); Julia, Nereus' sister (Rom. 16.15); Euodia and Syntyche – who are disagreeing with one another, (Phil. 4.2-3); Chloe, whose people carry news from Corinth (1 Cor.1.11) and Apphia our sister (Phlm. 2).

Nympha, by contrast, is not known to Paul personally (Col. 2.1). Margaret MacDonald states that:

> The reference to Nympha should not be downplayed, for patronage of a house church was arguably the most important leadership role for men or women in the Pauline churches. The reference should be compared, for example, to the

---

31. Such an imaginative engagement with the figure of Nympha has precedents. Brian J. Walsh and Sylvia C. Keesmaat, for example, have imagined the story of Nympha in their book *Colossians Remixed: Subverting the Empire* (Downers Grove, IL: Intervarsity Press, 2004), 49–57, 220–5. In terms of genre, one could call such stories haggadic Midrash; each imagining makes space for fresh hermeneutical engagement with the text.

32. Margaret Y. MacDonald, 'Can Nympha Rule This House? The Rhetoric of Domesticity in Colossians', in *Rhetoric and Realites in Early Christianities*, ed Willi Braun, Studies in Christianity and Judaism / Études sur le christianisme et le judaïsme 16 (Waterloo, ON: Wilfrid Laurier University Press, 2005), 99–120, 102.

reference to Gaius (Rom 16.23) who is described as the 'host to Paul and to the whole church'.[33]

Nympha's leadership of a house church was in keeping with common practices and leadership opportunities for prominent women in society at large, as Roman property law permitted women to own a household, including not only the physical property but also slaves.[34]

The prominence of Nympha forms an important counterpoint to the fact that the earliest of the New Testament Household Codes – which formalize the expectation that Christian family structures will mirror Greco-Roman patriarchal structures – is also found in Colossians (Col. 3. 18–4.1). How would Nympha have related to this code? This question will be explored further in the section on the code itself.

Nympha's name suggests that she had a pagan rather than a Jewish background. In the ancient world, nymphs were female deities living in rural areas (water or forests), and were the ones who crowned Apollo. Her name means 'bride', which has strong symbolic connections within the Johannine tradition with the symbolism of Christ as the bridegroom (e.g. Jn 3.29), though not in Paul's writings. The connection between the name Nympha and water is significant, as monumental fountains were called nymphaea.[35] Cities of the region had multiple nymphaea, piping water into the city via clay water pipes or carved travertine stone blocks and distributing it through the city by means of terminals and water towers. Nymphaea were valued![36]

All we know of Nympha is what we can glean from Col. 4.15:

> Give my greetings to the brothers and sisters in Laodicea, and to Nympha and the church in her house.

Were Nympha and her household in Laodicea? This is possible, if the word 'and' means 'and specifically'.[37] It is also possible that her house church was located in

33. MacDonald, 'Can Nympha Rule This House?' 104.

34. Richard P. Saller, 'Symbols of Gender and Status Hierarchies in the Roman Household', in *Women and Slaves in Greco-Roman Culture*, ed. Sandra R. Joshel and Sheila Murnaghan (London/New York: Routledge, 1998), 85–91, 86.

35. Erdal Yazici, *Hierapolis (Pamukkale), Laodicea and Surrounding Area*, trans. Uğur Ahmet Toprak, The Ancient Cities 3 (Istanbul: Uranus, 2014), 159.

36. Nymphaea were often adorned with ornate facades in this period in the cities of Asia Minor. As Barbara Burrell points out, their 'imported, colored marbles connoted luxury and up-to-date Urbanity, and were conspicuous gifts of the richest citizens to their beloved city. They made the entire city a theater, grander and more self-conscious than it had ever been before.' Barbara Burrell, 'False Fronts: Separating the Aedicular Façade from the Imperial Cult in Roman Asia Minor', *American Journal of Archaeology* 110/3 (2006): 437–69, 462.

37. Markus Barth and Helmut Blanke, *Colossians: A New Translation with Introduction and Commentary*, AB 34B (New York: Doubleday, 1994), 486.

Hierapolis, also part of this Letter's purview (Col. 4.13), or in or near Colossae.[38] The only hint we have is that in Col. 4.15-16 – before and after the mention of Nympha – all the focus is on Laodicea, so it does associate her with this area. However, if Nympha's household had been in the city of Laodicea, the general greeting to those in Laodicea would have included her. To be singled out in this way, Nympha must have been a woman of high status. This reading sets her in a rural context outside Laodicea, with business and personal connections with both that city and Colossae.

Nympha and her household may have been involved in textile production. The wealth of this region came from textile products, manufactured from the wool of the sheep raised in the area, which included raven-coloured, brown and grey as well as white sheep. The yarns were dyed various shades of red and purple, with dye obtained from the roots of a plant named *Rubai tinctoria L.* (madder), grown around the city. Together with the cities of Hierapolis and Colossae in the Lycus Valley, Laodicea founded a guild for marketing textile products.[39]

Just as Turkey is famous today for its beautiful handmade carpets, we know that such carpets were already in production in this region long before Nympha was born.[40] If she were involved in textile production – and perhaps the manufacture of carpets – Nympha and her household would have kept sheep and produced and dyed wool from natural roots and leaves.

Nympha will form an imaginative partner in this Eco-Stoic reading.[41] More will be said about her as a historical figure, but as a reading partner, her connection with the natural world will help in the process of *identification*. This is an interpretive step that helps us move from the *suspicion* that our readings have been anthropocentric, excluding Earth and focusing just on humanity. It will be through the step of identification that we can move towards *retrieval* – discovering the insights that we can find in the text that can point us towards becoming participants in God's love for all things.

38. MacDonald, 'Can Nympha Rule This House?' 183.

39. Yazici, *Hierapolis (Pamukkale), Laodicea and Surrounding Area*, 104.

40. F. W. Putzger, 'Wirtschaft des Römischen Weltreichs', in *Historisches Weltatlas*, ed. F. W. Putzger (Berlin & Bielefeld: Velhagen & Klasing, 1965), 28. A famous carpet belonging to a Scythian – the Pazyryk carpet (36 symmetrical knots per sq. cm) was excavated in 1949 from the grave of a Scythian nobleman in the Pazyryk Valley of the Altai Mountains in Siberia. It is dated to the fifth century BCE. Available online: https://hermitagemuseum.o rg/wps/portal/hermitage/digital-collection/25.+Archaeological+Artifacts/879870/?lng=en (accessed 30 July 2018).

41. C. Kavin Rowe has argued for the need for narrative juxtaposition using empathetic conceptual imagination in order to bring Stoic and Christian traditions into dialogue, *One True Life: The Stoics and Early Christians as Rival Traditions* (New Haven & London: Yale University, 2016), 199–204. This Eco-Stoic Reading seeks to do so in ways that are respectful of each tradition's integrity and claim upon its adherents. By contrast with Rowe's project, however, the issue of rivalry between the traditions is not emphasized, as Nympha's perspective is located firmly within Pauline Christianity, but depicted as shaped by the narrative patterns of Stoic philosophy and practice.

CHAPTER 1

Stoic philosophy: The 'soil' in which the Gospel took root

As a young person, I asked the well-worn question why God sent Jesus into the ancient world without all of today's benefits of speedy travel and communication. The answer I got had to do with the Roman Empire: with its system of roads, the *Pax Romana* and the advantages of common languages (Koine Greek across the Empire and Latin for administration), it was the ideal time and environment for the spread of the Gospel. It was a good response and it satisfied me then, but it was only half of the answer. What I wasn't told then was that in the first century CE, there was also a very widely accepted popular (Koine) philosophy – a way that people saw the world and their place in it – and it was common to many people across the Mediterranean world and beyond. That philosophy was Stoicism.

Stoic philosophy was widely known and discussed in first-century Asia Minor. In fact, according to David Hahm, 'more people in the Mediterranean world would have held a more or less Stoic conception of the world than any other' from the third century BCE to the second century CE.[1] Hahm argues that in this period, Stoicism was very likely the most widely accepted world view in the Western world, and 'it appealed to all classes, attracting slaves and laborers as well as kings and emperors. Its ideals infiltrated religion and science, medicine and theology, poetry and drama, law and government.'[2] Unlike the later Neo-Platonism, which was within the purview of elite thinkers, Stoic ideas were generally known; they formed a sort of philosophical Koine or common understanding that crossed social and national boundaries.

This chapter is intended to introduce the reader to the popular Stoicism which served as this cultural Koine of the Roman Empire around the beginning of the Common Era.[3] I also intend to show how Stoic ethics, world view and cosmology could provide a cultural and spiritual soil that was at least as important for the rapid, successful transmission and reception of the Christian Gospel across the

---

1. David E. Hahm, *The Origins of Stoic Cosmology* (Columbus, OH: Ohio State University Press, 1977), xiii.

2. Hahm, *The Origins of Stoic Cosmology*, xiii.

3. The focus of this volume is on the popular Stoicism of the Roman period, and makes no claim to being a comprehensive overview of the development of Stoic ideas.

Roman Empire as were the logistical advantages of its roads, common languages and stable administration.

Stoicism's highest value – Virtue – is expressed most fully in a life that is in harmony with nature, being prepared for self-sacrifice, and prioritizing generosity of spirit. This Stoic world view was a perfect pre-evangelistic preparation for anyone hearing the Gospel of Jesus Christ for the first time, even without the benefit of an association with a Jewish synagogue. Such an unprecedentedly widespread, common world view among the people of the Roman Empire – and one which shares some important parallels with the early Christian proclamation – made possible a more successful, widespread uptake of the Gospel than could have happened at any other time in history. And we know that this opportunity was something which Paul and his co-workers were well qualified and determined to bring to fruition. We will examine this later by way of a case study; Luke's account of Paul and the philosophers in Acts 17.

First-century Stoic philosophy, with its ethic of a virtuous, altruistic life, and its understanding of the material world, offered a cultural scaffold which enabled people in remarkable numbers to comprehend and accept the Gospel of a Christ who could die for others, and rise again from the dead. Stoic thought, with its value of life lived in harmony with nature, offers something to our very different cultural situation today, namely a lens through which we might read the Letter to the Colossians ecologically.

Stoic philosophy: The 'soil' of an ecological reading

This ecological commentary is being written at a time when the consequences of our *disharmony with nature* are unfolding exponentially. Rainfall and weather patterns are changing, fire is ravaging regions in unprecedented ways, and ecosystems are collapsing. It is no longer possible to deny that human disharmony with nature has set these things in process. Our world is experiencing the consequences of economic and political opportunism, the outsourcing of the real costs of our decisions to other places or future generations, and apathy and inertia in addressing these issues. Learning to live in harmony with nature has never been more pressing than it is today.

The Christian faith can be a pathway of learning to live in harmony with nature, as we are learning to live in harmony with God. So often, however, we read the biblical sources of our faith in ways that assume that the natural world is peripheral to God's purposes. We also assume that the early Christians shared this attitude to the natural world and pinned all their hopes on a heaven that was disembodied and disconnected with reality as they knew it. Recovering the substratum of Stoic ideas can enable us to read our sources in ways that are closer to the original hearers, and in ways that recover the ecological perspective and potential of the Letter to the Colossians. Stoic philosophy, as refracted through this Letter to people who had placed their hope in Jesus Christ, can be the 'soil' of an ecological reading of Colossians.

In Colossians, we are exploring a letter written to people living in a philosophical environment where the highest value in life is Virtue – which, as noted earlier, is measured as a life lived in harmony with nature, being prepared for self-sacrifice, and prioritizing generosity of spirit. By contrast, we are reading this Letter in a world which has little time for Virtue, and which teaches us to be pragmatic about what we offer of ourselves to others, and what we expect in return. Even our Christian faith is viewed pragmatically, as an assurance of eternal blessedness, while the natural world around us disintegrates. Now more than ever, our world needs Christians who perceive our call as a call to Virtue, living our lives in harmony with nature and God, who are willing to relinquish some of our privileges and prioritize generosity of spirit.

To this end, the Letter to the Colossians can be a bridge between two worlds – our present-day world and the world which received this text. Stoic philosophical ideas can help us read this Letter with greater clarity, so that we can recognize the consequences of our dominant, present-day culture's poverty of spirit, and learn ways of living in harmony with nature and with God.

Thinking about philosophy

Philosophy literally means 'love of wisdom'. Philosophy encompassed a great deal more in the Greco-Roman world of the first century than it does today. If one entered a philosophical school or academy, one might expect to hear rigorous discussion and debate not only about logic and ethics but about physics as well.[4] 'Love of wisdom' in that era was not partitioned in the same way as university faculties are today. Philosophy sought to establish first principles, upon which sciences such as geometry and mathematics could proceed. Seneca put it this way: 'Now philosophy asks no favours from any other source; it builds everything on its own soil' (*Epistles* 88.28, LCL 76: 364–7). Logic, related as it is to *Logos*, or reason, was understood to be core to all philosophical and scientific endeavour, not so much as a field or component of a field, but as the means through which the world and all its parts could be explored rationally and consistently.

Philosophers debated what areas of discussion rightly belonged to the 'curriculum' of philosophy, and in what order. One early Stoic philosopher of the third century BCE, Cleanthes, claimed that it has six parts: dialectic, rhetoric, ethics, politics, physics and theology (quoted by Diogenes Laertius in his *Lives* 7.41, L&S 158). More common was a tripartite division into logic, ethics and physics, although even then, theology was understood to be an integral part or goal of these studies. Plutarch cites the Stoic philosopher Chrysippus who, after reviewing the different fields of study, calls theology 'the fulfilment'.[5]

---

4. For a well-informed and imaginative tour of philosophical establishments, see L&S 1–6.

5. Plutarch, *On Stoic self-contradictions* 1035 (*SVF* 2.42, part) in L&S 159. Plutarch is critical of Chrysippus, as he perceives a lack of consistency in following this order rigorously.

It is apparent that philosophy and theology were understood to be closely linked fields of study in the ancient world. Yet according to Col. 2.8, philosophy and theology are not necessarily seen as useful partners:

> See to it that no one takes you captive through philosophy and empty deceit, according to human tradition, according to the elemental spirits of the universe, and not according to Christ. (Col. 2.8 NRSV)

Is this a warning to avoid philosophy as a pursuit that is incompatible with Christ and that it is closely aligned with 'empty deceit'? I think not. It is more accurate to translate this passage as a warning against particular types of philosophy rather than as a blanket condemnation of philosophy itself:

> Be careful not to allow anyone to captivate you through an empty, deceitful philosophy that is according to human traditions and the elemental spirits of the world, and not according to Christ. (Col. 2.8 NET Bible)

In fact, the Letter to the Colossians is very positive about the 'love of wisdom' (= philosophy!):

> For this reason, since the day we heard it, we have not ceased praying for you and asking that you may be filled with the knowledge of God's will in all spiritual wisdom and understanding. (Col. 1.9)

> It is he whom we proclaim, warning everyone and teaching everyone in all wisdom, so that we may present everyone mature in Christ. (Col. 1.28)

> I want their hearts to be encouraged and united in love, so that they may have all the riches of assured understanding and have the knowledge of God's mystery, that is, Christ himself, in whom are hidden all the treasures of wisdom and knowledge. (Col. 2.2-3)

> Let the word of Christ dwell in you richly; teach and admonish one another in all wisdom. (Col. 3.16)

Wisdom is something worth striving for, and '*all* wisdom' continually indicates the breadth of this quest. It is only those things that have the *appearance* of wisdom, without true foundation, that are rejected in this Letter:

> All these regulations refer to things that perish with use; they are simply human commands and teachings. These have indeed an appearance of wisdom in promoting self-imposed piety, humility, and severe treatment of the body, but they are of no value in checking self-indulgence. (Col. 2.22-23)

From all these passages in the Letter itself, it is clear that the recipients were keenly interested in cultivating a love of wisdom and knowledge. Their interest was so keen that they seem to have been in danger of being misled by some traditions that the writer names as 'empty and deceitful' (Col. 2.8). One focus of this commentary is to identify and examine the strands of philosophical thought that the recipients of the Letter may have known and embraced, including those which the writer may ultimately have needed to refute.

The early believers in Christ in Asia Minor participated in and were shaped by their context. We are at a much greater cultural distance from the Letter's original recipients than they were from their pagan neighbours, whether or not we share their faith in Christ. If we explore their frames of reference, particularly how these could have shaped their ideas, it will help us to understand the Letter more accurately. Philosophy embraces such questions as how to understand existence, substance and perception, all of which form a basis for being able to embrace a crucified and risen Lord, who is 'the image of the invisible God' (Col. 1.15).

What do we know about Stoic philosophy?

Answering this question is not as easy as it was back in Paul and Timothy's day. Only a few of the writings of Stoic philosophy which existed in the first century CE – perhaps 1 per cent – have been preserved and passed on into the present. Some of what has been preserved is embedded in the writings of others who did not share the Stoics' views, and who wished to refute them. For this reason we rely on collections of sources. An important collection was made by the German philologist Hans Von Arnim (1859–1931), whose three-volume collection *Stoicorum Veterum Fragmenta*, (*SVF*) with a supplementary index in a fourth volume is still used. A newer two-volume collection with translations and philosophical commentary was published in 1987 by A. A. Long and D. N. Sedley.[6] Their first volume will be an important source for this commentary – cited as L&S with page number(s). Other ancient sources have been preserved more fully. Many of the references here will come from the Harvard Loeb Classical Library editions – cited as LCL with volume and page numbers.

For the purposes of this commentary, I will refer not only to Stoic sources which predate the writing of Colossians but also to Stoic writings up to and including those of the second century CE, on the understanding that there was indeed a Stoic approach which the second-century exponents also represent. On this basis, I include the writings of Epictetus and Marcus Aurelius as well as those of Paul and Timothy's contemporaries, Seneca and Musonius Rufus. Each of these writers helps us glimpse the coherence of Stoic ideas, while contributing their distinctive voices to the philosophical discourse. In choosing to include these writers, I am not claiming that the works of Seneca and Musonius Rufus were known directly by the believers at Colossae. Rather, I am saying that the ideas reflected in them

---

6. Anthony A. Long and David N. Sedley, *The Hellenistic Philosophers*, 2 vols. (Cambridge: Cambridge University Press, 1987).

were the sorts of ideas that were circulating in first-century Asia Minor, not only in educated circles but also among those who listened in to public discussions and performances.

The distinctive features of Stoic philosophy will become more apparent through the Stoic Reading Contexts set out in this commentary. But to offer an initial summary of these features, we may mention the following:

- The world is an organic whole, animated and directed by intelligence/reason (*Logos*). The cosmos is permeated by the *Logos*, which is variously described as the world's soul, commanding faculty and spirit/breath/*pneuma*.
- The world is through and through providential, providing humanity and all creatures with all that we need for a good life.
- God, the ultimate cause of all things, is known in nature, *physis*, and Stoics can speak of God and nature interchangeably. 'Since the world is the "substance" of god, and god is the "nature which sustains the world and makes things grow", physics, in the final analysis, is theology' (L&S 267).
- In reflecting on God, they used various names and concepts, from the Highest God of the Roman pantheon, Jupiter, or the Greek equivalent Zeus, to Fate, Providence and the Universe, and of course Nature:

  - The ancient sages did not even believe that Jupiter, the sort we worship in the Capitol and in other temples, sent lightning by his own hand. They recognized the same Jupiter we do, the controller and guardian of the universe, the mind and spirit of the world, the lord and artificer of this creation. Any name for him is suitable. You wish to call him Fate? You will not be wrong. It is he on whom all things depend, the cause of causes. You wish to call him Providence? You will still be right. It is by his planning that provision is made for this universe so that it may proceed without stumbling and fulfil its appropriate functions. You wish to call him Nature? You will not be mistaken. It is he from whom all things are naturally born, and we have life from his breath. You wish to call him the Universe? You will not be wrong. He himself is all that you see, infused throughout all his parts, sustaining both himself and his own. The Etruscans had the same concept, and so they said lightning was sent by Jupiter because nothing is done without him. (Seneca. *Natural Questions*, Volume I: Books 1-3, LCL 450: 172–3)
  - The term universe or cosmos is used by [the Stoics] in three senses: (1) of God himself, the individual being whose quality is derived from the whole of substance; he is indestructible and ingenerable, being the artificer of this orderly arrangement, who at stated periods of time absorbs into himself the whole of substance and again creates it from himself. (2) Again, they give the name of cosmos to the orderly arrangement of the heavenly bodies in itself as such; and (3) in the third place to that whole of which these two are parts. Again, the cosmos is defined as the individual being qualifying the whole of substance, or, in the words of Posidonius in his elementary

treatise on Celestial Phenomena, a system made up of heaven and earth and the natures in them, or, again, as a system constituted by gods and humans and all things created for their sake. By heaven is meant the extreme circumference or ring in which the deity has his seat. (Diogenes Laertius 'Zeno' LCL 185: 240–3 modified)

- The true goal of humanity is an active life in harmony with nature. It follows that cultivating harmony with Nature/God gives peace of mind:
    - Zeno represented [this goal] as: 'living in agreement'. This is living in accordance with one concordant reason, since those who live in conflict are unhappy. His successors expressed this in a more expanded form, 'living in agreement with nature'. (Stobaeus 2.75.11–76.8, L&S 394)
    - Again, living virtuously is equivalent to living in accordance with experience of the actual course of nature, as Chrysippus says in the first book of his *De finibus*; for our individual natures are parts of the nature of the whole universe. And this is why the end may be defined as life in accordance with nature, or, in other words, in accordance with our own human nature as well as that of the universe, a life in which we refrain from every action forbidden by the law common to all things, that is to say, the right reason which pervades all things, and is identical with this Zeus, lord and ruler of all that is. And this very thing constitutes the virtue of the happy person and the smooth current of life, when all actions promote the harmony of the spirit dwelling in the individual with the will of the One who orders the universe. (Diogenes Laertius 'Zeno' LCL 185: 194–7 modified)
    - Marcus Aurelius put it very poetically: 'All that is in tune with thee, O Universe, is in tune with me! Nothing that is in due time for thee is too early or too late for me! All that thy seasons bring, O Nature, is fruit for me! All things come from thee, subsist in thee, go back to thee' (*Meditations*, 4.23. LCL 58: 80–1).

- Stoics believed that human beings have a natural capacity to perceive the world accurately and discriminate accurately about their sense perceptions. (Other philosophical schools, particularly the Sceptics, were not confident about this.)
- Stoics reject dualism (body/spirit); they reject Plato's theory of ideas, which thinks of reality as we experience it as a shadow of the true heavenly reality. The key difference between Platonic and Stoic cosmology is that Stoic cosmology sees the spirit – the divine – *permeating* all reality; a contrast with Platonic thought, which sees the divine at a *distance* from this world. To use our modern theological terms, the Stoics emphasized the immanence of God.
- Stoic logic deduced that for something to exist it must be capable of producing or experiencing some change, and that this condition is only met by bodies/matter, as only corporeal realities can affect other corporeal things. Therefore, for them, nature (and God) are necessarily embodied. The type of

embodiment is similar to the spiritual/pneumatic bodies of which Paul writes in 1 Cor. 15.44-54, contrasting them with the fleshly bodies.

- Many (though not all) Stoics believed that there was a cycle of ages, each of which ended in a conflagration. At that time God (Zeus) withdrew into himself, and created the universe afresh.
- Stoics believed that one needed to undergo a profound change from a self-interested, prudential world view to a virtuous, altruistic life in which one prioritized the good of all. This change they viewed as being brought about by *Logos*.

  – Seneca, (a Stoic), described Stoics this way: 'No school is more kindly and gentle, none more full of love to [human beings] and more concerned for the common good, so that it is its avowed object to be of service and assistance, and to regard not merely self-interest, but the interest of each and all' (Seneca, *On Mercy* 2.5. LCL 214: 438–9).

  – One person, who has done another a kindness, is ready also to reckon on a return. A second person is not ready to do this, but yet inwardly ranks the other as a debtor, and is conscious of what has been done. But a third is in a manner not conscious of it, but is like the vine that has borne a cluster of grapes, and when it has once borne its due fruit looks for no reward beyond, as it is with a steed when it has run its course, a hound when it has singled out the trail, a bee when she has made her honeycomb. And so a person who has done one thing well, does not cry it abroad, but progresses to a second good deed, as a vine to bear afresh her clusters in due season. (Marcus Aurelius, *Meditations*, 5.6. LCL 58: 102–5, modified)

- Stoics excelled at ethical reflection, and trained their followers in the wisdom that led to a Good Life. Particularly by the first century CE, they were known for their training in virtue.

  – Am I not wholly intent upon God, and His commands and ordinances? If you have these thoughts always at hand and go over them again and again in your own mind, and keep them in readiness, you will never need a person to console you, or strengthen you (Epictetus, *Discourses*, 3.24.114–15. LCL 218: 220–1).

  – Let us go to our sleep with joy and gladness; let us say: 'I have lived; the course which Fortune set for me is finished.' And if God is pleased to add another day, we should welcome it with glad hearts. That person is happiest, and is securely self-possessed, who can await the morrow without apprehension. When somebody has said: 'I have lived!', every morning that person arises is a bonus. (Seneca, *Letters* 12.9. LCL 75: 70–1, modified)

- Stoic ethics emphasized that some things are under our control, but other things are not. This distinction was crucial because we can be in charge of all those things that are under our control; all the things outside our control do not ultimately define us.

- Some things are under our control, while others are not under our control. Under our control are conception [the way we define things], choice [the voluntary impulse to act], desire [to get something], aversion [the desire to avoid something], and, in a word, everything that is our own doing; not under our control are our body, our property, reputation, office [or position] in society, and, in a word, everything that is not our own doing. (Epictetus, *Ench.* 1.1 LCL 218: 482–3)

- The criterion of happiness and a good life is virtue. While we naturally prefer some states to others – health rather than illness, comfort rather than poverty – these preferences are not essential to a happy life. They are in fact *adiaphora* (indifferent).

  - Chrysippus well says, 'As long as the consequences are not clear to me, I cleave ever to what is better adapted to secure those things that are in accordance with nature; for God has created me with the faculty of choosing things. But if I really knew that it was ordained for me to be ill at this present moment, I would even seek illness; for the foot also, if it had a mind, would seek to be covered with mud.' (Epictetus, *Discourses* 2.6.1. LCL 131: 242–3, modified)
  - If it has to do with some one of the things not under our control, have ready to hand the answer, 'It is nothing to me' (Epictetus *Ench.* 1.5, LCL 218: 484–5).
  - Do not seek to have everything that happens happen as you wish, but wish for everything to happen as it actually does happen, and your life will be serene (Epictetus *Ench.* 8, LCL 218: 490–1).
  - Not what you endure but how you endure, is important (Seneca, *On Providence* 2.4, LCL 214: 8–9).
  - Forget not in future, when anything would lead thee to feel hurt, to take thy stand upon this axiom: This is no misfortune, but to bear it nobly is good fortune (Marcus Aurelius. *Meditations* 4.49, LCL 58: 96–7).

We can see from this initial overview that Stoic thought resonated with many aspects of the Gospel of Jesus Christ: the world as providential, virtue as central, suffering as not ultimately affecting one's true self. The Stoic Reading Contexts at the beginning of each chapter will expand this introduction to Stoic thought, and offer a conceptual context for the section of the Letter to the Colossians that follows.

Stoics and Epicureans

Stoic philosophy was prominent in first-century Athens, which continued to be an important centre of philosophical study and debate. If we turn to Luke's account of Paul's visit to Athens in Acts 17.15-34, we find that Paul encountered both

Epicurean and Stoic philosophers there (Acts 17.18); philosophers representing other schools would have been there too, but are not explicitly mentioned. In Luke's account of Paul's visit to Athens, the Epicureans and Stoics are Paul's audience and debating partners.

Stoic and Epicurean philosophy developed in opposition to one another.[7] Epicurus and his school are known for their emphasis on pleasure as the greatest good and pain as the greatest evil, whereas the Stoics saw neither pleasure nor avoidance of pain, though preferable, as the ultimate end or motivator of human life. All philosophical schools reflected on what happiness is and how we achieve it. Happiness for Stoics was achieved by living in accordance with nature, and by cultivating and practicing virtue:

> They [the Stoics] say that being happy is the end, for the sake of which everything is done, but which is not itself done for the sake of anything. This consists in living in accordance with virtue, in living in agreement, or, what is the same, in living in accordance with nature. Zeno defined happiness in this way: 'Happiness is a good flow of life.' (Stobaeus 2.77, 16-27 (*SVF* 3.16) L&S 394)

For Epicurus, there was no overarching and benevolent purpose to existence or nature. He and his followers, whom he called friends, did not deny the existence of the gods, but held that they are not involved in human affairs and do not desire our worship:

> Now to say that they [the gods] conceived the wish to create a world wonderful in nature for the sake of [humans], and that for that reason the gods' work is praiseworthy, so that it is proper for us to sing its praises and consider that it will be everlasting and imperishable, and that it is wrong that what was built by an ancient plan of the gods for the sake of humankind, in perpetuity, should ever be disturbed from its foundations by any force, or assailed with words and turned upside down – to elaborate such a fiction, Memmius, is folly. For what profit could imperishable and blessed beings gain from our gratitude, to induce them to take on any task for our sake? (Lucretius 5.156–234, L&S 59 modified)[8]

For Epicurus and his friends, the study of philosophy was to eliminate pointless fears, particularly of death and of the gods, and to live tranquilly. They avoided political engagement and embraced a quiet life.

---

7. L&S 5.

8. We rely on Lucretius here (see also his *On the Nature of Things*, LCL 181), as most of Epicurus' own works are lost. The fullest account of Epicurus, including quotations from his works, is found in Diogenes Laertius' *Lives of Eminent Philosophers Volume 2*, LCL 185. For a fuller discussion of Epicurean and Stoic views in relation to Paul in Athens, see Craig S. Keener, *Acts: An Exegetical Commentary*, Vol. 3 (Grand Rapids, MI: Baker Academic, 2014), 2580–95.

When we consider Paul's interaction with the highly intellectual and devout community of philosophers in Acts 17.15-34, we find him addressing himself primarily to the Stoics. The Epicureans were not the ones who would have constructed or valued the altar to an unknown god, nor were they likely to be persuaded in terms other than purely physical ones. Instead, Paul addresses the people with phrases that would connect with a Stoic philosophical framework: 'For "In him we live and move and have our being"; as even some of your own poets have said, "For we too are his offspring"' (Act 17.28). Paul is shown to use phrases from the Greek poetic tradition, probably echoing the sixth-century BCE poet Epimenides, but in doing so, he is evoking Stoic philosophical ideas best known to us through the (later) work of the Stoic emperor Marcus Aurelius:

> Constantly regard the universe as one living being, having one substance and one soul; and observe how all things have reference to one perception, the perception of this one living being; and how all things act with one movement; and how all things are the co-operating causes of all things which exist; observe too the continuous spinning of the thread and the contexture of the web. (Meditations 4.40)[9]

Of course Paul (and Luke) did not know this particular articulation of Stoic ideas, but we can see that the choice of the phrase 'In him we live and move and have our being' is an apt one for interesting a Stoic audience.

Paul then goes on to quote from the poem *Phaenomena* by a Greek poet Aratus (*c.* 310–245 BCE): 'For we also are his offspring' (LCL 129: 206–7). Here, too, this phrase is well chosen as a Stoic 'teaser'. Aratus was an early Stoic, and his poem articulated Stoic views of divine providence. So Luke makes it clear that the Stoics were Paul's dialogue partners in Acts 17, and the ones he hoped to persuade.

Why would the Stoics be more open to listen to Paul and Timothy's Good News?

It is the contention of this commentary, and the contention of others working on Pauline and Stoic thought, that there are significant parallels between the two modes of thought – not just at the level of individual words or ideas, but at a deeper level. The premise of my approach is that Stoic concepts and values were widely spread in the Roman Empire in the first century, and formed a pre-evangelistic conceptual framework that enabled the Gospel to be comprehended and embraced by people, even by those who had little or no contact with Jewish traditions. Just as today we can see certain books and stories (like those of C. S. Lewis and J. R. R. Tolkien) as pre-evangelistic, setting out ideas that connect the

---

9. Marcus Aurelius, *The Meditations of Marcus Aurelius*, trans. George Long (London: Blackie & Son Ltd., 1910), 44. This translation is clearer than that in LCL 58: 90–1.

Gospel with contemporary culture, Stoic ideas and practices offered many points of connection with the Gospel. Stoic ideas and practices, in particular, made it possible for people with a pagan and polytheistic background to grasp the Gospel of a Saviour who suffers and dies for the sake of those in need and who embodies wisdom for those who are prepared to follow him.

There is a growing interest in Stoic thought among New Testament scholars, particularly among those who study Paul, because Stoic concepts can at times help us to understand aspects of Paul's thought and teaching which are otherwise opaque. Some interpreters of Paul want to read him simply in terms of his Jewish (or Hellenized Jewish) heritage, but others are investigating how the Greco-Roman context of his apostolic labours added to his thought and manner of expression. One particular scholar who has been studying this deeper connection between Stoic philosophy and Paul's thought is Troels Engberg-Pedersen.

Troels Engberg-Pedersen on the Stoic substructure of Paul's thought

In his first book on the topic, *Paul and the Stoics*,[10] Engberg-Pedersen argues that the foundational structure of Stoic ethics is directly comparable with Paul's concept of conversion and the Christian life. Both Paul and the Stoics share a belief that the goal of human life is to be reached only through a conversion; through a crucial event or decision to move from an individual, self-focussed, limited state of being to a state of being in which one is free to live a virtuous, altruistic, good life. Both systems recognize the reality (articulated earlier by Aristotle) that a fundamental weakness of will prevents us from living fully virtuous lives, and both recognize that a fundamental change must take place so that we may live in a way fully in keeping with the ultimate Good.

The crucial event or decision of course is different – for Paul, it is a conversion to Christ and finding in Christ the freedom to live for the common good. For the Stoics, it is the decision to live according to *Logos* or Reason – called *homologia* – and so move from a way of life characterized by egoism to a way of life that is devoted to the common good through the love and practice of wisdom. Different though they be, both pathways are focused on 'the phenomenon of conversion conceptualized as a story'.[11] Both systems involve a profound shift in what a person values. Both see this conversion as a change of identity.[12] Both see it as a move from babyhood to adulthood,[13] and envisage the formation of an ideal community where all socially based distinctions between people are abolished.[14]

---

10. Troels Engberg-Pedersen, *Paul and the Stoics: An Essay in Interpretation* (Edinburgh: T & T Clark, 2000).

11. Engberg-Pedersen, *Paul and the Stoics*, 36.

12. Engberg-Pedersen, *Paul and the Stoics*, 65.

13. Engberg-Pedersen, *Paul and the Stoics*, 62.

14. Engberg-Pedersen, *Paul and the Stoics*, 78–9.

Is this so very different from other philosophical or religious systems? Engberg-Pedersen's implicit answer is yes. Within the scope of this first book, he does not set this out in detail, except in relation to the contrasts with Aristotle. But he does demonstrate that the Stoics and Paul share a framework of discontinuity – change must begin by embracing a radically different perspective. As one eminent reviewer of Engberg-Pedersen's book puts it, 'such thinking is so close in structure to Stoicism and so alien to the traditions of Judaism and ancient Mediterranean culture more generally, that a genetic connection seems likely'.[15]

Not everyone is convinced that Engberg-Pedersen's model demonstrates a specific connection between Stoic and Pauline ethics, however. Kathy Gaca, a classicist, thinks that this model outlines the dynamics of conversion and group identity more generally, and might describe various groups – Stoics and Pauline Christians, but also Epicureans, Isis-worshippers or others. For her, Engberg-Pedersen did not sufficiently rule out other contenders who fit the model in antiquity and could have been Paul's sources, such as the Epicureans and mystery religions.[16]

Engberg-Pedersen responds to this criticism by stating that it is the conjunction of five distinctive features that demonstrates a distinctive Stoic connection.[17] Each of the features specifies an aspect of change:

1. a change in 'self-identification';
2. a change that is radical and complete and goes from seeing oneself in a way that is essentially tied to the self as individual to seeing oneself in a radically different way as belonging to some overarching entity outside oneself (Reason, that is, God);
3. a change that is thoroughly cognitive;
4. a change that results in behaviour on the part of the converted person that is always and only morally good;
5. a change that generates a group of people – those who have all undergone the change.[18]

---

15. Stanley K. Stowers, 'Review of Troels Engberg-Pedersen, *Paul and the Stoics*', RBL. Available online: http://www.bookreviews.org (2002) (accessed 18 May 2018).

16. Kathy L. Gaca, 'Review of Troels Engberg-Pedersen, *Paul and the Stoics*', RBL. Available online: http://www.bookreviews.org (2002) (accessed 18 May 2018).

17. Troels Engberg-Pedersen, 'Response to Reviews of Troels Engberg-Pedersen, *Paul and the Stoics*', RBL (2002). Available online: http://www.bookreviews.org (2002) (accessed 18 May 2018).

18. This encapsulates the Stoic theory of *oikeiōsis* (a technical term, signifying a change in perception from viewing something as foreign to viewing something as affiliated or kin, and variously translated as 'appropriation', 'orientation', 'familiarization', 'affinity', 'affiliation' and 'endearment'. Engberg-Pedersen has written a monograph on this aspect of Stoic philosophy: Troels Engberg-Pedersen, *The Stoic Theory of Oikeiosis: Moral Development and Social Interaction in Early Stoic Philosophy*, Studies in Hellenistic Civilization 2 (Aarhus: Aarhus University Press, 1990).

It is true that other groups in the ancient world had some of these features, but radical exclusivity was not a feature of Isis worship or other mystery cults. The structure of Epicurean group identity did have some of these features too, but the fourth, with its focus on the morally good, was not their foundational tenet. They placed the greatest good – the surest way to happiness and pleasure – in prudence: 'Of all this the beginning and the greatest good is prudence. Therefore prudence is even more precious than philosophy, and it is the natural source of all the remaining virtues' (Epicurus, *Letter to Menoeceus* 132. L&S 114). The prudential life was not one of discontinuity, but of increasing consistency, and this does distinguish it from the model set out above.

It is important to recognize that Engberg-Pedersen is not advocating interpreting Paul simply as a Stoic, overlooking the theological priority of Christ grasped in continuity (and at times discontinuity) with his Jewish heritage. He recognizes that there are interlocking aspects of Paul's identity:

> Paul was an apostle of Christ (as he insists) and a fortiori a Christ-believer (and fervently so). Paul was also an apocalypticist (as he would himself have been most willing to accept had he known the word). And Paul was a Jew (and proud to be so). Paul was also a Greco-Roman (though not so proud of being so). And Paul was a 'Stoic'. That last thing, however, he would probably have been loath to admit.[19]

Just how deeply Paul was influenced by Stoicism – whether superficially or profoundly – continues to be a topic for debate. Engberg-Pedersen has followed up his study of the shared ethics of Paul and the Stoics with a more recent study called *Cosmology & Self in the Apostle Paul: The Material Spirit.*[20] Here he turns to questions of cosmology, with a particular focus on the material, bodily understanding of 'spirit' both in Stoicism and Paul. In this book he sets out to see 'all the different ways in which bodiliness is an intrinsic part of everything Paul says on the *other* side of the fleshly body, that is, in Christ-believers who, like Paul himself, had precisely left behind the world of the fleshly body'.[21] His entry point is Paul's concept of the resurrection body as a 'pneumatic' (or spiritual) body (in contrast to a fleshly body) in 1 Corinthians 15. Engberg-Pedersen argues that Paul thought about the spirit as a material, bodily phenomenon – in close parallel to Stoic thinkers. While this may be a strange idea indeed to us, who are shaped by the non-materialist, dualistic categories of Neo-Platonism, it is worth asking the question: What did Paul mean when he wrote about bodies – fleshly, spiritual and corporate? What if for most of Paul's contemporaries, disembodied bodies were

19. Engberg-Pedersen, 'Response to Reviews of Troels Engberg-Pedersen, *Paul and the Stoics*', *RBL* (2002).
20. Troels Engberg-Pedersen, *Cosmology & Self in the Apostle Paul: The Material Spirit* (Oxford: Oxford University Press, 2010).
21. Engberg-Pedersen, *Cosmology & Self*, 3.

just a contradiction in terms? These cosmological (and ontological) questions will be important for our study of Colossians.

We will conclude our introduction to Stoic philosophy by considering two texts that give us insight into the place of philosophy in the first century CE as education and as entertainment: *Chion of Heraclea* and Dio Chrysostom's Tarsic Discourse 1.

Philosophy as ancient education: An example

One way of connecting with philosophy in Paul's day was to travel to its famous centre, Athens, and join a philosophical school there.

There is an ancient novel called *Chion of Heraclea*,[22] written as a series of letters set further back in the days of Socrates and his students Plato and Xenophon (late fifth and early fourth centuries BCE). *Chion* was probably written towards the end of the first century CE. This novel gives us a glimpse of what people thought about philosophy around the time that Acts 17 was written – the account of Paul and the philosophers on the Areopagus in Athens.

A young man, Chion, has set off from his home on the Black Sea coast of Asia Minor, and he writes letters back, mostly to his parents, who have encouraged him to go to acquire 'virtue' by studying philosophy. Chion had worried that this study would make him a less active and useful person, but he discovers the opposite. In his third letter to his parents he writes:

> 3.5 It will interest you to hear that I am now much more eager to sail to Athens and study philosophy. You will certainly recall that often when you exhorted me to philosophic studies, telling me in an admirable way about those who had devoted themselves to each branch of philosophy, you found that I agreed with you in most respects, but that on one point I was full of fear. For it seemed to me that philosophy made people more serious in other matters upon which it touched (in fact I thought that they drew soundness of mind and justice from no other source than philosophy), but highly enfeebled their power of action and made them timorous and meek. Inactivity and tranquility were, as you used to say, the subject of admirable eulogies by philosophers.[23]

> 3.6 It appeared to me deterrent that, even if by the study of philosophy I were to develop into a better man, I should not be able to become a brave man, a soldier, or a hero, if need be, but should renounce all that, bewitched by philosophy as by an enchanting song that made me forget every splendid deed. For I did not know that even when it comes to bravery, philosophers are better off, but I have only just learnt that from Xenophon, not only when he spoke to me about it, but

22. Chion, *Chion of Heraclea: A Novel in Letters*, translated and edited by Ingemar Düring (1951; repr., New York: Arno Press, 1979 modified).

23. Chion, *Chion of Heraclea*, 48–51.

because he showed in action what qualities he possessed. For although he spent considerable time on discussions with Socrates, he is capable of rescuing armies and cities. In no respect did philosophy make him of less use to himself or his friends.[24]

Chion spends five years in Athens, and intends to stay another five. But when he hears that his home is in the grip of a tyrant, Clearchus, he sets off to free them. In the thirteenth letter, he writes to his father Matris: 'I cannot stay living in freedom as long as my own city is under a tyrant. As to myself, my mind has not changed. Living or dying I shall remain good.'[25]

Philosophy has been an educational pathway for Chion to become a principled, decisive man of action. And it has shaped his ideas of freedom as well, as we read in his fourteenth letter, also addressed to Matris:

14.3 However, I regard as slavery that which subdues the soul together with the body, whereas, in my opinion, a subjection of the body that does not imply a subjection of the soul is no slavery. For if slavery involves evil, this evil affects the soul, or else it ought not to be called evil, since only to those who are not freemen is fear of suffering and sense of pain after having suffered the worst that can happen. How so? Can anybody be a slave who does not fear future and is not vexed by present evil? How can he be called a slave, not being affected by the evils of slavery?[26]

Chion is articulating characteristic Stoic ideas about suffering: we are only really slaves if our attitudes to suffering, evil or the future are fearful. If our soul, our inner disposition, is not intimidated by circumstances, then we are essentially free, whatever our condition. Chion's philosophy has shaped his attitude to freedom:

14.4 You must understand that, under the influence of philosophy, I have become such as not to be ever made a slave by Clearchus, even if he fetters me or whatever evil he makes me suffer. For he shall never subjugate my soul which determines freedom or slavery, since the body is always subject to the changes of fortune even though it be not subordinated to a tyrant. And if he kills me, he will grant me freedom in its highest form. For if the body cannot reconcile the soul with its slavery as long as they are united, do you really think that the soul will lack independence when separated from the body? No, not only am I free whatever I suffer, but Clearchus will remain a [slave], whatever he inflicts upon me, for he will act from fear, and fear is incompatible with freedom of the soul.[27]

24. Chion, *Chion of Heraclea*, 50–1.
25. Chion, *Chion of Heraclea*, 64–5.
26. Chion, *Chion of Heraclea*, 66–9.
27. Chion, *Chion of Heraclea*, 68–9.

Chion writes his sixteenth letter to the tyrant Clearchus, lulling his opponent into a false sense of security that a philosopher can have no political aspirations. But along the way we glimpse how Chion assumes – and expects his opponent to share the view – that the practice of philosophy helped you draw closer to the divine:

16.6 Since, on one hand, I had a good aptitude for the study of philosophy, and on the other hand I was not easy to convince in such matters [as politics,] I spent this time acquiring knowledge about God, who surveys all things, and about the state of the world, contemplating the principles of nature, learning to honour justice and what else philosophy teaches. And nothing is more worthwhile not only to know but also to investigate. For, to one who is of godlike nature and thus has a share in divine providence, what can be more beautiful than to devote one's leisure solely to one's immortal self and try to bring that part of oneself into closer contact with that which is akin? (For I hold that the godlike is akin to the Divinity.) 7 This is what I longed for and endeavoured to learn, but as to politics (you will excuse my speaking frankly), I did not even consider it worthwhile to remember.[28]

Chion's final letter in the novel is to Plato, where he writes that he has made the decision to attempt to free his fellow citizens from tyranny through an attempt to kill Clearchus. The seventeenth letter shows that Chion knows he will probably die in the attempt: 'I know that I shall be killed, and my only prayer is that I shall not suffer death until I have done away with the tyrant.'[29] We may be uncomfortable with this ancient heroic act as an example of philosophy, but such an act of self-sacrifice was something that ancient readers had no difficulty in valuing. The final words of the novel – still addressed to Plato – are about Chion's sacrificial death on behalf of those he will rescue:

17.3 After my heroic deed it is good for me to leave this human world ere I share its enjoyments any more. What I may happen to perform will be held greater than what I shall suffer, and I myself will be honoured more by those to whom I have done good, if I purchase freedom for them at the price of my own death. For it appears as a greater profit to those who have a kindness done to them, if he who did it takes no share himself. Though faced with this presage of death, I am thus in good spirits. Farewell, Plato, and may you remain happy until your old age. I am sure that I now speak to you for the last time.[30]

Chion of Heraclea tells us that ancient philosophy was not only about ideas of how the world could be understood but, more particularly, about the type of life that sought the good of others and was prepared to die for this Good. It was also

28. Chion, *Chion of Heraclea*, 74–5.
29. Chion, *Chion of Heraclea*, 78–9.
30. Chion, *Chion of Heraclea*, 78–9.

engaged in knowledge about God, and seeking to live a life in keeping with divine providence. Suffering and death were the true philosopher's lot, as they had been for Socrates. Philosophers who laid down their lives mirrored Socrates, and even surpassed Plato, who in the last lines of the novel is wished a comfortable old age. In such a world, the Good News of Jesus of Nazareth – one who fully embodied wisdom and was prepared to die for the sake of all people – was a message that people could hear and receive.

Philosophy as ancient entertainment: An example

There were some young men like Chion who were wealthy enough to take up residence in a city such as Athens with a small group of staff and friends and live there for years without financial constraint. But what about simple townsfolk, merchants, farmers and others who did not have the means to apply themselves to years of philosophical study? Were they able to connect with and be influenced by philosophical ideas?

Some philosophers lived as something like travelling entertainers, delighting crowds with their speeches, often for payment. From another first-century figure in Asia Minor, Dion of Prusa (also known as Dio Chrysostom, the Golden-Tongued), we get an amusing description of the public's expectations of such philosophers. In his thirty-third discourse, Dio begins by challenging his audience as to what they are expecting of him, and then he goes on to say what he thinks their answer might be:

> Well then, let me state my own suspicions. You seem to me to have listened frequently to marvellous orators (*theiōn anthrōpōn* = 'divine' people), who claim to know all things, and regarding all things to be able to tell how they have been appointed and what their nature is, their repertoire including not only human beings and demigods, but gods, yes, and even the earth, the sky, the sea, the sun and moon and other stars – in fact the entire universe – and also the processes of corruption and generation and ten thousand other things. And then, methinks, they come to you and ask you what you want them to say and upon what topic – as Pindar put it, 'Ismenus or Melia of the golden distaff or noble Cadmus' and whatsoever you may deem suitable, the speaker starts from there and pours forth a steady and copious flood of speech, like some abundant river that has been dammed up within him. Then, as you listen, the thought of testing these several statements or of distrusting one of such learning seems to you to be shabby treatment and inopportune, nay, you are heedlessly elated by the power and the speed of the delivery and are very happy, as, without a pause for breath, the speaker strings together such a multitude of phrases, and you are affected very much as are those who gaze at horses running at a gallop—though not at all benefited by the experience, still you are full of admiration (Dio Chrysostom, *Discourses* 33. Tarsic Discourse 1. LCL 358: 276–9 modified).

Dio is laughing at himself; after all, his nickname was Chrysostom, the Golden-tongued; he must have been just the sort of speaker to sweep his audience along and have them begging for more. But he is also having a jibe at his audience who, in their enthusiasm for hearing about anything and everything, let themselves be taught about the most wide-ranging topics, including cosmology and theology, without testing what is being said. In this light-hearted way, Dio is challenging his listeners to recognize that they enjoy being swept along by a sparkling rhetorical performance, but are not necessarily any the wiser about deeper philosophical truths.

What we learn here from Dio is that philosophy was not just a serious undertaking for specialists but also an ancient form of entertainment. Epicurus wrote that 'in philosophy enjoyment keeps pace with knowledge. It is not learning followed by entertainment, but learning and entertainment at the same time' (*Vatican sayings* 27, L&S 156).

Communities gathered to enjoy the performance, and came away marvelling at the philosopher's skill, and feeling a bit 'wiser'! There were speakers known as sophists who were prepared to argue either for or against something, as required. Various philosophers wrote against such practices, but in doing so they were criticizing them for disregarding the criterion of truth, not for performing their oratory for audiences. We know from archaeological remains in Turkey that each town valued having an open-air theatre. The arrival of a philosopher offering a skilful performance was something that attracted a wide-ranging audience. So philosophy was not limited to the Areopagus, the prominent marble hill next to the Acropolis in Athens, nor was it tucked away in colonnaded porticoes in the other great cities of the empire, but it fed into the social and intellectual life of ordinary communities throughout Asia Minor.

Nympha's notes

Already as a small girl, I knew that my father and mother honoured the Most High God, arising before dawn to light candles that would welcome the first rays of the sun, and praying for illumination. I sensed the beauty of the Most High God too as I played in the garden. My parents loved Wisdom and would often visit nearby Laodicea to hear the orators and philosophers who visited our region. At times, these philosophers would accept an invitation to join us at our villa, and I would hear them discourse about all manner of things. I remember my father clapping his hands when one of them quoted Plato on the topic of public education. Not only should every young man be educated, Plato had said, but 'for females too my law will lay down the same regulations as for men, and training of an identical kind'.[31] My parents had no sons that lived, and delighted in raising me according to Wisdom.

---

31. Plato, *Laws* 7.804 C–E. LCL 192: 56–9.

Some of these visitors would focus on Socrates, Plato and Aristotle, but for us, it was the Stoics who spoke most clearly to our life on the land – Zeno, Cleanthes and Chrysippus, Panaetius and Posidonius, to name my favourites. I loved the riddles that they posed, and the way that they encouraged me to believe that the *Logos* was not just in themselves, but in me and in all things as well. I learned to see divine Wisdom all around me – in the sprouting of a seedling, in the passing of the seasons, even in the ending of a life.

I became the head of my household all too soon. My mother and father passed away within a year of each other, and I now oversee the whole textile production. It was one of my slaves who excels at knotting fine carpet who told me nearly four years ago of a teacher who had come to stay for some months at Colossae – teaching that in the East, Wisdom had been fully incarnate in the Sage named Christ Jesus; one who had given up his life to rescue us from the darkness and then risen with the sun. This teacher, Epaphras, I invited to visit us as my parents used to invite other teachers, and he taught us how the Most High God has been revealed in Christ Jesus, the Sage from the Judeans who bridged all divides, and who now reveals the mystery of the ages to Jews and Gentiles alike. Through the teaching of Epaphras, I could recognize the full measure of divine Wisdom embodied in Jesus Christ. My whole household turned from placating the elemental spirits to serving the Most High God, known to us in Christ Jesus. We have all been immersed in water, and we now assemble in Jesus' name and sing hymns to Wisdom incarnate.

A few months after Epaphras left our region to return to Rome and his fellow teachers, we starting receiving other visitors who are also Christ-followers. Some of them have been teaching us about other spiritual practices, in the manner of the Judeans. Some of my cooks are now refusing to prepare the foods we have traditionally eaten, claiming that to do so is to transgress Wisdom. Others are refraining from work altogether on certain days, so as not to transgress Christ. And others of my household are having visions, and are claiming to be Sages themselves.

When the earthquakes began in our region, we were mercifully spared any severe destruction, as we took refuge in the fields with the other creatures of Earth. But many Christ-believers began to question whether we were living pious enough lives. They began to seek out other rites and practices to ensure their safety. I am hoping that we will soon receive the teacher Archippus, who was sent from Rome to help us. He has been in our region for some time now, but he is much taken up in the cities, particularly Laodicea, where the earthquakes have done terrible damage in the past months.

I know that some things are within my control and others are not. As the Earth rumbles and quakes at times as though in pain, I wonder at her fierce majesty – and try to stay calm. It reminds me that suffering is not just the human lot, but something that every creature and even Earth herself shares. We need to find compassion for all things and relieve suffering in every way we can. The rumbling and the quaking are not a sign of divine wrath, as some say. Like the pangs of childbirth, something new is under way, reminding us to value every moment and to give thanks for life itself. I rise before dawn and praise the Most High God through Christ for each new day.

CHAPTER 2

Stoic reading context: Happiness, heaven and hope

Happiness – living in harmony with nature – was at the heart of the Stoic way of life. Zeno defined happiness as 'living in agreement' and as 'a good flow of life', and his successors expanded this definition to 'living in agreement with nature'.[1] There are many aspects of ancient Stoic philosophy that have a contemporary feel. In particular, we resonate with the Stoics' desire for the sort of happiness brought about by living in harmony with nature and so with God.

Eudaimonia – a Greek word for happiness favoured by Stoics – implies that living in harmony with nature and with God is a spiritual thing.[2] This sort of happiness was a deep equilibrium and contentment achieved through paying attention to the big providential picture rather than the immediate and changeable context. This was living according to Logos, universal reason. It meant shaping one's attitude to external circumstances by accepting them rather than pitting oneself against them and so being subject to them. Stoics held that for the wise person, external circumstances were *adiaphora* – of no significance – in the face of the beneficence of a providential universe. This sort of happiness did not deny the reality of suffering, but sought to reframe one's experience of it. Even in the face of misfortune, the wise person cultivated the attitude that the important thing is not the circumstance itself, but how we respond to it. So while misfortune was beyond human control, for the wise person, suffering itself was under the control of the will. Even natural disasters appeared to be evil only when viewed from a limited perspective. The shape of reality was cyclical, with each age ending finally in fire, but even then, the new age arose from the ashes.

The Jewish philosopher Philo, a contemporary of Jesus, described the freedom of this attitude in Stoic terms:

> The person who, out of a low and slavish mindset, sinks to low and slavish actions despite their own better judgment, makes him or herself a slave. By contrast, the

---

1. L&S 394.

2. *Daimonia* (Spirits) has a wide range of meaning in ancient Greek writings, much as 'spirituality' does today (LSJ 365). The prefix *eu* ('good') specifies that the spirits referred to are positive and distinguishes them from the English terms 'daemon' and 'demon', with their negative connotations.

ones who willingly embrace their current circumstances persevere voluntarily and patiently in the face of misfortune and do not regard anything pertaining to the human condition as extraordinary. Such people will conclude, after careful examination, that all divine things are honoured by an eternal order and by happiness (*eudaimonia*). By contrast [with divine things], all mortal things are driven about by the surges and rough waves of events towards unfair and uneven decline. The one who nobly endures such vicissitudes is both a philosopher and a free human being.[3]

Stoics thought of God – Zeus – as a creative, even artistic fire who embraced all things, and 'in' such a god, even misfortune was not ultimately evil. The other gods as they were known were ciphers for other parts of reality – parts of the whole – and so Stoics were not at odds with their pantheistic neighbours. Nevertheless, Stoics did not court favour with the gods, seeking good fortune. Instead, they sought to live in agreement with whatever happened, and by their attitude, to achieve a good flow of life. This was living according to nature, or universal law, guided by the authentic Logos (*orthos Logos*) and so by God.[4] God, nature, universal reason and universal law were so closely aligned as to be synonymous.[5]

The most vivid articulation of Stoic theology is the *Hymn to God* by Cleanthes, the second leader of the Stoic school of philosophy following on from its founder, Zeno of Citium. Cleanthes, from the same region as the city of Colossae, western Asia Minor, lived *c.* 330–230 BCE.

Hymn to God by Cleanthes[6]

(1) Most majestic of immortals, many-titled, ever omnipotent Zeus,
prime mover of nature, who with your law steer all things, hail to you.
For it is proper for any mortal to address you:
we are your offspring,
and alone of all mortal creatures which are alive and tread the earth
we bear a likeness to god.
Therefore I shall hymn you and sing forever of your might.
(2) All this cosmos, as it spins around the earth, obeys you, whichever way you
    lead,
and willingly submits to your sway.
Such is the double-edged fiery ever-living thunderbolt

---

3. Philo, 'Quod omnis probus liber sit' (Every Good Person Is Free) 1.24. Translation mine.

4. Diogenes Laertius 7.87-9, L&S 395.

5. For a discussion of Stoic theology, see Dirk Baltzly, 'Stoic Pantheism', *Sophia* 42/2 (2003): 3–33. With a personal, providential view of God, Stoic pantheism differed from other types of pantheism. Baltzly canvasses the concept of panentheism (p.4), but prefers to nuance pantheism to describe Stoic concepts.

6. L&S 326-7 (modified).

which you hold at the ready in your unvanquished hands.
For under its strokes all the works of nature are accomplished.
With it you direct the universal reason (*Logos*) which runs through all things
and intermingles with the lights of heaven both great and small … .
(3) No deed is done on earth, god, without your offices,
nor in the divine ethereal vault of heaven,
nor at sea, save what bad people do in their folly.
But you know how to make things crooked straight and to order things disorderly.
You love things unloved.
For you have so welded into one all things good and bad
that they all share in a single everlasting reason.
It is shunned and neglected by the bad among mortals,
the wretched, who ever yearn for the possession of goods
yet neither see nor hear god's universal law,
by obeying which they could lead a good life in partnership with intelligence.
Instead, devoid of intelligence, they rush into this evil or that,
some in their belligerent quest for fame,
others with an unbridled bent for acquisition,
others for leisure and the pleasurable acts of the body …
<But all that they achieve is evils,> despite travelling hither and thither in burning
    quest of the opposite.
(4) Bountiful Zeus of the dark clouds and gleaming thunderbolt,
protect humankind from its pitiful incompetence (*apeirosunē* = ignorance).
Scatter this from our soul, Father.
Let us achieve the power of judgement
by trusting in which you steer all things with justice,
so that by winning honour we may repay you with honour,
for ever singing of your works, as it befits mortals to do.
For neither humans nor gods have any greater privilege than this:
to sing for ever in righteousness of the universal law.

This is not a hymn to an impersonal deity, but one that addresses God as Father and affirms that we are God's children and bear God's likeness. This hymn not only affirms God's power, but also God's personal interest and involvement with all people and all things. Much of the vision of this hymn resonates today; 'we are your offspring, and alone of all mortal creatures which are alive and tread the earth we bear a likeness to God' is reminiscent of Ps. 8.5 (LXX 8.6): 'Yet you have made them a little lower than the divine beings, and crowned them with glory and honour.'

Cleanthes' hymn confidently affirms God's love even of the unlovely. It acknowledges that many mortals do not live according to reason – God's universal law – and so bring about their own evils through incompetence or ignorance.

This hymn calls on humans to attune themselves to God, to reject the quest for fame and an 'unbridled bent for acquisition', and to live according to reason, Logos. It sees this as within the reach of every person to decide to do so. No matter what our circumstances, the hymn implies that we can be in agreement with nature and so in control of our own happiness.

Heaven

Stoics had a view of God's indwelling and shaping of the universe that can best be described as 'biological'.[7] God acts on matter from within, not from outside. This is in contrast to Plato's model set out in *Timaeus*, according to which the demiurge (a celestial being distinct from the Most High God) acts from outside matter to create the cosmos, like an artisan creating an artefact. For Stoics, the divine artisan permeates matter through the universal Logos, enlivening and shaping the world from within, not according to an external paradigm. God's presence is deeply embedded within matter, though not identical with matter.[8]

For this reason, Stoics have a strong sense of divine immanence – the presence of God permeating all things – whereas other philosophical schools emphasized divine transcendence – God far above and beyond us. This influences how one thinks about heaven. For those who emphasize divine transcendence, heaven is at a distance and stands in contrast to the earth. Heaven and earth are two separate realms, with a gulf between them, and God is a far distant reality. For Stoics, however, heaven and earth are full of the divine presence, not as two separate realms, but as a universe infused with divine presence and guided by universal reason.

Stoics name the world's 'commanding-faculty', the divine Logos, as heaven. Diogenes Laertius states that this was how three of the foremost Stoic thinkers, Cleanthes, Chrysippus and Posidonius, spoke of the Logos that directs the world:

> The world is directed by intelligence and providence, since intelligence pervades every part of it, just like the soul in us. But it pervades some parts to a greater extent and others to a lesser degree ... Chrysippus in his *On providence* book 1 and Posidonius in his *On gods* say that the world's commanding-faculty is the heaven, and Cleanthes the sun. Yet Chrysippus in the same book has a rather different account – the purest part of the aether; this they say, as primary god, passes perceptibly as it were through the things in the air and through all animals and plants, and through the earth itself by way of tenor. (Diogenes Laertius 7.138–9 (including *SVF* 2.634) L&S 284).

Heaven is mentioned twice in Cleanthes' hymn, in vv. 2 and 3. In the first reference, universal reason runs through all things and intermingles with the lights of heaven.

7. Jean-Baptiste Gourinat, 'The Stoics on Matter and Prime Matter: "Corporealism" and the Imprint of Plato's *Timaeus*', in *God and Cosmos in Stoicism*, ed Ricardo Salles (Oxford: Oxford University Press, 2009), 46–70, 50.

8. For a comparison of Stoic concepts of matter and causation with those of Plato and Aristotle, see Gourinat, 'The Stoics on Matter and Prime Matter', 48–58.

Heaven is part of the universe and signifies the skies, with the heavenly bodies governed by the same Logos that we know on earth. In the second reference, the vault of heaven is described as divine and ethereal, yet it is juxtaposed with the realms of earth and sea, and God's presence is equally guiding all three realms.

In summary, when we read 'heaven' in a text influenced by Stoic thought, we need to think of it not as a separate realm, but as referring to the presence of the divine, the world's commanding faculty (or 'soul').

Hope

Hoping for a different set of circumstances, a different outcome or a different world runs contrary to a fundamental attitude of Stoicism, namely 'living in agreement'. Hope is, for the Stoic, a distraction from virtue. It is here that we find a significant difference between Stoic ideas and the Christian Gospel.

Stoic philosophy did not offer a means for breaking the hold that old ways of seeing and living have over a person, such as the Christian Gospel offers through the power of Christ. All rests with human decision or choice. There is no gift of grace or liberation instilling hope for something better. Despite the affirmation that God loves (even) the unloved, good and evil are fitted into an overall system – a closed system. In this vision there is no pathway to move from evil to good; no pathway to salvation. Cleanthes may entreat 'Bountiful Zeus of the dark clouds and gleaming thunderbolt' to instil within humans the power of judgement/knowledge, but there is no expectation of divine grace implied, enabling and prompting the profound change that is needed. The problem of evil, for Cleanthes and the other Stoic philosophers, was a problem of the weakness of human will. Human beings brought about their own suffering through their own folly and weakness, and they further failed as they experienced suffering by giving it attention. Here is a story of a Stoic philosopher, Posidonius, who through sheer force of will refuses to give pain his attention.

The Story of Posidonius and Pompey[9]

The Roman general Pompey[10] attended a lecture by the Stoic philosopher Posidonius before he set out on his campaigns. Posidonius sent him on his way with a quotation from Homer to 'ever fight bravely and to be superior to others'.[11] On his triumphant return in 62 BCE, Pompey once more visited Rhodes, where

9. Cicero, *Tusculan Disputations* 2.61, LCL 141: 214–17; Plutarch, *Pompey* 42, LCL 87: 224–5; Pliny the Elder, *Natural History* 7.112, LCL 352: 578–81.

10. Pompey is the Roman General who intervened in the conflict between the Hasmonean brothers Hyrcanus II and Aristobulus II, and who laid siege to and took Jerusalem in 63 BCE.

11. Strabo, *Geography* 11.1.6 (C.492), LCL 211: 186–9. This was the instruction given to Glaucus by his father Hippolochus when setting out for Troy – Homer, *Iliad* 6.208, LCL 170: 288–9.

he heard Posidonius, along with other orators, deliver a polemical display speech. He also paid a personal call on the old philosopher at home, leaving his lictors (bodyguards) outside as a mark of respect. Posidonius, even though he was laid low by a painful attack of arthritis, insisted on giving Pompey a lecture from his sickbed on the theme 'Only the honourable is good.' This long private lecture was punctuated by cries of agony, demonstrating the Stoic philosopher's refusal to admit pain as an evil.

The Stoic world view cultivated the ability to disengage with the reality of suffering. In identifying this attitude with God, there is a downplaying of compassionate engagement with the suffering of others. There is no hope for changing one's circumstances now, nor hope for a future that will be better than the present.[12] The overall framework may be proclaimed as beneficent, but the individual was not offered personal hope in this world, nor in a life beyond the grave.

In fact, Stoic philosophy canvassed the idea that there would be an everlasting recurrence of the world, so that everyone and everything will take place again. What we are and what we experience will be just the same in the world to come as it is now, even down to the smallest detail.[13] For those who longed for something better, this is a frightening doctrine! In the closed Stoic system, there was no such thing as hope for profound change, except in one's own attitude and allegiance to Logos. So in fact, rejecting hope or anything external was considered a virtue, which leads to happiness. Diogenes Laertius, quoting Cleanthes, put it this way:

> Virtue is a consistent character, choiceworthy for its own sake and not from fear or hope or anything external. Happiness consists in virtue since virtue is a soul which has been fashioned to achieve consistency in the whole of life.[14]

Hope – like fear, or anything 'external' – is, for the Stoic, a distraction from virtue.

Despite the many similarities between Stoic thought and the Gospel in theological and ethical areas, they differed profoundly with regard to hope. Hope

12. Recent scholarship is questioning whether it is right to go further and speak of 'cosmic pessimism', 'enslaving', 'tyrannical' and 'inexorable' fate, as earlier scholarship has done by way of characterizing the second and third centuries and explaining the attraction of the Christian Gospel. See N. Denzey Lewis, *Cosmology and Fate in Gnosticism and Graeco-Roman Antiquity: Under Pitiless Skies* (Leiden: Brill, 2013), 22.

13. Marcus Aurelius wrote: 'Always remember, then, these two things: one, that everything everlastingly is of the same kind and cyclically recurrent, and it makes no difference whether one should see the same things for a hundred years or for two hundred or for an infinite time. Two, that the longest-lived and the quickest to die have an equal loss. For it is the present alone of which one will be deprived, since this is the only thing that he has, and no one loses what he does not have.' *Meditations* 2.14. L&S 310.

14. Diogenes Laertius *Lives of Eminent Philosophers* 7.89 (*SVF* 3.39) L&S 377. *Lives* Book 7, Chapter 1, 'Zeno' 7.1.89; LCL 185: 196–7.

for a different and better future was a distraction for the Stoics, whereas for Paul and his associates, it was a quintessential expression of God's gracious purposes for all creation. It is perhaps not surprising, then, that hope features so prominently in the opening of the Letter, and is linked so closely to the true Logos – the Gospel.

Eco-Stoic commentary on Col. 1.1-8

Translation of Col. 1.1-8[15]

Paul, apostle of Christ Jesus by the will of God,
and Timothy the brother,
[2] To the saints and faithful brothers [and sisters] in Christ in Colossae:
Grace to you and peace from God our Father.
[3] We give thanks to the God and Father of our Lord Jesus Christ for you always as
we pray,
[4] having heard of your faith in Christ Jesus and of the love that you have for all the
saints.
[5] [This faith and this love] arise from the hope laid up for you in heaven, which
you have already heard about in the true Logos, the Gospel [6]that has come to
you.
Just as it is bearing fruit and growing in the whole world,
so it has been also bearing fruit among yourselves from the day you heard it and
came to know the grace of God in truth.
[7] In just this way you learned [the true Logos, the Gospel] from Epaphras, our
beloved fellow slave. [8]He is a faithful servant of Christ on our behalf, and he
has made clear to us your love in the Spirit.

The Letter opens with the formal naming of the senders as Paul and Timothy. Paul does not know the believers at Colossae personally (2.1), and there is no indication that Timothy does either. The personal connection is through Epaphras, who is strongly affirmed in 1.7 and again in 4.12. Chapter 4 is the context for more personal greetings and communication, and the letter bearer, Tychicus, is to fill the recipients in on 'all the news' (4.7).[16] Here at the opening, then, the formal identity of the senders is foremost, together with their source of authority – 'Christ Jesus, by the will of God'. The believers at Colossae are named as 'saints and faithful brothers [and sisters', which is implied in the Greek].[17] Their identity as saints is not based

---

15. The translations of Colossians from here on and throughout the commentary are mine. Text in square brackets indicates what is implied by the grammar or logic of the text, and is supplied to make the meaning clearer.

16. At times Paul sent Timothy in this capacity (1 Cor. 4.17; Phil. 2.19-23), but that has been to places where Timothy is already known (1 Thess. 3.2; 2 Cor. 1.19; Phil. 2.22).

17. The Greek word implies 'brothers and sisters' (see BDAG 18 s.v. *adelphos* 1, where substantial nonbiblical evidence is cited for the plural *adelphoi* meaning 'brothers and sisters').

on the writers' knowledge of their saintly behaviour, but on the conviction that those who have embraced the Gospel are set apart or sanctified by God. Their sanctity is by God's grace, and not by anything that they have done. This grace also makes them family to one another, which accounts for the use of the familial language of brothers and sisters in Christ, with the one Father (v.2).[18] As such, by God's grace they share an inheritance with all the saints (1.12).

The opening greeting also flags that the recipients are sanctified and faithful because they are 'in Christ' (v.2). The Letter will set out what being 'in Christ' means, challenging the recipients to see that the concomitant is also true: 'Christ [is] in you' (1.27). The Letter offers some rich reflections on the significance of being 'in Christ', often in categories that resonate with Stoic thought. Being 'in Christ' and having 'Christ in you' is reminiscent of the divine Logos permeating reality, but it specifies the divine Logos as known and experienced in and through Christ.

Verses 3-23 of ch. 1 can be viewed as an extended thanksgiving. Many of the features of thanksgiving found in the undisputed letters of Paul are spread out across these verses. These include thanks to God for the community and their faith,[19] their embrace of the Gospel[20] and their love,[21] the spread of the Gospel[22] and the eschatological horizon of judgement, from which the community will be preserved (Col. 1.22).[23] This extended thanksgiving is made up of only three sentences in the Greek (1.3-9, 9-20, 21-23), which contributes to the section's expansive, 'big-picture' view of the spread of the Gospel. Its lofty vision of the reality into which they have been transferred serves to lift their gaze from what they themselves can achieve, and refocus it on what God has been doing throughout the whole world (Col. 1.6).

Epaphras has presented the Colossians – and others in the region, both at Hierapolis and Laodicea – with Good News; with an invitation to *hope*, by placing their trust in Jesus Christ, the Anointed One, who has broken open the closed Stoic system of eternal repetition through his death and rising to new life. In the cults of Asia Minor, it was believed that priests or censors could open up a connection between the human world and the divine. Paul and Timothy expect that the new Christ-believers can, in a comparable way, conceptualize Jesus as anointed to bring God's word of grace, thus enabling a better future, beginning here and now. The injustice of a world in which some were born to power and privilege, and others to slavery, exploitation and misery was no longer simply *adiaphora* – of no significance. God's anointed One had joined all who were shamed, despised and tortured; in his sacrificial death and rising to new life, he introduced hope where there was none.

---

18. No other Pauline salutation uses 'brothers in Christ' in quite this way. 'Brothers' is often used as a form of address in the Pauline letters, but not 'brothers in Christ'. The theme of being 'in Christ' and hence being part of God's household will be discussed in Chapter 6.

19. Compare Rom. 1.8; 1 Thess. 1.3; Phlm. 6.

20. Compare 1 Thess. 1.5; Phil. 1.5; Gal. 1.6.

21. Compare Phlm. 5; 1 Thess. 1.3; Phil. 1.5.

22. Compare Rom. 1.8; 1 Thess. 1.7; Phlm. 5.

23. Compare 1 Cor. 1.8; Phil. 1.10-11; 1 Thess. 1.10.

The trajectory of hope

Stoics saw the universe as a providential and interconnected place indwelt by a loving, omnipresent God. The new believers in Christ did not reject this idea, but through the Gospel, it was now possible to envisage the divine presence as not simply perpetuating what is and giving strength to endure, but as intervening to bring about a better, more just and equitable future. The good news of the loving God intervening personally and corporeally in this world in the person of Jesus Christ engenders hope for a more just and loving future. Such hope is compatible with Stoic cosmology, though not with its cyclical deterministic eschatology.

To have hope is to express dissatisfaction with what is, and to cultivate the conviction that a better world is possible. Hope recognizes that goodness, virtue and happiness are not found in ourselves alone, but depend upon the one in whom we hope, namely God.

Paul and Timothy write that the hope that the Colossians have now embraced is securely 'laid up for [them] in heaven' (v.5). I suspect that the lens that we bring to understanding this phrase is a Platonic one, in which heaven is the realm of God, and earth is but a shadow of that separate transcendent realm. Hope then comes to signify participating in that realm after death, and so we assume that 'hope laid up in heaven' means hoping for something better in the afterlife.

Our 'default' understanding of the phrase would not have been the default understanding of those influenced by Stoic thought.

Stoic cosmology does not have a dualistic view of heaven and earth, with the two as separate realms – heaven as God's realm and earth as a separate shadow of that realm. How would those steeped in Stoic ideas understand 'hope laid up in heaven'?

As we have seen in Cleanthes' hymn, heaven, earth and sea are all part of the one reality permeated by the presence of God. The vault of heaven is described as divine and ethereal, yet it is juxtaposed with the realms of earth and sea, and God's presence is guiding all three realms through the universal Logos. For Colossian believers shaped by Stoic ideas, hope laid up in heaven means hope preserved and sustained in God, who permeates all reality. Heaven is then a metonym for God's presence. The believers' hope is not distant nor exclusively future, but present, enlivening and guiding them.

We will see this articulated again in Col. 3.3, where we read: 'For you have died, and your life is hidden with Christ in God.' The believers' life – and hope – is hidden with Christ in God, not simply in the future, but already, as they have already 'died' and they are already experiencing the divine life here and now. In this cosmology, there is no chasm between present and future, nor between heaven and earth. The divine presence permeates and connects all.

The 'hope laid up in heaven' (= in the God whose presence permeates all things) is bearing fruit and growing here and now, as it gives people access to hearing and comprehending the grace of God (v.6). By emphasizing hope, Paul and Timothy teach that suffering and death are not *adiaphora* – of no significance. These realities are neither cyclical nor eternal, but framed within the grace of God.

Hope is a useful entry point to see how the Gospel was heard against a Stoic background, which did not offer hope for a better life now or in the future. We know from an earlier letter of Paul, 1 Thess. 4.13, that having hope could and should make a profound difference to believers in the face of death:

> [3] But we do not want you to be uninformed, brothers and sisters, about those who have died, so that you may not grieve as others do who have no hope.

Hope is described further in Col. 1.23 and 27. In v. 23 it is 'the hope promised by the Good News that you heard'. Hope is closely associated with the Gospel, because it reveals that God is known in the person of Jesus Christ, whose death on the cross spelt release from the system (Col. 2.13-15). The imagery here is of release from imperial bondage, but release from the rulers and authorities evokes release from the spiritual as well as the political system.

God is at work not only creating and sustaining a beneficent universe but is also engaged in confronting injustice and bringing about a better world both for the greater human good, and for 'every creature under heaven' (1.23). For the purposes of this commentary, this is a very important claim, as it shows that both hope and the Good News are not just for humans, but for every creature under heaven. A fuller discussion of this will follow in the discussion of v. 23.

The content of this hope is then described in 1.27 as 'the hope of glory'. Glory is a key term in the Hebrew Bible and refers to the visible manifestation of God's presence. For example, in Psalm 29, God is hailed as the storm god (like in Cleanthes' hymn), whose glory (Heb. *kabod*) is manifest over the flood.[24] Isa. 6.3 proclaims that the whole earth is full of God's glory. This resonates with the Stoic concept of God's presence permeating all things. Nevertheless, glory is also an object of hope in Col. 1.27. God's presence is visible throughout the earth, yet in order for us to perceive and participate in that glory, something further needs to take place: the revealing of God's gracious purposes in and through the person of Jesus Christ. The hope of glory is a concise way of saying that we and all creatures can, through the Good News of Christ, participate in the very life of God, visibly and tangibly.

These three concepts (hope, Good News, glory) are connected together by vv. 5, 23 and 27 and mutually inform one another (see Figure 2.1).

At the centre of this is 'Christ in you' (Col. 1.27). This is the mystery that has been hidden but which has now been revealed to the saints (Col. 1.26). Against a Stoic background, which saw the universal Logos permeating reality, the Logos is here identified with the Gospel of Christ. The authors are articulating a Christological 'logic', Logos, which finds expression in these interrelated concepts.

This constellation of concepts is also found in Rom. 8.18-25. There we find a discussion of 'the *glory* about to be revealed to us' (Rom. 8.18). We also find

---

24. Norman C. Habel and Geraldine Avent, 'Rescuing Earth from a Storm God: Psalms 29 and 96–97', in *The Earth Story in the Psalms and the Prophets*, ed. Norman C. Habel (Sheffield: Sheffield Academic Press, 2001), 42–50.

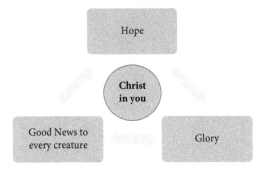

Figure 2.1 'Christ in you': Hope, Good News, Glory.

articulated there the '*hope* that the creation itself will be set free from its bondage to decay and will obtain the freedom of the *glory* of the children of God' (Rom. 8.20-21). In a similar way to Col. 1.27, Romans indicates that Paul conceptualizes the Good News as 'the revelation of the mystery that was kept secret for long ages' (Rom. 16.25), which Romans 8 articulates. And significantly, in Rom. 8.19-22, creation waits with eager longing, groaning to obtain the freedom of the glory of the children of God, while in Col. 1.23, this Gospel has been proclaimed 'to every creature under heaven'. 'Creation' and 'every creature' are metonyms, articulating that the Good News embraces the world not only of humans but also of all things. In both Romans 8 and Colossians 1, then, glory is God's visible and tangible presence, which, in and through Christ, God's children will share with every creature under heaven.

The ideas of salvation that are expressed in Rom. 8.18-25 (and are mirrored in Col. 1.5, 23 and 27) have often been seen as tangential to the Gospel, rather than an articulation of it.

> Like an island in a vast ocean, this passage [Rom. 8.19-25] and its focus on creation has mostly been viewed as an isolated phenomenon and hence tangential to the central narrative of salvation. By contrast, more recent scholarship has recognized this 'island' as connected with the deeper structures of Paul's thought.[25]

---

25. Vicky Balabanski, 'Pauline Letters: Paul's Vision of Cosmic Liberation and Renewal', in *The Oxford Handbook on Bible and Ecology* (forthcoming). See also Richard B. Hays, *The Faith of Jesus Christ: The Narrative Substructure of Galatians 3:1–4:11*, 2nd edn. (Grand Rapids, MI: Eerdmans, 2002), 33–117; Edward Adams, 'Paul's Story of God and Creation: The Story of How God Fulfils His Purposes in Creation', in *Narrative Dynamics in Paul: A Critical Assessment*, ed. Bruce W. Longenecker (Louisville, KY: Westminster/John Knox Press, 2002), 19–43; Sigve K. Tonstad, 'Creation Groaning in Labor Pains', in *Exploring Ecological Hermeneutics*, ed. Norman C. Habel and Peter Trudinger (Atlanta, GA: Society of Biblical Literature, 2008), 141–9.

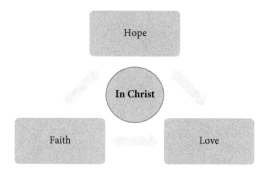

Figure 2.2 Pauline triad of faith, hope and love.

Hope for all creation is a bigger, more integral concept in Pauline thought than is generally recognized. It is closely connected with the mystery of the Good News, its deeper substratum, and with glory, God's presence and our participation in it. The Good News, hope and glory derive their content and contours from Christ and Christ's presence 'in us'.

There is another more obvious Pauline triad in these opening verses (Col. 1.4-5): faith, hope and love (Figure 2.2).

Here in Col. 1.4-5 we glimpse the familiar Pauline triad of faith, hope and love, known to us in 1 Thess. 1.3, 5.8; Gal. 5.5-6; 1 Cor. 13.13; Rom. 5.1-5 (see also Eph. 4.2-5). Again, we can see that the source of these three is Christ, or more specifically being 'in Christ' (Col. 1.4). There are also many instances where two of the three are linked in Pauline writings.[26] This combination of faith with hope and love is much less frequent outside the Pauline writings, though we may note some similarities in Heb. 6.10-12; 10.22-24 and 1 Pet. 1.3-8, 21-22.[27] Scholars have speculated that this is a pre-Pauline Christian triad,[28] but given the Pauline influence in the Petrine tradition (2 Pet. 3.15), and the probable post-Pauline date of Hebrews,[29] this is hard to substantiate. It seems to have the 'thumb-prints' of Paul, Timothy and their co-workers.

The triad is often understood ethically or missionally as a means of exhorting a community to practise these qualities, and it certainly lends itself to this

26. Faith and love: 1 Cor. 13.2, 13; 2 Cor. 8.7; Gal. 5.6; Eph. 1.15; 3.17; 6.23; 2 Thess. 1.3; 1 Tim. 1.14; 2.15; 4.12; 6.10, 11; 2 Tim. 1.13; 2.22; 3.10; Tit. 2.2; 3.15; Phlm. 5. Elsewhere only Jas 2.5; Rev. 2.19. Faith and hope: Rom. 5.2; 2 Cor. 10.15; Gal. 5.5; 1 Thess. 1.3, 5.8. Elsewhere only Pss. 33.18, 22; 130.7; 147.11.

27. Outside the NT we find it in *Barn.* 1.4, 11.8; Polycarp, *Phil.* 3.2-3.

28. See A. M. Hunter, *Paul and His Predecessors* (London: SCM, 1961), 33–5.

29. The dating of Hebrews is contested, but texts such as Heb. 10.32, which looks back on 'those earlier days', suggests that it post-dates the initial spread of the Gospel in the 40s and 50s.

purpose.[30] However, the triad itself seems to have been distilled by Paul and his associates into their quintessential summary of the Christian faith, on the basis that in Christ, God is shown to be revealed in these ways. God is faithful (*pistis*)[31], and so evokes faith – the 'thankful recognition of the gracious God' – among people.[32] God is the One in whom the Gentiles and all creation can have hope (*elpis*).[33] God is demonstrated as love (*agape*).[34] There is no one scriptural source for this triad; rather, the connecting point between the three appears to be Christ, seen in the light of his death, resurrection and Parousia.[35] Faith, hope and love are the three paradigmatic 'marks' of God as revealed in Christ, and they are known as the marks of communities – and people – who are 'in Christ'.

The most prominent of these three marks in Col. 1.4-5 is hope.[36] We do not normally think of the Pauline faith-hope-love triad as orientated towards hope – in fact, we may even overlook the affirmation that faith, hope and love *all* 'abide'[37] (1 Cor. 13.13) in favour of the promised triumph of love. But Paul's great meditation on love in 1 Cor. 13 – having touched on many aspects of love (including believing and hoping in v.7) – distils the qualities down to three that remain or abide (*meno*). Hope abides, together with faith and love. If we take this to mean eternally, then the future aspect of hope, though vital to our present reality, does not fully encompass the meaning of this concept.

Hope is eschatological, looking forward to the full participation of humanity and all creation in the life of God. Hope is also an articulation of dependence, so that even as we conceive of our relationship with God beyond the constraints of

---

30. See Michael J. Gorman, *Becoming the gospel: Paul, Participation and Mission* (Grand Rapids, MI: Eerdmans, 2015), ch. 3, 63–105.

31. For example, 1 Cor. 1.9; 10.13; 2 Cor. 1.18; 1 Thess. 5.24; 2 Thess. 3.3; Pss. 31.5; 145.13.

32. C. K. Barrett, *The First Epistle to the Corinthians*, 2nd edn. (London: A & C Black, 1971), 309.

33. See, for example, Ps. 65.5, for the breadth of this hope, and Ps. 71.5 for God addressed as Hope.

34. See Rom. 5.5, 8; 2 Cor. 13.13; 2 Thess. 3.5. One might have expected another term for love to be used rather than *agape*, namely *eleos* (mercy, loving-kindness, steadfast faithfulness) given its rich biblical heritage. Perhaps this term was too closely associated with covenantal nomism to serve the Pauline mission – the term is often associated with God's covenant with Israel and with the Law as the means of maintaining the covenantal relationship. However, see Rom.11.31.

35. For a similar argument, see Gorman, *Becoming the gospel*, 65–6.

36. This is true of 1 Thess.1.3 and 5.8 as well, where hope, as the last of the marks, receives greatest emphasis.

37. Scholars are divided as to whether this reference in 1 Cor. 13.13 to hope 'abiding' means for the present life of the church, or whether an eschatological meaning ('forever') is intended. For a defence of a present rather than an eschatological view, see Gordon D. Fee, *The First Epistle to the Corinthians* (Grand Rapids, MI: Eerdmans, 1987), 650.

chronological time, our participation in God is a gift. We continue always to 'hope' in God, even as we come to know God 'face to face' (1 Cor. 13.12). Understanding hope this way brings it close to the meaning of 'depend' or 'rely' on God.

For the present, however, hope is directed towards a future reality that is not yet seen. As Michael Gorman states,

> For Paul hope is not merely anticipation of the future but a present, anticipatory participation in the future, specifically in God's eschatological promise of glory. (e.g. Rom. 8.17-39; 2 Cor. 3.18; 4.17-18; 1 Thess. 2.12)[38]

Seen in this way, hope is not simply future-directed faith. It is current 'investment' in the future inheritance. Hope is something we practise, a decision to live in the light of what God has done in Christ, while at the same time, it is something that we do not yet fully possess. This hope gives us deep connection with God the Father and the Lord Jesus Christ (v.3) in the Spirit (v.8), and also with fellow believers not only nearby but also across the world (v.6).

Hope should not be seen individualistically. It is not just for ourselves or for fellow believers, but for all creation. Such hope turns the gaze outwards towards the wide horizon of God's grace. This type of hope is the opposite of self-centredness; rather, it breaks open the boundaries of who we understand ourselves to be. It prompts us to view our fellow creatures in the light of God's future, looking for them to be more than they now are, and to become all that they could be. It raises our view of all creatures.

The entry point for the Colossian believers is this hope, which has inspired in them a faith in Christ Jesus. On the basis of this faith, their connection with each other has become one of love (v.4); a love grounded and enabled in the Spirit (v. 8). This loving relationship implicitly extends to all creatures, who are also recipients of the same Gospel (v. 23).

The Stoic word *eudaimonia*, happiness, has a spiritual dimension; *daimonion* of Greek mythology is a natural spirit, with the prefix *eu* indicating good spirits. The reference to the Spirit in v. 8 reminds the Colossians that their happiness is not dependent on just any spiritual forces, but is enabled by the Holy Spirit of God, and expressed in their love – in particular the love that they have for all the saints (v. 4).

The True Logos, namely the Gospel

I have translated the phrase 'the word of the truth of the Gospel' in v. 5 as 'the true Logos, the Gospel', highlighting both the parallel and the contrast that this forms with Stoic thought.[39] As we have seen, the Stoics believed that happiness – or living

---

38. Gorman, *Becoming the gospel*, 100.

39. The true Logos, or word of truth, is very similar to an expression we find in 2 Cor. 6.7, although there, it is one of a list of qualities that characterize Paul and his fellow workers, and is better translated as 'truthful speech'.

in harmony with nature and with God – was found by living according to Logos; universal reason. Epaphras had been able to build on this understanding that was widely held in Asia Minor in the first century.[40] He had been able to affirm their desire to live in harmony with God and their desire to do so according to the universal Logos. But he had also been able to go further and communicate that the *means* of living in harmony with God had been provided by the grace of God (v. 6). Through faith in Christ Jesus they were enabled to live according to the true Logos, namely the Good News. In vv. 13-14 we have a brief summary of this Gospel:

> He has rescued us from the authority of darkness and transferred us to the kingdom of his beloved Son, in whom we have redemption, the forgiveness of sins.

God has provided the access to this grace. As we read vv. 5-6, we can see how it draws Logos and Gospel into the closest relationship, stressing that this Logos is indeed the true one:

> [This faith and this love] arise from the hope laid up for you in heaven, which you have already heard about in the true Logos, the Gospel that has come to you.

The term 'Logos' has many nuances in Koine Greek, ranging from 'word', 'message', 'speech' – the subject or matter of what is spoken or meant – through to 'reason' or 'rationality' – the logic of what is meant. For Stoics, it is the rational principle permeating all reality, and in that sense divine. For the Johannine tradition, it is God's full self-revelation through Jesus Christ the Word (Jn 1.1). For Timothy and Paul in v. 5, it is the true logic of divine self-revelation; namely, the Good News of salvation in Jesus Christ. The true Logos, the Gospel, is the 'Speech Act' of God, into which we are drawn, and by whose logic we live.

This true Logos is currently present among them (v. 6), resident and abiding. It is, then, this true reason or logic of the Gospel that is bearing fruit and growing throughout the world, and is also doing so among them. In vv. 5-6 the Colossians are being reminded of what they already know and believe: what is true in the whole world is also true among them; namely, the Good News of the grace of God is growing and bearing fruit.

Timothy and Paul have chosen an image of fruitfulness to articulate the way in which the true Logos, the Gospel, is expanding. The image of an earthy, nourishing, thriving tree bearing delicious fruit is apt. The grace of God has come to them abundantly, without their having had to earn it or produce it. Living in harmony with nature and so with God allows God's abundant goodness to flourish, not only across the world, but among them. These residents of the fertile Lycus Valley knew something of this flourishing fruitfulness, and they are reminded to perceive the grace of God this way – abundant grace.

40. Balabanski, 'Stoic Echoes in Non-Stoic Sources', 11–26.

Hermeneutical reflections

When we read of 'hope laid up in heaven' in our default Platonic understanding, it may sound impossibly otherworldly or even downright dangerous. It sounds as though we can despoil the present blithely confident of an otherworldly future. We know of people who are so invested in the next world that they are prepared to do unspeakable things in the name of it, and hasten their own end as well. Placing this phrase into a Stoic framework, by contrast, communicates that hope is to be found in the God who is present to us in Christ, here and now. What can we then make of the hope that is spoken of in Col. 1.4-5, 23 and 27?

1. This hope has a particular content.

This hope is part of a Pauline triad consisting of faith, love and hope, appearing in various orders. This threefold constellation distils what the God of Jesus Christ is like and what we are to be like. It articulates confidence that at the heart of reality there is the truth of God's abundant grace that comes to us in Christ, but also that we do not yet experience this grace in full. So hope articulates both confidence in what God has done, and dissatisfaction with the evils and limitations of the present. The sort of hope articulated here is lived out in life-giving, grace-filled ways, and cannot be co-opted into behaviours that are contrary to the logic of the Gospel, articulated in the faith, love and hope triad.

2. This hope is inclusive of all creation

The deeper meaning of the Good News is not limited to the well-being of individuals. If it is good news at all, it encompasses the well-being of the world, the cosmos, and brings hope to the Earth. As Cleanthes' *Hymn to God* states, the world is encumbered by the pursuit of fame, unbridled profit and acquisition, or short-term pleasure. With the parallel we see between Colossians 1 and Romans 8, we recognize that every creature under heaven is in need of the hope promised by the Gospel – for the children of God to be revealed as those who live out the Gospel as grace which passes grace on to others.

There are some Pauline ethical principles for living a Christ-like existence and participating in God's reconciliation of all things.[41] The first can be called 'other-regard', and can be understood as a call on the stronger to prioritize the interests of the weaker.[42] Elsewhere Paul uses the language of freely offered service to describe this attitude.[43] The ecological challenge is to extend 'other-regard' to all creatures, even those that we do not recognize as useful to ourselves. Anticipating the hope of

41. David G. Horrell, Cheryl Hunt and Christopher Southgate, *Greening Paul: Rereading the Apostle in a Time of Ecological Crisis* (Waco, TX: Baylor University Press, 2010), 178–80.

42. 1 Cor. 8.4-13; Rom. 14.1–15.7.

43. 1 Cor. 9.19 and Gal. 5.13.

the Gospel means choosing to live as faithful servants, caretakers and custodians of Earth; choosing the sometimes onerous or challenging path of living simply.

Praying is central to this simple way of living. It acknowledges that we do not have all spiritual wisdom and understanding, or full knowledge of God's will. It opens us to the Spirit's presence and guidance. It is profoundly countercultural to stop and commit oneself and all creation to the goodness of the Creator.

The imagery of bearing fruit invites us to reflect on our interconnectedness with non-human creation. The image pictures us as part of the biosphere – fed by the fruitfulness of Earth and choosing to enhance the fruitfulness of Earth by how we live. The practical choices we make are not irrelevant to the logic of the Gospel – quite the contrary. In Christ, we must seek to make all of our choices life-giving and enhancing. Whether that means shifting to a plant-based diet, choosing public transport and foregoing as much air travel as we can, or engaging in political processes to call for greater compassion for and inclusion of those who are disadvantaged by climate change, it is all part of the Gospel logic. The grace of God gives us the impetus to change for the better.

3. Hope is necessary; it is foundational to action

Hope is not optional. There is a mounting rhetoric of pessimism in ecological discourse in the face of climate change and the political-industrial behemoth which seems unstoppable. Pessimism can lead to hopelessness and apathy and drain people of their will to take action. This sort of fatalism can lead to various types of escapism, including hedonism. This is not a new problem, but one that has precedents in many eras and contexts.

One example is the saying: 'Let us eat and drink, for tomorrow we die' (Isa. 22.8). Its context was the threat of invasion in the eighth century BCE, and we find it quoted mockingly by Paul in 1 Cor. 15.32 in a discussion of future hope.

The emphasis on hope in Colossians shows that it is necessary; it lifts our gaze from ourselves to a wider horizon. It is also foundational to action; only if we believe that there is a future can we invest ourselves in bringing it about. Of course, the hope laid up for us in heaven (=in God) is not a future under our control, but it is a trajectory that gives perspective to the present.

4. Hope is lived out through our participation

As stated above, the sort of hope set out in Colossians 1 is not *merely* anticipation of the future but a present, anticipatory *participation* in the future, specifically in God's eschatological promise of glory.[44] In that sense it is a present reality and commitment, by which we can be known as those who share 'the hope promised by the Gospel … which has been proclaimed to every creature under heaven' (Col. 1.23). The Spirit of God enables this action, which is none other than love (Col. 1.8).

---

44. Gorman, *Becoming the gospel*, 100.

Nympha's notes

It never ceases to surprise me how generous the natural world is – the abundance of grain that sprouts from just a few kernels, the grapevines changing in a few short weeks from bare and empty, to green with delicious leaves and then weighed down with fruit; the ewes with their lambs. We may work hard as we prune the vines or plough the fields, but the return is out of all proportion to the work we put in. The stories I grew up with were all about Demeter and Persephone and the gods giving us these things, or sometimes withholding them from us. Many of us lived in fear that we might inadvertently do something to displease them.

Epaphras showed us that nature's generosity has another name – grace. God pours out abundant grace and we are invited to partake without fear, because we are 'in Christ': citizens and heirs of God's kingdom in Jesus Christ – not just now, but eternally. I think I have begun to comprehend the grace of God in truth. This God whom we have met – truly the Most High God – cares for us personally. Grace and peace are truly ours!

CHAPTER 3

Stoic reading context: Living consistently and with integrity

Of all the ancient philosophies, Stoicism made the greatest claim to being utterly systematic.[1] In fact, the concept of philosophy as 'system' (*episteme*) is distinctively Stoic.[2] Stoics endeavoured to integrate all aspects of philosophy, including the division of topics and the sequence in which they were studied, as part of living according to Logos, universal reason, and thus as living in harmony with nature and so with God. They also understood all parts of the pursuit of wisdom as useful and practical, leading to virtue. 'The Stoics said that wisdom is scientific knowledge (*episteme*) of the divine and the human, and that philosophy is the practice of expertise in utility. Virtue singly and at its highest is utility.'[3]

So for Stoics, the pursuit of wisdom must lead to utility – being of benefit and bringing about virtue – or it is nothing. Outward action and inward disposition must be in tune with one another, so that the pursuit of wisdom (philosophy) leads to practising virtue, and is of use to oneself and the world.

Stoics understood science and ethics as inseparable. Wisdom consisted in bringing the fields of knowledge together and acting upon them consistently. Stoicism was more like a way of life than a set of ideas. Living consistently and with integrity *was* living according to Logos.

How does one come to live consistently, rather than being pulled in various directions by our desires? This is a valid philosophical question, and in dialogue with the various philosophical schools of their day, Stoics pondered the nature of desire and how our sense perceptions of the world – which they called 'impressions' – lead on to our impulses and actions. Stoics were confident that our impressions accurately reflect reality (not all ancient philosophical schools were confident about this). However, before our impressions lead to action, the human being has a choice to assent (or not to assent) to the impulse arising from the impression. We may see a delicious apple hanging on a tree in our neighbour's garden, and our sense perception or impression is that it would be good to eat. However, before

1. L&S 160.
2. L&S 160, 256.
3. Aetius *Placita* 1, Preface 2, L&S 158; (*SVF* 2.35).

reaching out to pluck it, there is another step; we move from impression (delicious apple) to impulse (the choice to pluck it) to action (plucking and eating). As rational beings we can break this sequence (impression – impulse – action) by not assenting to the impulse. We can acknowledge the presence of the apple and our own desire for it but decline to assent to the impulse to pluck it.

In this way, Stoics held that for rational human beings, all impulses – including desires and aversions – are acts of assent. Our sense perceptions or impressions of the world do not force us to particular actions. We have a choice in what we do with those impressions. We can choose to regard them or disregard them. As rational human beings we are responsible for making these choices. Our actions and even our desires are a choice.[4]

The Stoic philosopher Epictetus calls assent 'the power to use impressions':

> What does Zeus say? 'Epictetus, if it had been possible, I would have made your wretched body and trappings free and unhindered. But as it is, please note, this body is not your own, but a subtle mixture of clay. Since, however, I was not able to do this, I gave you a portion of myself, this power of impulse and repulsion, desire and aversion – in a word, the power to use impressions. If you take care of it and place in it everything you have, you will never be blocked, never hindered. You will never complain, never blame, never flatter anyone.'[5]

For Epictetus, the power to use impressions is a divine attribute, reflecting God's own agency. In a deterministic, though beneficent universe, this was understood as real power to shape oneself, even if not one's circumstances. By exercising this power, Stoics expected a wise person would show consistency between the inner and the outer person – their desires and their actions. Paul and Timothy expected such consistency too, but because the closed system had been opened from God's side through the death and resurrection of Jesus Christ, the gracious work of God and prayer are proclaimed as shaping the world and the believer towards a better future.

Eco-Stoic commentary on Col. 1.9-14

Translation of Col. 1.9-14

9 Therefore we also have not stopped praying for you from the day we heard [about you].
We are [constantly] asking that you may be filled full with the knowledge of [God's] will in all wisdom and spiritual insight

---

4. L&S 322. Diogenes of Babylon saw this ability as having matured by the age of fourteen, according to Diogenes Laertius 7.55–6, L&S 197.

5. Epictetus, *Discourses* 1.1.10–12, L&S 391–2.

[10] to live [your] lives worthily, desiring to please the Lord in every way,
bearing fruit in every good work and increasing in the knowledge of God,
[11] being empowered in every capability according to his glorious strength
for all steadfast endurance and patience.
And [may you] joyfully [12] give thanks to the Father who has made you fit to
receive a share in the saints' inheritance in the light.
[13] He has rescued us from the authority of darkness and transferred us to the
sovereignty[6] of his beloved Son,
[14] in whom we have redemption, the forgiveness of sins.

This passage is a description of the prayer that Paul, Timothy and their associates
offer on behalf of the Colossians: that they may

- be filled full with knowledge of God's will in all wisdom and spiritual insight
- live consistently with that fullness
- desire to please the Lord
- bear good fruit
- be empowered
- be steadfast and patient
- give thanks joyfully

All of these are connected, because there is a *consistency* between their knowledge,
wisdom and insight on the one hand, and on the other, their way of life, impulses
and outward actions – their inner desires, their source of strength, their behaviour
under suffering and their impulse to thanksgiving and joy.

Timothy and Paul's prayer for the Colossians shows that they expect there to be
a connection between wisdom as knowledge of God and the practical outworking
of this knowledge in how people live. They pray for the believers at Colossae not
only to be filled with the knowledge, wisdom and spiritual insight of God but also
to live it out in an integrated and consistent way. Using language reminiscent of
Jewish *halakhah* (walking) to refer to all aspects of how one lives one's life (v. 10),
they pray that the Colossians will demonstrate an inward and outward integrity.[7]

---

6. The term *basileia* is often translated as kingdom, reign, realm or empire. Some terms
such as 'realm', have spatial connotations. In an Eco-Stoic reading, the divine presence is in
all places, so a translation needs to convey that the transfer to Christ's *basileia* has to do with
allegiance, rather than any place. I have chosen 'sovereignty' rather than the alternatives,
as 'reign' has connotations of time limitation, 'kingdom' can, in common usage, imply one
among others, and 'empire' has overtones of violence.

7. An Eco-Stoic reading does not assume that the confluence of Jewish and Stoic ideas
in Colossians is surprising or problematic. Both Paul and Timothy operated across cultural
and conceptual boundaries, as did most of their contemporaries. The contention that the
new Christ-followers in Colossae and neighbouring areas were shaped by Stoic ideas is not
negated by the inclusion of distinctively Jewish concepts in this Letter.

The passage opens in a way that knits it tightly to what has gone before. In vv. 7-8, Epaphras is named in close connection with Paul and Timothy as 'our fellow-slave', 'beloved', 'faithful servant of Christ on our behalf'. Epaphras' ministry is none other than the ministry of Paul and Timothy.[8] The thanksgiving that follows builds on this by connecting their impulse to pray continually for the Colossians to their shared ministry with Epaphras.

Verse 9 echoes the language of v. 6: 'From the day we heard it.' Since that day, the writers have not ceased praying for the believers in Colossae, which in turn recalls v. 3 – they are 'always' praying for them. In a similar way, the imagery in v. 10 of the Colossians 'growing and bearing fruit' echoes the way in which the Gospel – the true Logos – has been growing and bearing fruit in all the world (v. 6). What is going on among the Colossians is closely linked with what is going on in the wider world (v. 6). The believers in Colossae are being encouraged to know that the spread of the Gospel in their midst mirrors the universal scope of this Gospel's spread.

Plerophory (being filled full) through prayer connects us with the God who fills all

Verses 9-14 – and indeed onwards to v. 22 – are one long sentence in the Greek, all dependent on the main verb 'that you may be filled full' in v. 9. There is a string of prepositional phrases:

> [9] Therefore we also have not stopped praying for you from the day we heard [about you].
> We are asking that you may be filled full with the knowledge of [God's] will
> in *all* wisdom and spiritual insight, [10] to live [your] lives worthily,
> in *every way* desiring to please the Lord
> in *every* good work bearing fruit and increasing in the knowledge of God,
> [11] in *every* capability being empowered according to his glorious strength
> for *all* steadfast endurance and patience. [Emphases mine.]

'All' or 'every' – the Greek word *pas* in various grammatical forms – is very prominent in this description of their prayer. It is found once in v. 9d, twice in v. 10, and twice again in v. 11. The same term was already used in vv. 3, 4 and 6. The concentration of this term, particularly in vv. 9-11, is striking. It calls on the readers or hearers to notice the big picture of God's work, and see how the integrity of their lives is connected with everything else.

Scholars describe this style as rhetorical 'plerophory', a style that emphasizes the use of synonyms (knowledge, wisdom, insight, v. 9), cognates (being empowered with all power, v. 11), genitive attributes (strength of his glory, v. 11) and the

---

8. Epaphras is mentioned in Col. 1.7-8; 4.12-13 and Phlm. 23. He is to be distinguished from Epaphroditus in Phil. 2.25-30, who is well known to the community at Philippi.

frequent use of the word *pas* (all/every).[9] One could describe plerophory as a verbal depiction of abundant fullness.

Paul and Timothy's prayer uses this plerophoric style, particularly in vv. 9–11. The main verb of this section is *plērothēte* – may you be filled full – and all the subsequent phrases describe and depict this fullness.[10]

There seems to be a connection between the genre of prayer and the plerophoric style. This style is reminiscent of the language of the Psalms, which often refer to God in the superlative (the most High = *ho hupsistos*), and emphasize that God is over all the earth and all the gods. For example:

> For you, O LORD, are most high over all the earth; you are exalted far above all gods. (Ps. 97.9, LXX 96.9)

Or again:

> [11] Let the heavens be glad, and let the earth rejoice; let the sea roar, and all that fills it (*to plērōma*); [12] let the field exult, and everything in it. Then shall all the trees of the forest sing for joy [13] before the LORD. (Ps. 96.11-13, LXX 95.11-13)

These are examples of plerophoric style, with their use of synonyms and parallels and their repetition of 'all'. Such expansive language seems particularly appropriate in communal worship, exhorting one another to lift the gaze beyond their immediate context to glimpse the interconnectedness of all things, and so experience being filled with God's glory.

An example of plerophory which is comparable to Col. 1.9-11 is found in Eph. 6.18, where *pas* is used four times in the one verse:

> Pray in the Spirit at *all* times in *every* prayer and supplication. To that end keep alert and *always* persevere in supplication for *all* the saints. [Emphases mine]

Although this is an exhortation to prayer rather than a prayer itself, the connection between the subject matter and style evokes and reflects the prayer of the writer.

Returning to Col. 1.9-11, Paul and Timothy's prayer for the Colossians is that they may be 'filled full', and what follows evokes the plerophoric, associative language of prayer. Some scholars refer to the liturgical character of the language,[11]

---

9. Bujard, *Stilanalytische Untersuchungen zum Kolosserbrief*, 146–7. It is one of the features of Colossians that distinguishes it from the undisputed letters of Paul.

10. As discussed in Chapter 2, being 'filled full' evokes Isa. 6.3, which proclaims that the whole earth is filled full with God's glory. This resonates with the Stoic concept of God's presence permeating all things.

11. So, for instance, in reference to the plerophoric language of Ephesians, see Michael Theobald, 'Der Epheserbrief', in *Einleitung in das Neue Testament*, ed. Martin Ebner and Stefan Schreiber (Stuttgart: Kohlhammer, 2008), 415.

but that might be retrojecting the more formal and structured communal worship of later eras. It seems to me that this plerophoric language of prayer is closer to the Spirit-filled, and at times unpredictable, prayer of the Corinthians (1 Cor. 12–14). Even so, plerophoric style does not mean that the content of the prayer is not significant. As Paul wrote in 1 Cor. 14.15, he understood prayer as involving both the spirit and the mind.

Paul and Timothy are constantly praying, as is reflected in the present participle as well as the affirmation that they do not stop (v. 9). Being 'filled full' spans all aspects of life, beginning with the knowledge of God's will. We have already noted in this chapter the Stoic definition of wisdom as *knowledge* of the divine and the human. Both in Col. 1.9 and for the Stoics, knowledge of the divine is possible, and is fundamental to living. It affects all aspects of life, including lifestyle (literally 'how we walk' – [Heb] *halakhah*) and also what we desire. Stoics thought of humans as being responsible for what we desire, as we have seen, and here in Col. 1.10, Paul and Timothy pray that the believers may desire all (and only) those things that are pleasing to God. A fully integrated Christian life is one that grows and increases, reflecting outwardly the knowledge of God. The fact that the knowledge of God (v. 9) is repeated in v. 10 emphasizes the connection between each element:

Knowledge of [God's] will
    In all wisdom and
       spiritual insight
         Living worthily of the Lord
       In all things desiring to please [the Lord]
     In all good works bearing fruit and increasing in the
    Knowledge of God

The prayer goes on to ask that all this may lead to a fundamental attitude of joyful thanksgiving – gratitude to God. In Colossians, gratitude leading to thanksgiving is shown to be the foundational disposition of the Christian life (Col. 2.7; 3.15, 17; 4.2). It also reminds the reader that it is the fundamental starting point for Paul and Timothy too (Col. 1.3).

Joyful thanksgiving rests on the fact that an integrated life is grounded on the reality of God's grace. It is by this grace that the one who is in Christ has been made worthy to receive a share or portion of the 'inheritance' of the saints. We are not able to do this ourselves; it is God who enables us to do so (cf. 2 Cor. 3.5-6). The share or portion might remind the reader of the biblical tradition of the land, but for a Gentile community it would be particularly evocative of kinship, and of their adoption as 'heirs'. This is not explicitly stated in Colossians, but is made explicit in Eph. 3.6.

The inheritance of the saints is qualified by the phrase 'in the light'. Light (and its contrasting darkness) is a familiar image in Pauline writings (e.g. 1 Thess. 5.5; 2 Cor. 4.4, 6; 6.14; Rom. 13.12) and is used more extensively in Eph. 5.8-14. It refers to the light of God's presence and the Gospel, and so functions as a metonym for salvation.

Darkness is described as a power from which we have been rescued (v. 13). The verb 'rescue' or 'deliver' (*rhuomai*) is the same verb that we find in the Lord's Prayer (Mt. 6.13), in the phrase 'deliver us from evil'. The timing of the deliverance is viewed differently in these two traditions. In Matthew's Gospel it is something not yet realized, for which we pray. In Col. 1.13, it is an accomplished reality, yet still something to be named in the context of prayer. The differing perspectives are not necessarily contradictory; they reflect the eschatological tension between the 'already' and the 'not yet' of salvation. Colossians 1.13 states that we have been transferred into the sovereignty of God's beloved Son, in whom we now have redemption, the forgiveness of sins. The transfer is viewed as being in the past and the redemption and forgiveness are already ours. While in the undisputed Pauline letters this realized perspective is rarer, it is not unknown. In Rom. 8.28-30, where Paul writes from God's perspective, he refers to believers already being justified and already being glorified.

The more realized aspect of this eschatology in Colossians is also to be seen in Col. 2.12-14 and 3.1. In these later passages, the baptismal context and perspective of these affirmations becomes clearer. One can speak of already having been rescued and transferred into Christ's sovereignty by virtue of having received baptism. The future aspect – the hope laid up in heaven in 1.5 – is understood as the final outworking and culmination of what has already taken place. Again, the experience of prayer, worship and meditation is evoked, where the boundaries of time and space are not so defined.

In vv. 13-14 we have four soteriological affirmations with diverse associations:

- Rescue (with its associations of danger)
- Transfer into the sovereignty of God's beloved Son (with associations of citizenship)
- Redemption (with its associations of being freed from slavery)
- Forgiveness (with its associations of relationship breakdown)

What we do not have here is sacrificial or Temple imagery of atonement, presumably as this may not have been as potent for the Gentile believers of the Lycus Valley as the other conceptual frameworks. The dense cluster of these diverse ways of thinking about the salvation they have received in Christ reminds the Colossians of the Gospel as their hope, which is grounded in God's gracious action in Christ's death and resurrection.

Hermeneutical reflections

This passage describes what Paul and Timothy pray and long for: that the believers in the Lycus Valley, as part of an eco-wide sovereignty of Christ, may be filled full with the knowledge of God's will, and may live it out with integrity. This sovereignty is both spiritual and practical, putting allegiance and priorities into practice. They pray that the believers' lifestyle and desires may be integrated with their knowledge of God, leading to wisdom and spiritual insight. They pray that this integration results in 'worthy' lives that are marked by joy and gratitude. Consistency between the outer and the inner person, leading to virtue that benefits others, is the mark of lives that reflect the knowledge of God, who has enabled us to live as free and whole citizens of Christ's reign.

We know from another Pauline writing that these are the very things that Earth longs for as well:

> For the creation waits with eager longing for the revealing of the children of God. (Rom. 8.19)

Earth longs for the children of God to be revealed not only eschatologically or in the future but also as people who are truly and consistently living out the knowledge of God now. From Earth's perspective, such consistent, integrated living would include a keen desire to live in harmony with the natural world. This desire would not be separate from Christian – or indeed Stoic – wisdom and spiritual insight, but would be understood as part of the knowledge of God.

I will turn to one aspect of the passage, namely the concept of 'desiring to please the Lord in every way' (v.9). One of the difficulties that all of us who are part of the technological age face is the way our connectedness exposes us to the manipulation of our desires. Consumerism is the engine that drives the economic system of the 'first world' – and increasingly also of the 'majority world'. Our desires are both blatantly and subtly shaped by advertising in all its forms towards more consumption not only of goods and services but also of experiences. The messages we receive from our consumer culture are that we should desire to have more success, popularity, confidence, beauty, wealth, independence, leisure and freedom and that these 'virtues' are to be found through the purchase of things or experiences. Our desires are co-opted. This happens to the detriment of the natural world, which bears the brunt of the ceaseless pursuit of these things. The concept of sustainability – and its corollary of the choice to self-limit – is necessarily dependent on a different way of seeing and experiencing desire.

For Earth's sake, learning to desire to please the Lord in every way gives a different platform from which to view what is truly good. From this vantage point, one of the differences is that what is good is no longer simply what is good for me. 'I' am no longer the reference point, but rather God – whom we know in and through Christ – becomes that reference point. The vista is expanded beyond myself and my immediate family or network to the wider world, including other 'saints'. The horizon does not finish there either, as God's concern is for the whole cosmos, human and non-human. Desiring to please the Lord in every way is desiring the flourishing of all God's creation. This may at times mean curbing my own personal desires – not assenting to every impulse as it arises.

Stoic philosophy teaches that it is only with our assent that desires can shape or direct us, and that we are free to grant or withhold our assent. Paul and Timothy were constantly praying that the believers would be filled full with all the qualities that would enable them to 'assent' only to those things that are pleasing to God.

Bearing fruit and growing is a metaphor for the integrated life, which stands in contrast to the counterfeit growth of consumerism. In this metaphor, we glimpse the truth that it is God who brings about growth and flourishing, not only in the natural world but also in ourselves. The trees, bushes and grasses outside are not so very different from ourselves, after all.

Nympha's notes

Epaphras' home was once in the Lycus Valley too, not so far from here. You could still say he is 'one of us', though there are some in my household who think that only the Valley folk who have never ventured as far as Hierapolis qualify for that description. It's strange to think of him now more than a thousand miles away over land and sea in Rome. Seeing Rome was a dream of mine as a child. Famous Rome, centre of the world, I used to think: all people bow down to you. But since Epaphras preached the Gospel among us – and since we have been baptized – we are now citizens and heirs of a much greater realm, the realm of God in Christ. Rome is not the centre anymore. A network of divine grace is growing and bearing fruit all across the countryside, connecting us through prayer with Epaphras, Paul, Timothy and all their co-workers. Nothing and no one is outside the ambit of God's grace. Even the groves and cliffs where deities are revered are not outside God's grace – I have no hesitation in strolling there.

Paul and Timothy's letter was so welcome, telling us of their close friendship with Epaphras, of their care for us, and reminding us that despite the need for so much endurance and patience, we can always be joyful and thankful.

CHAPTER 4

Stoic reading context: Embodiment and cosmos

The hallmark of existence for Stoics was embodiment.

When Plato and his successors looked out on the world and on things that exist, they gave priority to the *idea* of what they saw rather than to material phenomena; they valued mind over matter. To put it another way, they gave ontological primacy to the intelligible (things grasped by the mind) over the sensible (things perceived by the senses). That may seem very normal to us, as we stand in the intellectual pedigree of this type of thought, with mind and all its concomitant values ranked more highly than matter.

Stoics lined up the world differently. For them, it was matter that counted, and matter was embodied – embodied in a far wider sense than we understand it to be.

The starting point for Stoics was not the high and lofty thought world grasped by the mind, with universals or ideals as the most appropriate topics of discussion. They started from the other end – from the particular, the embodied. They called that particular 'something'. In Greek, (the language the early Stoics shared), 'something' is the tiny word *ti*. This referred to a specific thing that could be the subject of thought and discussion, like the tiniest building block in a great structure of reality.[1]

Every*thing* that acted upon other *things* was understood as corporeal or embodied; only bodies could affect other bodies. For Stoics, reality was made up of embodied *things*, interacting causatively with other *things* in the great cascade of existence.

However, Stoics also recognized that there were some *things* that did not have a bodily presence and hence did not act upon other *things* or on themselves. The *things* in this small subgroup were called *asomata* – incorporeals – or things without bodily substance.[2] One of them was void or emptiness: the absence of things (conceptually real, but not embodied).

More surprisingly, another incorporeal was time. Time was a *ti*, something conceptually real and significant for thinking about reality, but not an embodied

---

1. L&S 162–5.

2. 'They [the Stoics] say that of somethings some are bodies, others incorporeals, and they list four species of incorporeals – sayable (*lekton*), void [*kenon*], place [*topon*] and time [*chronon*].' Sextus Empiricus *Against the professors* 10.218, L&S 162.

thing in itself. Stoics did not reify time into 'Old Man Time', an 'everlasting stream' or something to be 'devoured'.[3] Time was a *thing*, but did not strictly 'exist'. We may be inclined to divide the world up into things that exist and things that do not exist, on the assumption that our senses give us a good basis for making this primary distinction. However, the Stoics were more subtle than this. For them, there were *things* in the world that had an effect on other *things*, even while they themselves did not strictly exist. Some *things*, like time, do not have an independent existence of their own, but only *subsist* in relation to something else. Days pass, the sun rises and its height can be measured, but the time that is indicated by its position subsists rather than exists. By relegating time to the small group of '*asomata*' or incorporeals, the Stoics anticipated what contemporary physicists do with time as well, viewing it as a type of 'dimension', relativizing it and recognizing that it is dependent on other phenomena.

There are two other *asomata* or incorporeals that the ancient Stoic sources mention. Place is one of them. The place or location of an object, its *topos*, subsists rather than exists. Just as time is relative, so too is place – the location of a thing is not independent of that thing. Once again, place is a dimension.

The final thing that was deemed incorporeal, without its own embodied reality, seems to be the odd one out in our list (which has included void, time and place). This one was called a 'sayable', or 'expression' (*lekton*, singular, and *lekta*, plural). This referred to something that can be said, but which doesn't exist in reality, like a mythical creature such as a centaur. A centaur is a thing, a *ti*, but it does not exist, except in stories that tell of mythical creatures or in artistic representations of it. For Stoics, a *lekton* did not exist, but it subsisted; it was dependent on the story or the artwork. The sound of the story exists, as does the stone or the clay of the artwork, but the expression 'centaur' subsists.[4]

Chrysippus, the third leader of the Stoic school, posed this riddle to show the difference between something corporeal and something incorporeal:

> If you say something, it goes through your mouth. But you say: A wagon.
> Therefore a wagon goes through your mouth.[5]

Clearly wagons exist, and are embodied. However the word 'wagon' is not the wagon itself, but an expression or a 'sayable', a *lekton*, and therefore incorporeal, and as such, it doesn't trouble the jaw nearly as much to allow it to go through the mouth!

You may be wondering why they bothered with these fine distinctions and word games. One answer may be that they were fun! However, they had a serious

---

3. Andrew Marvel's poem 'To His Coy Mistress' depicts time as the enemy to be devoured.

4. L&S 195-202.

5. Diogenes Laertius, *Lives of Eminent Philosophers*, 7.187, 'Chrysippus', L&S 228 (spelling modified).

side too. The Stoics aspired to being utterly systematic in their account of reality, with philosophy not excluding any part of it. All scientific investigation of reality requires a set of first principles upon which a methodology is built; it is just as true today that the scientific methodology we adopt determines what results we reach in an experiment.

So for the Stoics, '*something*', *ti*, is the basic unity of reality. Most '*somethings*' are embodied and thus exist. Some *things* are not embodied, and so subsist, namely the semantic aspect of speech (though not the sound of it), void/emptiness, place and time.

The key thing about the embodied *ti* is its power to act, to effect change, in a great chain or cascade of causation.

Clearly Stoics thought about bodies differently from the ways that we do. They can ascribe the term 'body' to anything that shares in the vitality of the cosmos:

> Justice, passion, reason, truth, virtue, vices, judgments, the soul. All of them are bodies, not in the sense of exhibiting specifically defined surfaces, but in the sense of sharing the materiality of the whole. That materiality is, thanks to the pneuma, in large measure animate rather than inert. Events are corporeal, and so are their causes.[6]

Being invisible (to the eye or intangible to the other senses) did not disqualify something from being embodied. Visible and invisible things were interwoven in the fabric of reality. The ancients knew that there was much about reality that was not perceptible to the senses. They knew very well that there were invisible forces that had the power to kill or to heal. The Plutonium (the Temple to Hades) in Hierapolis is a famous example of that, where gases were emitted from underground fissures that had the power to kill birds and other creatures, or to give worshippers visions of healing. These gases, though invisible and undetectable, have the power to effect change, and so were seen in the Stoic framework as embodied.

So where did God (or the gods) fit into this framework? The Stoic insistence on embodiment did not disqualify the existence of God, or relegate God to the subgroup of incorporeals that subsist, like time. Quite the opposite in fact; they saw God as existing and permeating the whole of reality and nature. In effect they saw God much more biologically than we do. If *Bios* (life) and *Logos* (the reasoning/ logic about it) is the energy that permeates all of existence, they identified these two elements with the divine presence. Even though the Stoics took the tiny unit *ti*, *something*, as worth discussing and analysing, their interest ultimately lay with all the *somethings* as they related to one another. All things were bound together and followed a *logic* by means of a unified impulse, a *Logos*. Logic connected the cosmos together because Logos was present in all things. It was here that they saw the divine at work, in and through nature.

---

6. Thomas G. Rosenmeyer, *Senecan Drama and Stoic Cosmology* (Berkeley: University of California Press, 1989), 95.

Stoics are often thought of as pantheists – those who believe that everything is divine. But there is a term that is more suitable: the Stoics were pan*en*theists – they believed that the divine indwells all things.[7] There is a crucial difference between these views. Panentheism allows for the possibility that the divine indwells all things but is not coterminous with them or limited to them. God is not the sum total of all things, but indwells all things.

Zeno is reported to have said that the whole world and heaven are the substance (*ousian*) of God.[8] Such a pithy, aphoristic claim needs to be understood alongside other Stoic sayings that distinguish between two principles of the cosmos: that which acts – the divine prime mover – and that which is acted upon, namely elements (*stoicheia*), which pass away. Stoics equate the energy or power that moves or shapes matter as divine. They also call the divine energy 'seminal reason' – *Logos spermatikos*.

In distinguishing between these two principles, the Stoics indicate that God, though embodied, is not fully identified with matter. This is particularly clear in relation to the cosmic cycles, which expect the periodic dissolution of the world. When the world is destroyed in cosmic conflagration, God is not destroyed; at that time, God reposes in God's self.[9] This was a difficult concept to understand, particularly for those who held to the unchangeability of God, as we see in this comment from Origen:

> The god of the Stoics, in as much as he is a body, sometimes has the whole substance as his commanding-faculty; this is whenever the conflagration is in being; at other times, when world-order exists, he comes to be in a part of substance.[10]

One further word about definitions: the word 'cosmos', which we translate as 'world', is not the same as 'universe'. In the quotation below from Sextus Empiricus, we see that Stoic philosophers distinguished the concepts of the whole/the world, from the all or infinite:

> The Stoic philosophers suppose that there is a difference between the 'whole' and the 'all'. For they say that the world is whole, but the external void together with the world is all. For this reason they say the 'whole' is finite, since the world is finite, but the 'all' is infinite, since the void outside the world is such.[11]

---

7. For a fuller discussion of panentheism, see the Conclusion.

8. Diogenes Laertius *Lives of Eminent Philosophers*, 7.148–9, 'Zeno' (*SVF* 2.1022), L&S 266. See also in Long and Sedley's commentary on the Greek text, 'The term [*ousian*] … helps to state the thesis that the entire world is god.' L&S vol. 2, 264.

9. Seneca, *Letters* 9.16, L&S 277.

10. Origen, *Against Celsus* 4.14, L&S 276.

11. Sextus Empiricus, *Against the professors* 9.332, L&S 268.

We can set this out in the following way:

> The whole (*holon*) = the world (*ho kosmos*),
> The all/infinite (*to pan*) = the *kosmos* + the void
> All things (*ta panta*) = the world, the infinite and the void, every *ti* (visible,
>   invisible, embodied and incorporeal)

For interpreting Colossians, then, we note that every time the neuter terms *pan* (all) and *ta panta* (all things) in various forms are used, they refer to something greater than the cosmos (the world), namely the infinite.

Eco-Stoic commentary on Col. 1.15-20

Translation of Col. 1.15-20

[15] He [who] is the visible embodiment (*eikon*) of the unseen God
> 'Firstborn' of *all* creation
> > [16] For *all things* in the heavens and on the earth were created in him
> > > The things[12] seen and the things unseen
> > > Whether thrones or dominions or rulers or authorities
> > *All things* were created through him and for him.
> > [17] And he is before *all things*
> > And *all things* hold together in him

[18] And he is the head of the body of the church

He [who] is primacy (*archē*)
> 'Firstborn' from the dead
> So that he might become preeminent in *all things*
> [19] For in him *all* the fullness [of God] was pleased to live
> [20] And through him to reconcile *all things* to him [God]
> Having made peace through the blood of his cross through him –
> > Whether things on the earth or things in the heavens.

Jesus Christ is here spoken of as the visible, tangible embodiment of God. We encountered plerophoric language in the previous Chapter, with its overtones of worship and prayer; here we have it even more clearly, in a section identified by

---

12. 'Things' (not italicized) in vv. 16 and 20 is the translation of the Greek neuter plural definite article *ta*, rather than the indefinite pronoun *ti* (some*thing*). These specific 'things' are all subcategories of *ta panta*, all things.

most scholars as a hymn to Christ.[13] Because of the focus on 'all things' in these verses, we might call this a hymn to the coherence of all things in Christ. It is through this visible, tangible, somatic coherence revealed in the Logos of Christ that the unseen God can be known.

The structural elements of vv. 15-20, indicated in the layout of the translation, suggest two stanzas, each beginning with an affirmation concerning Christ's revelation of God. Each is introduced as a relative clause with the words 'who is ...' (1.15, 18b). Other hymns or hymnic fragments in the New Testament also open with a relative clause (Phil. 2.6; 1 Tim. 3.16; cf. also 1 Pet. 2.22; Heb. 1.3). This suggests that such forms of praise in a worship setting may have been preceded by a call to bless Christ with such words as 'Blessed be the beloved Son, who is...' (Col. 1.13).[14] The importance of such communal praise is indicated in Col. 3.16, where it is described as letting the 'Word of Christ dwell in them richly [through singing] psalms, hymns and spiritual songs to God'. Through participation in praise and worship, then, the Logos of Christ gives access to the unseen God.

There are clear structural elements evident in vv. 15-20, with repetitions of phrases and motifs ('firstborn of...', 'all things', 'things in heaven and on earth'), and the extended focus on Christ. Nevertheless, this section is not divided grammatically from the preceding verses (9-14), but continues the one long sentence which ends at the close of v. 22. Paul and Timothy's prayer that the Colossians may be filled with the knowledge of Christ (vv. 9, 10) is still the governing concept, and the Christological hymn is incorporated as a means for this to be realized/experienced.

In the broadest terms, the first stanza concerns Christ in relation to creation, and the second concerns Christ in relation to reconciliation. Christ is 'firstborn' of all creation, v. 15; Christ is 'firstborn' from the dead, v. 18c.[15] In two divine 'movements', Christ's work in creation and redemption are summed up.

The choice of 'firstborn' to articulate Christ's leadership in both divine movements is significant for an ecological reading.[16] Birthing is an image that

13. See particularly Matthew Gordley, *The Colossian Hymn in Context*, WUNT 2/228 (Tübingen: Mohr Siebeck, 2007) and his subsequent study *Teaching through Song in Antiquity*, WUNT 2/302 (Tübingen: Mohr Siebeck, 2011).

14. So Eduard Lohse, *Colossians and Philemon*, Hermeneia (Philadelphia, PA: Fortress Press, 1971), 38, n. 45.

15. Wisdom is described in similar ways in Prov. 8.22-26 and Sir. 24.9, but the word *prōtotokos* is not used. Ps. 89.27 (LXX 88.28) uses *prōtotokos* of David. The closest parallel usages of this term outside the NT are *Pss. Sol.* 18.4 – which speaks of Israel as God's 'unique firstborn son' – and Philo *De Agricultura (On husbandry)* 1.51 – where he names God's *Logos* with a similar term: *protogonon*, firstborn (LCL 247: 134–5).

16. The word *prōtotokos* is used in Rom. 8.29 to refer to Christ as the firstborn among many brothers and sisters, placing it in the framework of salvation. In Rev. 1.5, Christ is 'the firstborn of the dead', also associating Christ's work with the second movement. However in

connects Christ with physical reality, blood and all. The materiality of this word prohibits us from simply spiritualizing it and so cutting it off from creation. Christ as 'firstborn' both of creation and of the dead is the pioneer who opens up the way that connects the invisible, unknowable divine reality with the material world. The blood of his cross is named as the means of making peace in v. 20; this too insists that we understand the firstborn not as quarantined from creation, but as connected with material, tangible reality.

As we come to notice how prominent material reality is in these verses, the word *eikon* 'visible embodiment' in v.15 stands out. This term can refer to the image, representation or likeness of something (cf. Mt. 22.20), but this sense is too weak. I have translated the Greek word as 'visible embodiment'. Christ is no mere likeness, in the sense of a portrait or artistic representation; Christ is proclaimed in this hymn as God's active agent in creation. As we have seen, for those influenced by Stoic ideas, only embodied reality can be causative and can *effect* things. If Christ is the visible, tangible embodiment of God who is not seen, Christ is both the revealer and the agent of the unseen God.

This first stanza also places Christ in the closest connection with creation as the One in whom through whom and even for whom the universe came into being. The concept of a living Being as the one through whom the universe came into existence has a long history in philosophical thought, going back (at least) to Plato. Plato wrote a discourse 'concerning the universe' (*peri tou pantos* 'Concerning all things')[17] known as *Timaeus*, in which Socrates and Timaeus discuss cosmology, cosmogony (how the world came into being), time and eternity. This discourse was very influential across the philosophical schools, including Stoicism, and also shaped Hellenistic ideas more generally.

The key idea was that prior to the creation of the heavenly bodies or humanity, the cosmos was brought into existence as a 'Living Creature endowed with soul and reason owing to the providence of God.'[18] 'God desired to make it resemble most closely that intelligible Creature which is fairest of all and in all ways most perfect, [so] He constructed it as a Living [Being], one and visible, containing within itself all the living creatures which are by nature akin to itself.'[19]

Stoics gave this image of the cosmos as a Living Being a revised and more central position in their cosmology, seeing the universe as permeated by an

---

Heb.1.6, Christ is named 'firstborn' in contrast to the angels, indicating pre-eminence; this reference suggests that the word may have been used as a title for Christ.

17. Plato, *Timaeus* 92 C, LCL 234: 252–3.

18. Plato, *Timaeus* 30 B–C, LCL 234: 54–5.

19. Plato, *Timaeus* 30 D. LCL 234: 56–7. For a more detailed account of this, see V. Balabanski, 'Hellenistic Cosmology and the Letter to the Colossians', 94–107. I have modified the Loeb translation to read 'Living Being' rather than 'Living Creature', as the Greek word *zōon* literally means 'living One'.

all-pervasive fiery spirit (*pneuma*) that connects all things and holds them together. Marcus Aurelius put it this way:

> Constantly regard the universe as one living being, having one substance and one soul; and observe how all things have reference to one perception, the perception of this one living being; and how all things act with one movement; and how all things are the cooperating causes of all things that exist; observe too the continuous spinning of the thread and the structure of the web.[20]

There are close parallels and also crucial differences between Stoic cosmology and the hymnic material of Col. 1.15-20. Colossians affirms that there is indeed One in and through whom all things came into being, who is prior to creation, and in whom all things hold together. Colossians shows that 'all things' – the universe – embrace the world as we know it, including things on earth, the powers that be and all that is visible. But it also includes those aspects of the universe beyond our grasp or knowledge – things invisible, spiritual powers. Nothing is outside the authority of the One through whom all things came into being and in whom all things are sustained. Colossians affirms that this One makes visible and tangible the unseen God. All of these affirmations are conceptually comprehensible within a Stoic Timaean framework.[21]

What stands in contrast to the Hellenistic understanding of the Living One is the affirmation in stanza two which links this One with divine redemption. In Stoic thought, there is no redemption from the providential universe as God has constructed it. There will be a conflagration that will destroy and remake the world, but the reborn cosmos will replicate what exists now in every respect.[22] This was a grim horizon for the majority of humans, not to mention the fate of all creatures.

20. Marcus Aurelius, *The Meditations of Marcus Aurelius*, 4.40, translated by George Long (London: Blackie & Son Ltd. 1910) 44.

21. They are also comprehensible in a Jewish Wisdom framework, though a discussion of this is beyond the scope of this reading. Philo of Alexandria had already made connections between Jewish Wisdom traditions and Hellenistic philosophical concepts; he calls divine Wisdom the 'image' of God (*Allegorical Interpretation of Genesis* 1.43, LCL 266: 174–5) and elsewhere he names the divine Logos as the image of God (*On the Special Laws* 1.81, LCL 320: 146–7): 'And the image of God is the Word through whom the whole universe was framed [made].' We see here Jewish Wisdom categories explicitly translated into Hellenistic categories.

22. The concept of repeated cycles of destruction is found in Plato's *Timaeus* 22 C–D, LCL 234: 32–5. Not all Stoics continued to hold to this eschatology. Philo states that Boethus of Sidon (second century BCE), Panaetius of Rhodes (*c.* 185–*c.* 110 BCE) and his student Posidonius (*c.* 135–*c.* 50 BCE), and Diogenes [of Babylon], (early to mid-second century BCE) rejected the concept of conflagration and regeneration in favour of the incorruptibility of the world (Philo, *On the Eternity of the World* 1.76–7, LCL 363: 238–9).

The two-stanza structure in Col. 1.15-20 indicates that there are two movements in which Christ is central: creation and reconciliation. Creation, though perfectly made and sustained, is beset by death and by conflictual forces that require reconciliation. The 'making peace' that is set out in stanza two restores the integrity and balance of creation. The cosmic story behind this is only alluded to, but the movement from creation to restoration in Christ is not only one that restores creation but one that also reveals Christ as 'head' (*kephalē*) of creation.

The second stanza opens with naming Christ as '*archē*', a word with a rich set of associations. It can mean 'beginning', and is generally translated this way, given the associations it evokes with the Greek of Gen. 1.1 and Jn 1.1, 'in the beginning ...'. It can mean rule or ruler; this meaning stands in contrast to the so-called rulers named in Col. 1.16 (thrones, dominions, rulers, authorities). These rulers and authorities have been stripped of their claim to ultimate authority (Col. 2.15), as Christ is indeed the true Ruler or Sovereign.

The word '*archē*' can also mean 'first principle', as opposed to the derivative principles, the elements or *stoicheia*, which are named in Col. 2.8.

The Christ Hymn affirms that Christ is not only the beginning but also the Ruler and first principle of creation. I have chosen to translate '*archē*' as primacy, to hold these various meanings in tension. Primacy indicates a similar expansiveness: it means the 'state or position of being prime in order, rank, importance or authority ... pre-eminence, precedence, superiority, sovereignty'.[23]

The second stanza proclaims Christ's primacy even over death: 'firstborn from the dead'. The salvific work of crucifixion, resurrection and exaltation is distilled here in a few words to convey the Good News that all things are reconciled and restored to God. This restoration – or gathering up under Christ's headship – later comes to be known as 'recapitulation', *anakephalaiōsis*. The word is not mentioned in Colossians, but the verbal form of it appears in Eph. 1.8-10.

There is much debate about the meaning of this verb *anakephalaioō* in Ephesians, which can mean sum up, renew, head up, unite or indeed recapitulate.[24] For our purposes, it is sufficient to note that the hymnic/poetic material in Col. 1.15-20 makes a very similar claim, namely that in Christ, creation and 're-creation' (reconciliation) are seen to be two corresponding parts of the one great story.

At the intersection of the two stanzas, Christ is proclaimed as the *head* (*kephale*) of the body of the church (*hē kephalē tou sōmatos tēs ekklēsias*, Col. 1.18). In the light of the preceding discussion, the affirmation of Christ as head is notable, but not surprising. It is also not surprising to read that Christ is the head *of the body*, given the Hellenistic view going back to Plato of the world as an embodied Living

---

23. Herbert Coleridge, F. J. Furnivall, James A. H. Murray, Henry Bradley, William A. Craigie, Charles T. Onions et al., *The Compact Edition of the Oxford English Dictionary*, Vol. 2 (New York: Oxford University Press, 1971), 1357.

24. See, for example, Markus Barth, *Ephesians*, vol. 1, AB 34 (Garden City, NY: Doubleday, 1974), 89–92; contra Andrew Lincoln, *Ephesians*, WBC 42 (Dallas, TX: Word Books, 1990), 32–3.

Being. What does stand out as unexpected is the phrase 'of the church' in this context, as these hymnic verses do not otherwise name the church. Many scholars consider the words 'of the church' to be an addition to the pre-Pauline hymnic/ poetic material, and that seems probable.[25] Without the addition, 'he is head of the body' would refer to the cosmos. Adding 'of the church' shifts the meaning of the body of Christ away from the understanding of 'body' as a localized and communal expression of Christ (e.g. 1 Cor. 12.12-27) towards the church as a cosmic and universal reality (cf. Eph. 1.22-23). Colossians 1.18 appears to be an interim stage between the communal concept of the body of Christ in 1 Corinthians and the cosmic concept in Ephesians. With the church placed in this way between the two stanzas of Christ's universal work, the reader is reminded that the whole hymnic vision is being used to articulate a prayer that the church at Colossae may be filled full with the knowledge of God.

All the divine *fullness* (*to plērōma*) was pleased to live in Christ (Col. 1.19). This is referred to again in Col. 2.9. It is the same fullness that the writers pray may fill (*plēroō*) the recipients of the Letter (1.9). As there are eight uses of this term and its cognates in Colossians, this concept is clearly of great significance to the writers.[26] Please see the further discussions of fullness in Chapters 3 and 7, and later in this Chapter.

Ecological reading of the passage

The theology of Col. 1.15-20 is conveyed in two distinctive ways: the repetition of *all things* and the extensive and highly sophisticated use of prepositions.

All things This expression articulates the universal scope of the One who embodies the unseen God. All things were created in him and in him all things hold together. This One is preeminent even in those things that are beyond the scope of mortals – namely death – and nothing is outside the purview of this One's reconciling work.

This is a word picture of universal proportions; it cuts no one and no *thing* adrift. We find a similar word picture at the end of Rom. 8.38-39, which spans spatial, temporal and political boundaries, and in this Colossian hymn, the perspective reaches back before all time. By repeating 'all things' six times and extending this further with the words 'all the fullness', the recipients of the Letter are drawn into a perspective where they share the embrace of the divine life – Christ's own love for

---

25. See for example Lohse, *Colossians and Philemon*, 42–3, citing Ernst Käsemann, 'A Primitive Christian Baptismal Liturgy', in *Essays on New Testament Themes*, tr. W. S. Montague, Studies in Biblical Theology 41 (London: SCM Press, 1964), 150–3. Lohse sees it as a gloss by the author of Colossians, on the basis of Col. 1.24, which refers to the body of Christ as the church.

26. Col. 1.9, 19, 24, 25; 2.9, 10; 4.12, 17.

the whole world. We have seen that plerophoric rhetoric evokes the experience of worship, and this is clearly evoked here. But the repetition of 'all things' also invites the gathered community to move beyond the tendency to dissociate themselves from their surroundings, and instead to see themselves as connected with all things. The natural world is God's world – in fact Christ is experienced in and through it. If all things were created in him, through him, for him, and all things hold together in him, then the world is imbued with Christ.[27]

Christian theology constantly shies away from anything that might be perceived as pantheism, on the very real basis that humanity has always tended towards idolatry. No sooner do we glimpse something of the divine beauty in nature than we tend to make it into an object of our worship. Salvation history is riddled with human attempts to make for ourselves 'little gods' to which we bow down. The danger of the vision of all things created in, through and for Christ is that our tendency to idolatry can run rampant. So to avoid that very real danger, we cut ourselves off from the rest of creation, indeed from all things, and reject what we perceive as pantheism.

However, in this Colossian hymn we do not have a vision of pantheism (equating all things with God), but pan*en*theism (in Christ), pan*dia*theism (through Christ), pan*eis*theism (for Christ) and pan*sun*theism (held together by Christ). If God sustains the world in every moment in and through Christ, then we humans can and must embrace the world as kin.

Theological prepositions In Col. 1.15-20, we have seven different prepositions used multiple times to articulate the way in which Christ's presence permeates reality.[28] All things were created *in* Christ, *through* Christ and *for* Christ. Christ is *before* all things and they stand together *with* him (*sunistēmi*). We also have the prepositions *on* and *from* in these verses: Christ is before all things *on* the earth, Christ is firstborn *from* the dead.

The use of prepositions to encompass and convey truth was taking place in various contexts in the ancient world, including in philosophy, Jewish reflection on Wisdom and also in Christian liturgy.[29] We find it elsewhere in Paul's letters, such as in Rom. 11.36: 'For *from* him and *through* him and *to* him are all things. To him be the glory forever. Amen.'

27. See Figure 7.1, Chapter 7, p. 123.

28. In (*en*) – vv.16 twice, 17, 18, 19, 20; through (*dia*) – vv.16, 20 three times; for (*eis*) – v. 16, also v. 20, where 'him' presumably refers to God; before (*pro*) – v. 17; with (*sun*) – v. 17; on (*epi*) – vv. 16, 20; from (*ek*) – v. 18.

29. Gregory E. Sterling 'Prepositional Metaphysics in Jewish Wisdom Speculation and Early Christian Liturgical Texts', in *Wisdom and Logos: Studies in Jewish Thought in Honor of David Winston*, ed. David T. Runia and Gregory E. Sterling, The Studia Philonica Annual 28: Studies in Hellenistic Judaism 9, BJS 312 (Atlanta GA: Scholars Press, 1997) 219–38.

Or in 1 Cor. 8.6: 'For us there is one God, the Father, *from* whom are all things and *for* whom we exist, and one Lord, Jesus Christ, *through* whom are all things and *through* whom we exist.'

Early Christological debates made reference to these prepositions in order to reflect on the relationship between the Father and the Son, but they also recognized that they are not used in a consistent technical way.[30] This is the language of praise, which seeks to cross and dissolve boundaries, rather than to establish them.

This way of using language to reflect on cosmology and ontology is called 'prepositional metaphysics'. The approach goes back to Aristotle, Plato's most famous pupil. Aristotle distinguishes four causes: the material cause, the formal cause, the efficient cause and the final cause.[31] For Stoics, however, while there are subordinate causes, there is essentially one primary cause – that which makes – and this cause is identified with reason, which is none other than God. Seneca writes: 'Now, however, I am searching for the first, the general cause; this must be simple, inasmuch as matter, too, is simple. Do we ask what cause is? It is surely Creative Reason—in other words, God'.[32]

We have various examples of Stoic praise for God, nature or the cosmos, which in Stoic thought are closely aligned. The most famous is that of Marcus Aurelius:

> All that is in tune with you, O [Cosmos], is in tune with me! Nothing that is in due time for you is too early or too late for me! All that your seasons bring, O Nature *(physis)*, is fruit for me! All things are from you *(ek sou)*, all things are in you *(en soi)*, and all things are for you *(eis se)*.[33]

The second-century BCE author of *De mundo* known as Pseudo-Aristotle wrote: 'All things are from God and through God hold together for us' (*De mundo* 397b).[34] Aristides, the second-century CE orator who influenced Marcus Aurelius, wrote: 'For all things everywhere are through you *(dia sou)* and have become for us on account of you *(dia se)*.[35] Philo, the first-century Jewish philosopher, used

---

30. See Sterling's discussion of Basil of Caesarea, 'Prepositional Metaphysics', 219–20.

31. The most famous illustration is of a bronze statue, whereby the material cause is the bronze, the formal cause is the specific shape that the statue takes, the efficient cause is the artist and the final cause is the purpose of the creation, be it reward, fame or piety. See, for example, Seneca, *Epistles.* 65.4-6, LCL 75: 446–7, Alexander of Aphrodisias, *De Fato* 3 (cited by Eusebius in *The preparation for the Gospel*; see *Die Praeparatio Evangelica* 6.9.3–6, ed. Karl Mras and Édouard des Places, Eusebius Werke 8/1, Introduction and books 1–8; (Berlin: Akademie, 1982), 328–9), and Clement of Alexandria in *Miscellanies (Stromata)* 8.9.26.2-3; 8.9.28.2.

32. Seneca, *Epistles* 6.12, LCL 75: 450–1.

33. Marcus Aurelius, *Meditations* 4.23, LCL 58: 80–1, (modernized).

34. Sterling, 'Prepositional Metaphysics' 223.

35. As translated, by Sterling in 'Prepositional Metaphysics', 223–4. For the original saying in its context, see Aelius Aristides, *Eis ton Sarapin*, in *Aristides*, vol. 1, 8.51, line 4, ed. Wilhelm Dindorf (Leipzig: Reimer, 1829), 87.

a similar expression: 'Through the causative word (*dia rhēmatos tou aitiou*) ... through whom also the whole cosmos was made.'[36] In all these instances, the prepositions are used as a way of speaking about the cause and origin of all things and connecting them with God – often with a sense of awe and wonder.

The Colossian hymn identifies one cause that brings into being and unifies all things, namely Christ. These verses affirm that Christ is the Reason permeating the universe. If all things were created *in* Christ, *through* Christ and *for* Christ, and if Christ is *before* all things and they stand together *with* him, the claim that these prepositions make is that Christ effectively encompasses all things, the universe. This is nothing less than a cosmic Christology.

Cosmic Christology has direct ecological implications. The Jesus of the Gospel traditions models a lifestyle of simplicity and respect for all creatures, and the Cosmic Christ gives a framework for reconfiguring our relationship with Earth – humanity and Earth together are kin, part of 'all things' that are in Christ and embraced in every dimension by Christ. There is no dualism between material and spiritual reality in this Christology – all material reality is imbued with the life of God. A cosmic Christology does not allow us to view creation merely as a backdrop to the divine story or as spiritually irrelevant. Nature is not merely the arena for God's dealings with humanity.

In embracing a cosmic Christology, Christian practice cannot remain an individual piety, which takes no responsibility for just dealings with other species, because 'all things' were created in Christ and for Christ. All things are not our property and right, but Christ's. It is incumbent upon human beings to reflect on the ethical basis upon which we build our way of living, our use of Earth's resources and our treatment of other creatures.

Cosmic Christology is largely foreign to Western Christianity. Jesus is proclaimed as 'Lord', 'Saviour' and 'Friend', but not as the one through whom and for whom the world was created, nor as the reconciler of a broken and exploited cosmos. It is precisely Western protestant theology that scholarship has implicated in some of the damaging practices of the transnational corporations; these practices have been justified by an eschatology that looks for a new (as in replacement) heaven and new Earth.[37]

Cosmic Christology remains problematic for many, perhaps most, Western evangelical Christians. It seems as though proclaiming a Christ who is 'bigger than Jesus'[38] is seen to be relativizing the particularity of the revelation in the crucified

36. Philo, *Sacrifices* 1.8, LCL 227: 98–9. See also *On the Special Laws* 1.81, LCL 320: 146–7.

37. So Harry O. Meier 'There's a New World Coming! Reading the Apocalypse in the Shadow of the Canadian Rockies', in *The Earth Story in the New Testament*, ed. Norman C. Habel and Vicky Balabanski, The Earth Bible 5 (London, New York: Sheffield, 2002), 166–79.

38. This is a phrase of J. A. T. Robinson's, in *The Human Face of God* (London: SCM Press 1973), 10.

and risen Jesus. The authors of Colossians would vigorously disagree, given that the 'blood of his cross' (1.20) is cited as the instrument of cosmic reconciliation. Other contemporary evangelical thinkers also disagree.[39] Yet the fact remains that contemporary Western Christians have significant difficulty in connecting the individual and historically particular with the universal and transcendent. The role of the Cosmic Christ has therefore largely been occupied by the third person of the Trinity in Western theology.

However, one very significant development is Pope Francis's Encyclical *Laudato si' … On Care for Our Common Home*. In ch. 2, #99–#100, drawing explicitly on Col. 1.16, and then Col. 1.19-20, Pope Francis links the destiny of all creation with the 'mystery of Christ'.

> From the beginning of the world, but particularly through the incarnation, the mystery of Christ is at work in a hidden manner in the natural world as a whole, without thereby impinging on its autonomy. The New Testament does not only tell us of the earthly Jesus and his tangible and loving relationship with the world. It also shows him risen and glorious, present throughout creation by his universal Lordship: 'For in him all the fullness of God was pleased to dwell, and through him to reconcile to himself all things, whether on earth or in heaven, making peace by the blood of his cross' (Col. 1.19-20). This leads us to direct our gaze to the end of time, when the Son will deliver all things to the Father, so that 'God may be everything to every one'. (1 Cor. 15.28)

Pope Francis goes on to state that the creatures of this world no longer appear to us under merely natural guise because the risen One is mysteriously holding them to himself and directing them towards fullness as their end. The very flowers of the field and the birds which his human eyes contemplated and admired are now imbued with his radiant presence.[40]

Pope Francis uses the language of 'the mystery of Christ' rather than Cosmic Christology; mystery is a concept familiar to those in the Roman Catholic tradition from liturgical and Eucharistic settings. This brief section of the encyclical links the pre-incarnate mystery of Christ, the incarnate Jesus and the eschatological future of creation. It calls for a profound shift in our perception of the creatures of the world – they are valued and loved by God. It also calls for a shift in eschatology; Christ is also directing all creatures towards 'fullness'.

There are some precedents in Western Christianity for such a mysterious, cosmic vision of Christ, particularly in the Celtic tradition. An ancient Lorica

39. Compare Richard Bauckham, 'Where Is Wisdom to Be Found? Colossians 1.15-20 (2)', in *Reading Texts, Seeking Wisdom*, ed. David Ford and Graham Stanton (London: SCM, 2003), 134–5.

40. Francis, *Encyclical letter Laudato si' of the Holy Father Francis on Care for Our Common Home*, 2.99–100.

(a prayer for protection) attributed to St Patrick includes the use of prepositions in a way that is comparable to their use in the Colossian hymn:

> Christ with me, Christ before me, Christ behind me,
> Christ in me, Christ beneath me, Christ above me,
> Christ on my right, Christ on my left … .

Similarly there are other early Hebridean/Gaelic prayers:

> Be thou a bright flame before me
> Be thou a guiding star above me,
> Be thou a smooth path below me,
> And be a kindly shepherd behind me,
> Today, tonight, and forever.[41]

Cultivating a theology of Christ's presence, such as came naturally to ancient Celtic Christians, is one way to begin to recover a sense of the sacredness of all things.

Nympha's notes

As a child, I remember being cared for by a slave named Klaros. I was a cheeky child, and used to laugh at her name, saying 'Klaros is a boy's name! You should be Klara!' She used to smile and say to me 'I am not bright or famous, little mistress. I am from Klaros, the place of the oracle.' 'What oracle?' I would say, but she did not answer. Then one morning before dawn, I woke up to see her at the window facing east. She had lit a tiny oil lamp, and its flame cast strange shadows across her face. Then she began to chant these words:

> Self-generate, without teacher, without mother, unshaken, a name not contained in a word, dwelling in fire, this is God; we angels are a small portion of God.

As the dawn began to break, I realized that she was praying – to a god without teacher or mother, a god without origin or name. She was praying to a god who dwells in light – not the tiny flame of the lamp, but the light of the world as it broke

---

41. Attributed to Bishop Serf (*c.* 500), in *Celebrating the Saints: Daily Spiritual Readings to Accompany the Calendars of The Church of England, The Church of Ireland, The Scottish Episcopal Church and The Church in Wales*, ed. Robert Atwell (Norwich: Canterbury Press, 2016), 245.

across the valley. She saw herself as a spark of that same fire. She was praying to the Most High God, whom she did not know but whom she nevertheless revered.[42]

I now know that Most High God in and through the unique Son Jesus Christ. I now know that all things are a small portion of God, because they were created in and through and for Christ and have been reconciled to God through Christ. All things need the light of God to flourish. I like to remember the smell of the tiny oil lamp, think of Klaros praying and know that Christ was watching over her, even though she did not know it.

42. Joan Riley, 'Beyond the Mainstream: The Cultural Environment of Asia Minor as a Matrix for Expressions of a Highest God', PhD dissertation 2017, Flinders University of South Australia, ch. 8.

CHAPTER 5

Stoic reading context: Cognition, cosmic sympathy and oikeiōsis *(restoring kinship)*

Part of 'living in accordance with nature' for Stoics is the conviction that we have the *ability* to do so. According to nature's plan, all creatures, and particularly those endowed with reason, have the mental equipment to discriminate accurately between what is real and what is not. Our minds are stocked with preconceptions, which enable us to conceptualize something new or surprising when we encounter it. Stoics held that our senses give us a cognitive impression of something, but this cognitive impression may or may not be an accurate reflection of reality. With the help of reason, we assent to the cognitive impression or withhold our assent to it. The outcome of assent to a cognitive impression is 'cognition'.[1]

A wise person, says Stobaeus, is not quick to assent to a cognitive impression:

> So precipitancy and assent in advance of cognition are attributes of the precipitate inferior human being, whereas they do not befall the person who is well-natured and perfect and virtuous.[2]

Another Stoic writer states:

> Wise people are incapable of being deceived and of erring, and ... they live worthily and do everything well. Therefore they also give greater attention to ensuring that their assents do not occur randomly, but only in company with cognition.[3]

The Stoics added a further attribute to the concept of cognitive impression: it must be 'of such a kind as could not arise from what is not'.[4] This means that only real

---

1. L&S 250–1.

2. Stobaeus, *Eclogae* 2. 112, 5-8 (*SVF* 3.548, part), L&S 256 (modified).

3. Anonymous Stoic treatise, *Herculaneum papyrus 1020* col. 4, col. 1 (*SVF* 2.131, part), L&S 255 (modified).

4. Sextus Empiricus, *Against the professors* 7.252 (*SVF* 2.65, part), L&S 243. The LCL reference is *Against the Logicians* 1.252 in LCL 291: 134–5.

things as they really are can produce the clarity and distinctness necessary to reach cognition.

Rising from the dead is a case in point; Stoic preconception states that it does not happen. As Sextus Empiricus reports, 'one who is dead does not rise again':

> For there are times when a cognitive impression occurs, but it is incredible owing to the external circumstances. (2) Thus when Heracles stood before Admetus, having brought Alcestis back from the dead, Admetus then took in a cognitive impression of Alcestis, but did not believe it … for he reasoned that Alcestis was dead, and that one who is dead does not rise again though certain spirits do sometimes roam around.[5]

So the resurrection of Jesus Christ would have been highly disputed, given the great value Stoics placed on withholding assent from things that 'could not arise'. One could only give credence to the apostles' claim that they had seen the resurrected Christ with their own eyes if one was convinced that those making the claim were wise, 'incapable of being deceived and of erring, and that they live worthily and do everything well'.[6] In the contemporary world, we do not associate accurate cognition with a virtuous character, but this was current in the Colossians' context, and makes the issue of who brought them the Gospel much more crucial to their acceptance of it. They knew Epaphras personally – he was 'one of them' (Col. 4.12), so his character was crucial to their embrace of the gospel. Similarly, the great respect in which Paul and his associates were held was foundational in the legitimacy of the gospel's claim that God has brought about reconciliation through Christ's death.

Cosmic sympathy

The cosmic scope of reconciliation set out in Colossians – all things, whether on earth or in heaven, v.20, 22 – can be understood against the background of the Stoic concept of cosmic sympathy. The concept of the world as a living being goes back to Plato's *Timaeus*, and became central to the early Stoics. It was used and extended by the Stoic polymath Posidonius (c.135–c.50 BCE), who made use of scientific observations to argue that there is a sympathetic relationship between all parts of the world – what affects one part affects all.[7] Just as the height of the tides correlates with the phases of the moon, just as the life-giving force of the

---

5. Sextus Empiricus, *Against the professors* 7.253–6, L&S 246.

6. Compare 1 Cor. 15:3-12, where Paul recounts the witnesses to the resurrection, culminating in himself and his own credentials. He sets this in contrast with the claim 'of some' that there is no resurrection of the dead.

7. Everett Ferguson, *Backgrounds of Early Christianity*, 3rd edn (Grand Rapids, MI: Eerdmans, 2003), 361–3.

sun shapes different peoples in different places, so the cosmos functions as a living being, with every part interconnected with the rest.[8] Similarly, all beings are interconnected according to their level of being; some with the power of growth and nourishment, the next level with the power of motion, and humans with the power of reason and speech.[9] In a way reminiscent of Plato's *Timaeus*, the whole universe is a being, with every part contributing to the whole. When one part is dysfunctional, other parts suffer; when reconciliation takes place, through cosmic sympathy, all things are affected.

Oikeiōsis *(restoring kinship)*

A key Stoic concept is *oikeiōsis* – to make someone or something to be of the same household, family or kin as oneself.[10] This means to make a person one's friend, and so 'reconciliation' is one of the ways of translating this term.[11] The term has overtones of affiliation and affection, and is sometimes translated as 'appropriation', in the sense of making something 'one's own'. In Stoic philosophy, the concept was not limited to other human beings, but meant recognizing oneself as 'endeared by nature' to all animals, as well as humans.[12] So beginning with Chrysippus, some Stoics and those influenced by Stoicism wrote of the concept of *oikeiōsis* as characterizing the whole of nature, not just humanity.[13] See the further discussion of this in Chapter 8.

Eco-Stoic commentary on Col. 1.21-23: Reconciliation in his body of flesh

Translation of Col. 1.21-23

[21] And you who were at one time strangers and enemies in your mind-set as expressed through your evil actions,[22] he [Christ] has now reconciled in the body of his flesh by his death, in order to present you holy and blameless and irreproachable before [God].

---

8. Ferguson, *Backgrounds of Early Christianity*, 361–3. Posidonius himself engaged in methodological studies of these phenomena.

9. Ferguson, *Backgrounds of Early Christianity*, 363.

10. On the importance of this term, see Ilaria Ramelli, 'The Stoic Doctrine of Oikeiosis and its Translation in Christian Platonism', *Apeiron* 47/1 (2014):116–40.

11. LSJ, 1202.

12. LSJ, 1202 *oikei-oō* II.1.b., citing Chrysippus, 3.43.

13. Chrysippus *Fragmenta logica et physica,* fragment 724 line 4, *SVF 2,* 206 cited in Plutarch's *Moralia,* 1038, LCL 470: 454–5; Posidonius *Fragmenta* Fragment 416 line 58; Hierocles, as quoted by Stobaeus, cited in Chapter 8. See also Philo *De opificio mundi,* 1.10, LCL 226: 10–11.

[23] Since this is so[14] remain securely established and steadfast in the faith, without shifting from the hope promised by the Gospel that you heard, which has been proclaimed in all creation under heaven.

It is of this Gospel that I, Paul, became a servant.

In these verses, Timothy and Paul make the claim that through his death, in his body of flesh, Jesus Christ has reconciled those who were at one time strangers and enemies both in their mindset and their actions. This reconciliation has made the believers holy, blameless and irreproachable before God. It has also reconciled them to each other, so that they are no longer strangers and enemies. It has profoundly reshaped who they are as individuals: they now count among those who are virtuous and at peace with each other.

Against the background of our reading context, the Colossian believers are now able to count themselves among those who perceive reality as it truly is; they are able to receive cognitive impressions, assent to them and reach reliable cognition. As such, they are no longer estranged from reality, resorting to evil actions. They see things as they really are, and are now able to live accordingly. This means they see reality with new eyes – the eyes of those who are fully virtuous before God, fully reconciled with God.

The image of salvation as reconciliation is central in Colossians. Among the various Pauline ways of articulating the salvation effected by Christ's death, that of *reconciliation* refers to the restoration of right relationship between God and humanity as well as between God and creation. Relationships that have been disordered by wrong attitudes and behaviours are reinstated and reconfigured through Christ's reconciling death.

More particularly, this monumental shift has taken place through the death of Christ in the body of his flesh. Although the word 'resurrection' does not occur here, nor indeed anywhere in Colossians, it is implied when Christ's reconciling death is mentioned, and is presented explicitly in Col. 2.12:

Having been buried with him in baptism, you also have been raised with him through faith in the power of God who raised him from the dead. (Col. 2.12)

The Colossians, together with all believers, are those who know that Jesus Christ was raised by God from the dead, and who participate in that cosmic act through baptism. This is reiterated also in Col. 3.1. The cosmic significance of Christ's death and rising affects everything, but it is at work most actively in those who have been baptized into Christ's death. The (new) harmony between different parts of the cosmos is most visible in the believers.

---

14. The reasons for this translation are set out in Vicky Balabanski, 'Colossians 1:23: A case for translating ἐπιμένετε (continue) as imperative, not indicative', in *TynBul* 70/1 (2019), 85–94.

They are the ones who have entrusted themselves to the Logos of the Good News and to the hope of salvation. They have reached cognition of the truth of Jesus Christ's death and resurrection and its cosmic significance because they have rightly perceived the wisdom and virtue of Epaphras, who brought them the Gospel. It is no less a figure than Paul himself who vouches for Epaphras, and for the message of the Gospel itself:

It is of this Gospel that I, Paul, became a servant. (Col. 1.23)

The Stoic background makes the personal imprimatur of the apostle more vivid: the reputation of Paul for wisdom and virtue makes the news of Christ's death on the cross and being raised from the dead no mere cognitive impression of some distant group of 'inferior' men and women, but a reliable cognition of many apostles, and of Paul himself.

Verses 21-22 continue the long grammatical unit that began at v. 9 and incorporated the Colossian hymn in vv. 15-20. It is not until v. 23 that we have a new finite verb: *epimenete* (continue, remain, persevere). This makes v. 23 stand out as an important rhetorical transition, from the prayer of Paul and Timothy that the Colossians may be filled full (v.9) right through to the exhortation in v. 23. The verbal form *epimenete* is generally understood as indicative, which would mean that all of the preceding was provisional upon the believers continuing on with practising their faith: 'If you remain …'. However, the form of the verb may be imperative, and I have taken it in this sense, on the basis that the six most ancient manuscripts all indicate some sort of break between vv. 22 and 23, and imply a new sentence is starting at v.23.[15] This makes the word *eige* an enclitic particle, meaning '"since this is so", remain securely established and steadfast in the faith …'. This is a more appropriate translation, as the rich picture of salvation in vv. 9-22 is not dependent on the believers' behaviour; rather, it forms a secure basis for their faith and hope.

There are two matters of particular ecological significance in these verses.

1. Reconciliation in the body of his flesh
2. Proclaimed to all creation under heaven

Reconciliation in the body of his flesh In Chapter 4 we saw just how important embodied reality is for this remarkable Letter. Embodied reality is the only sort of reality that can affect anything, so even spiritual realities are understood by the Stoics not as disembodied, but as embodied, though unseen. Disembodied things (such as emptiness, time or place) subsist rather than exist, always dependent on other realities. For those influenced by Stoic thought, virtues are embodied. Given

---

15. Balabanski 'Colossians 1:23: A case for translating ἐπιμένετε (continue) as imperative, not indicative', 88–9.

this way of categorizing reality, the most important act of all – the reconciliation of all things to God in Christ, *exists* (not subsists). It is embodied, and not only that, it is embodied in and through the body of Christ's flesh. Christ's death was embodied, and his being raised from the dead was also embodied. This leads Timothy and Paul to emphasize the locus of this salvation squarely in the incarnate body of Jesus Christ. This reconciliation happened in Christ's real, visible, embodied flesh.

Together with the reference in Col. 1.20 to 'the blood of his cross', this focus in Col. 1.22 on the physical body of Christ as the locus of reconciliation is significant. By emphasizing the physical body and the real blood that was shed, it insists that the material world is crucial to God. It is in and through the material world that reconciliation – salvation – takes place. The Christian tradition that we have inherited keeps the doctrines of creation and salvation as separate movements of God, but Col. 1.15-22 sees them as inextricably bound together in a material spirituality, or a spiritual materiality.

For those shaped by Stoic thought, this physicality was not a problem as it was in more Platonic circles and in Docetic and Gnostic thought.[16] The affirmation that all things are reconciled to God through the peace-making of Christ's blood on the cross (v.20), and the application of this act to the believers in vv. 21-22 is a claim that this reconciliation is embodied and therefore real. The embodied spiritual significance of Christ's death and being raised to life has affected believers and the cosmos alike. Through cosmic sympathy, Christ's reconciling work yields resonances throughout the world.

Proclaimed to all creation under heaven With the concept of cosmic sympathy – the interconnectedness of all things – as part of the Koine of people's cosmological world view, we can better understand the claim in v.23 that the Gospel 'has been proclaimed to all creation under heaven' (or 'every creature under heaven'). Traditional exegesis tends to see this as simply a variation on the description of the spread of the gospel that we have in Col 1.5-6.[17] Some scholars note the parallel between Col. 1.23 and Mk 16.15: 'Go into all the world and proclaim the Good News to the whole creation.'[18] This verse from the longer ending of Mark, which is not found in the earliest manuscripts of Mark, is an imperative to proclaim the Gospel to the whole creation, but implies that this is yet to take place. The statement in Col. 1.23 says that this has already taken place (aorist passive participle, dependent on the aorist verb 'you have heard'). The difficulty of interpreting this phrase is

---

16. Compare 1 Jn 4.2, 'Every spirit that confesses that Jesus Christ has come in the flesh is from God'. Docetic views held the real fleshly embodiment of Jesus Christ to be false.

17. See, for example, James D. G. Dunn, who notes a 'degree of hyperbole' in this claim, *The Epistles to the Colossians and to Philemon*, 111–12.

18. Schweizer, *The Letter to the Colossians: A Commentary*, 96; Robert McL. Wilson, *Colossians and Philemon: A Critical and Exegetical Commentary* (London: Bloomsbury/ T & T Clark, 2005), 166.

twofold: What does 'all creation under heaven' mean, and how can one say that proclaiming the Gospel to all creation has already taken place?

Scholars have tended to interpret every creature as 'humankind', claiming this reflects a Jewish usage.[19] An ecological reading resists replacing the inclusive term 'all creation' with the anthropocentric term 'humankind' so readily, on the basis that there are many choices the author/s could have made to specify humanity, had this been what they meant.[20] The choice of the inclusive *ktisis* (creation or creature) and the descriptor *pasē* (all) embraces the non-human world. It lays claim to the significance of Christ's reconciling work for non-human creation as well as for humanity.

The Stoic concept of *oikeiōsis* (restoring or recognizing kinship), and in particular its inclusion not only of people but also of animals and indeed 'all creation', makes v. 23 much clearer. Although the word *oikeiōsis* does not appear in Colossians, the concept of reconciliation as restoring kinship across all divides, including with non-human creation, is central. Reconciliation is at work cosmically, in the community of believers and in all creation.

The Gospel of this reconciliation has been proclaimed not only to the Colossians but also (literally) 'in all creation under heaven'. Because of the preposition 'in', I think the Greek is best rendered as a collective – 'creation' – rather than 'every creature'. The words 'under heaven' might seem to limit this proclamation to the earthly sphere.

The concept of 'heaven' – and the difference between Stoic and Platonic ideas of heaven – has been raised in Chapter 2, in relation to Col. 1.5. There I interpreted heaven as a metonym for God's presence, drawing on Stoic usage of naming the world's commanding faculty as the heaven.[21] Heaven is named five times in Colossians (1.5, 16, 20, 23 and 4.1). In the Colossian hymn, twice it is paired with earth (1.16, 20), so that heaven and earth are grouped together as a unified whole. The reference to 'heaven' in Col. 1.23 and 4.1 might seem to make a distinction between heaven and earth, but in these instances too, 'under heaven' and 'in heaven' make God's presence their reference point. As we will see in the discussion of Col. 2.9, we have imagery in this Letter that evokes the permeation of the divine throughout reality. So when Col. 1.23 states that the Gospel has been proclaimed

---

19. See Lohse, *Colossians and Philemon*, 67 fn. 46, citing *Aboth* 1.12. 'Hillel said, "Be ... one that ... loves the creatures"', which he takes to mean '[hu]mankind.' That is a very circular claim.

20. Scholars who use an approach called Systemic Functional Linguistics point out that 'a text is a product of ongoing selection in a very large network of systems – a systems network'. M. A. K. Halliday and C. M. I. M. Matthiessen, *An Introduction to Functional Grammar*, 4th edn (London: Routledge, 2014), 23. The choice of 'to all creation under heaven' is distinct from 'to all people under heaven'.

21. Diogenes Laertius, referring to Chrysippus and Posidonius, 7.138–9 (including *SVF* 2.634), L&S 284.

'in all creation under heaven', no clear distinction is being drawn between earthly and heavenly proclamation. Heaven is a metonym for God's presence.

How can the author/s of the Letter state that the proclamation of the Gospel to all creation under heaven has taken place? One could put this down to the plerophoric tone of the opening of the Letter, making a doxological but non-specific claim that *in some sense* all creation has heard the Gospel proclaimed. But such a claim must have a basis in the writers' and recipients' cosmology to have meaning. It seems to imply that in the death and rising of Christ, the proclamation to all creation has been effected. The Stoic notion of cosmic sympathy enables us to conceptualize this claim. The profound dysfunction of the universe, the creation being at odds with the Creator, has been fundamentally changed by the death and rising of the One through whom and for whom all things came into being. Just as Ps. 19.1-4 affirms that the knowledge of God's glory goes forth without speech, words or voice, so through cosmic sympathy the proclamation of the Good News in all creation has taken place through the cross and resurrection and their reconciling power.

Hermeneutical reflections on Col. 1.21-23

The Stoics believed that living in harmony with nature expressed living in harmony with God. The Christian Gospel welcomes this insight, but also has a greater sense of the reality of dysfunction, evil and sin, as it affects both nature and humanity. In our own strength, we are not able to live in accordance with nature nor in accordance with God who, through Christ, brought all things into being. The dysfunction is greater than the Stoics allowed, and the solution required is also far greater – the death of the One through whom all things came into being.

An ecological reading of this passage recognizes that the scale of the dysfunction between humanity and the rest of nature is much greater than might first appear. The extent to which our estrangement from nature, from God and from one another leads to evil deeds is palpable when we view the self-interested systems in place that ensure the richer get richer at the expense of nature and the poor.

Reconciliation requires profound change in human beings. The shift from estranged and hostile attitudes leading to evil actions, to a community that is holy, blameless and irreproachable before God requires an intervention of cosmic proportions. The writers of Colossians look at this intervention as having been perfected and completed, but they also recognize that the believers must act on it for it to be effective (v. 23). The key terms used to describe this are: remain securely established (literally 'having been founded', perfect passive participle), steadfast in faith (literally seated or stable), without shifting (literally 'being shifted', present passive participle) from the hope promised by the Gospel.

What would such secure confidence look like in the contemporary world? One might think that only those who are so convinced of their own point of view that nothing can sway them might qualify for this description. But this does not sit well with an ecological way of reading Colossians, which embraces an inclusive rather than an exclusive posture towards all things. What is being called for in the believers is a great sense of gratitude and trust in the God who not only called into being an intricate, beautiful, interdependent world but also gave humanity a key role in its care. The long unit running from vv. 9 to 22, and culminating in the transitional v. 23, shows that being 'filled full' with the knowledge of God has been enabled by God's own initiative, making Godself known to us through Jesus Christ. Verse 23 returns the focus to the hope with which the Letter opened (Col. 1.5). What remains to us is an appropriate response to the knowledge of God's great two-part movement of creation and salvation, and to the hope that springs from it. What is called for is a truly mature and adult response, without dismissing child-like trust in the hope of the Gospel.

The concept of cosmic sympathy has a contemporary counterpart in Deep Ecology, such as that we find in the philosophy of the Norwegian Arne Naess, who is recognized as one of the most eminent and influential philosophers of our time.[22] Naess calls his approach 'Ecosophy', and defines the approach as 'a philosophy of ecological harmony or equilibrium'.[23] Naess sees the universe as a whole that is being substantiated in every single being, irrespective of whether the being is rational or not. All things are constituted by their relations to other things; organisms are knots in the biospherical net or field of intrinsic relations.[24] Deep Ecologists such as Naess, Warwick Fox,[25] Bill Devall[26] and others are seeking on a non-theistic basis to establish a philosophical foundation for the valuing of all things as one extended, all-encompassing organism. By identifying with every other being, we can learn to perceive other beings as part of our 'extended Self'.

The providential views of Stoicism, and of the Gospel, appear to be tenaciously anthropocentric, and thus sit uneasily with the core values of Deep Ecology.[27] However, when we recognize our extended or ecological Self in the natural world, what is good for the human person cannot be separated from what is good for

---

22. See Evangelos D. Protopapadakis, 'The Stoic Notion of "Cosmic Sympathy" in Contemporary Environmental Ethics', in *Antiquity, Modern World and Reception of Ancient Culture*, Антика и савремени свет (Antiquity and Modern World) Series, vol. 6, ed. Ksenija Maricki-Gaďanski (Belgrade: Scientific Publications of The Serbian Society for Ancient Studies, 2012), 290–305, 295.

23. Naess' definition continues: 'A philosophy as a kind of *sofia* wisdom, is openly normative, it contains both norms, rules, postulates, value priority announcements and hypotheses concerning the state of affairs in our universe. Wisdom is policy wisdom, prescription, not only scientific description and prediction.' Arne Naess, 'The Shallow and the Deep, Long-Range Ecology Movement: A Summary', *Inquiry* 16/1–4 (1973): 95–100, 99.

24. Naess, 'The Shallow and the Deep', 95.

25. Warwick Fox, 'Deep Ecology: A New Philosophy of our Time?' *Environmental Ethics*, ed. Andrea Light and Holmes Rolston III (Malden: Blackwell, 2003).

26. Bill Devall, 'The Ecological Self', in *The Deep Ecology Movement: An Introductory Anthology*, ed. Alan Drengson and Yuichi Inoue (Berkeley, CA: North Atlantic Publishers, 1995), 101–23.

27. See Baltzly, 'Stoic Pantheism', particularly 15–18.

Earth. Providence cannot remain confined to what is narrowly beneficial for human beings. As Elizabeth Johnson puts it, 'Ultimately divine purpose is cosmocentric and biocentric, not merely anthropocentric.'[28]

Recognizing ourselves as profoundly embedded in the natural world does not solve the ethical dilemmas of how we make use of the Earth's resources – 'self'-interest still needs to make decisions about priorities, just as regular self-interest prioritizes one's own needs. Nevertheless, it can be a valuable perceptual shift. What is still necessary is a further step – that of willingness to self-limit and self-empty; these draw us closer to the Gospel values.

Nympha's notes

Isn't prayer the most important demonstration of cosmic sympathy that there is? Paul, Timothy and our own Epaphras are praying constantly for us, and the God of the cosmos, whom we know in and through Jesus Christ, connects us with them. Their prayers are effective over the hundreds of leagues that separate us. That's true cosmic sympathy!

I grew up with my little lyre, learning not only the sounds the strings made but also the mathematical proportions of the strings. Those same proportions shape the heavenly spheres. There is correspondence between the great realities of the world and the sound of a string vibrating. I used to think of this correspondence between the macro and the microcosm as controlling me, so the harmony of the spheres – or their disharmony – unleashed good or evil upon us mortals.

But now I think differently. The cosmos is through and through the good creation of the One through whom it came into being. It is only when we are estranged from God that disharmony and evil deeds result. Jesus Christ has overcome that disharmony and restored our kinship with all things. So the prayers of those whose virtue is known to us and to everyone are effective, and each prayer is a cosmic act!

---

28. Elizabeth A. Johnson, 'Jesus and the Cosmos: Soundings in Deep Ecology,' in *Incarnation: On the Scope and Depth of Christology*, ed. N. H. Gregersen (Minneapolis, MN: Fortress Press, 2015), 133–56, 150.

CHAPTER 6

Stoic reading context: Suffering as 'indifferent'

One of the key differences between the Stoic and Epicurean schools of philosophy was their attitude to suffering. Epicureans saw pleasure and pain as primary motivators and viewed them as the standard for all choice and avoidance respectively: all creatures maximize pleasure and avoid pain.[1]

Stoics saw things differently. They relegated pleasure and pain to a lower level of significance; they acknowledged that pleasure is preferable to pain, but did not allow that either of them was objectively good or bad. Virtue is good, the opposite of virtue is bad, and all else is ultimately neither good nor bad, but indifferent. Diogenes Laertius put it this way:

> (1) They [the Stoics] say that some existing things are good, others are bad, and others are neither of these. (2) The virtues – prudence, justice, courage, moderation and the rest – are good. (3) The opposites of these – foolishness, injustice and the rest – are bad. (4) Everything which neither does benefit nor harms is neither of these: for instance, life, health, pleasure, beauty, strength, wealth, reputation (*doxa*), noble birth, and their opposites, death, disease, pain, ugliness, weakness, poverty, low repute, ignoble birth and the like … . For these things are not good but indifferents (*adiaphora*) of the species 'preferred' (*proēgmena*). (*Lives* 7.101-3, L&S 354)

This is the attitude for which the Stoics are best known: suffering is not bad, but indifferent. Life, health, pleasure, strength are all preferable, but not in themselves good. We know from our own experience that the sort of pain that we experience during or after a session of strenuous physical exercise is worth the effort it takes to extend our endurance and achieve a goal. That does not make the pain 'good', but it does mean that it is not something to be avoided. Viewing pain this way relegates it to something less important than the ultimate goal, namely virtue; it relativizes the pain in comparison with that for which one is striving.

The key is to discern what is ultimately worth striving for – what is ultimately good.

---

1. L&S 90. See Diogenes Laertius *Lives* 10.34, LCL 185: 564–5; Cicero, *On ends* 1.37–9, LCL 40: 40–5.

Diogenes Laertius, in the quotation above, summarizes some of what the Stoics see as virtues, in contrast to the 'indifferents'.

Given that suffering belongs to the category of indifferents, few Stoic philosophers wrote at any length about it. Seneca is an exception; he experienced chronic illness (asthma) as well as many other illnesses, setbacks and losses.[2] His Epistle 78 reflects extensively on the endurance of illness, and elsewhere he writes about many other types of suffering as well, including natural disasters, interpersonal violence and torture, war and political upheaval.[3] Seneca argues that suffering has educational value and even a divine purpose; God 'does not make a spoiled pet of a good person; God tests that person, hardens and fits him or her for God's own service'.[4]

As we saw from the example of Chion of Heraclea (see Chapter 1), suffering and even dying on behalf of one's community for the sake of justice was understood as Good. It was this foundational distinction between what is truly good and what is indifferent that shaped Stoic philosophy in particular and was widely understood and admired in the Greco-Roman world. It was also this distinction that enabled people who had no prior association with Jewish synagogues to grasp the concept that a Saviour could willingly embrace death for the sake of the people. This was not just a noble death in the tradition of Socrates, to remain true to one's values. For people shaped by Stoic ideas, the willingness to embrace death for the sake of others had salvific overtones.

In this section of the Letter, we have both Paul's suffering and Christ's suffering presented as necessary for the sake of the church, and therefore not only indifferent, but rather a cause for rejoicing. This reflects a close similarity with Stoic attitudes to suffering.[5]

At the end of this passage, the writer 'rejoices' again – this time in the Colossians' 'good order' (*taxis*) and 'stability' (*stereōma*). Good order was a mark of all the other qualities of a good life; according to Cleanthes, the verbal form of good order appears first in his list of what is good:

> You ask me what the good is like. Listen then. Well-ordered (*tetagmenon*),[6] just, holy, pious, self-controlled, useful (*chrēsimon*), honourable, due, austere, candid, always useful (*aiei sumpheron*), fearless, undistressed, profitable, unpained, beneficial, contented, secure, friendly, precious < ... > consistent, fair-famed, unpretentious, caring, gentle, keen, patient, faultless, permanent. (Cleanthes in Clement, *Protrepticus* 6.72.2 (*SVF* 1.557), L&S 373)[7]

---

2. Brian J. Tabb, *Suffering in Ancient Worldview: Luke, Seneca and 4 Maccabees in Dialogue* (London: Bloomsbury/T & T Clark, 2017), 24.

3. Seneca, *Epistles* 14.3, LCL 75: 84–5; *Ep.* 67.3-4, LCL 76: 36–7; *Ep.* 91.8, LCL 76: 436–7.

4. Seneca, *De Providentia* 1.6, LCL 214: 6–7 (modified).

5. Paul Foster disagrees. See his *Colossians*, Black's New Testament Commentaries (London: Bloomsbury, 2016), 219.

6. Perfect passive participle of *tassō*, cognate with *taxis*.

7. Clement quotes these as Cleanthes' revelation concerning the nature of God, L&S vol. 2, 372.

Table 6.1 Virtues deemed 'good' and the 'indifferents'

Virtues deemed good	Indifferents
Prudence, justice, courage, moderation	Life, health, pleasure, beauty, strength, wealth, reputation/glory, noble birth; Death, disease, pain, ugliness, weakness, poverty, low repute, ignoble birth.

Being of benefit to others is key to all of these qualities – synonyms for 'useful' are even repeated. But there was also room for joy and pleasure in their framework of 'goods', though they did not qualify as virtues or the highest good. Stobaeus put it this way:

> Of goods, some are virtues but others are not. Prudence, moderation, <justice> and courage are virtues; but joy, cheerfulness, confidence, well-wishing and the like are not virtues. (Stobaeus 2.58, 5–15 (*SVF* 3.95, part) L&S 372)

If we were inclined to think of Stoics as people who are withdrawn and indifferent to emotional engagement with others, these quotations suggest otherwise – 'friendly, caring, gentle, patient' and 'joyful and cheerful' paint a different picture. What they also show is that Stoics sought to give a 'taxonomy' to their thinking about virtues, feelings and values – to evaluate their order (*taxis*) and relationship to each other. We will conclude this Stoic Reading Context with Diogenes Laertius' summary of Stoic thinking on good feelings:

> (1) They [the Stoics] say that there are three good feelings: joy, watchfulness, wishing. (2) Joy, they say, is the opposite of pleasure, consisting in well-reasoned elation (*eparsis*); and watchfulness is the opposite of fear, consisting in well-reasoned turning aside (*ekklisis*). For the wise person will not be afraid at all, but will be watchful. (3) They say that wishing is the opposite of appetite, consisting in well-reasoned desire (*orexis*). (4) Just as certain passions fall under the primary ones, so too with the primary good feelings. Under wishing: kindness, generosity, warmth, affection. Under watchfulness: respect, cleanliness. Under joy: delight, sociability, cheerfulness. (Diogenes Laertius, *Lives* 7.116 (*SVF* 3.431) L&S 412, modified)

Stoics are known for bearing adversity with fortitude. What they are less well known for is the way they sought to recognize and value what is truly good, and to live by it. Paul shows a similar commitment; having recognized what is truly good in the death and resurrection of Jesus Christ, he willingly suffers, labours and strives in continuity with Christ's suffering. He does so joyfully for the sake of Christ's body, the church, though as we will see, the scope of the mystery of God is much greater than the small communities of believers in the Lycus Valley and beyond may realize. The scope is universal.

Eco-Stoic commentary on Col. 1.24–2.5

Translation of Col. 1.24–2.5[8]

[24] Now I am rejoicing in [my] sufferings for your sake, and in my turn I am *filling up* (*pler-*) what is needful of Christ's afflictions in my *flesh* for the sake of his body, which is the *church*.

   [25] I became a servant [of the church] according to the economy of God – a role given to me for you – to *fill full* (*pler-*) the Logos of God,

      [26] the *mystery* that has been hidden from the ages and generations but has now been revealed to his *saints*.

         [27] It is to the saints that God chose to make known what an abundance of *glory* this *mystery* among the Gentiles means:

            Christ in you, the hope of *glory*.

               [28] Him we proclaim, exhorting all people and teaching all people in all *wisdom*, so that we may present all people mature in Christ.

               [29] For this I also labour, *striving* according to his power that is powerfully at work in me.

               [2.1] For I want you to know how greatly I am *striving* on your behalf, and for those in Laodicea, and for all who have not seen me face to face,

            [2] so that, having been united in love, their hearts may be comforted and so [they may have] all the riches of *fully* (*pler-*) assured understanding leading to knowledge of the *mystery* of God, the Father of Christ,

         [3] in whom are hidden all the treasures of *wisdom* and knowledge.

      [4] I am saying this so that no one may deceive you with persuasive words.

   [5] For though I am absent in the *flesh*, yet I am with you in spirit,

rejoicing to see your good order and the stability of your faith in Christ.

Paul's self-introduction and mission speech

In this next major section of the Letter, we are presented with the persona of Paul as the servant of the Gospel and of the church.[9] Here is Paul's self-introduction and mission presented as a rhetorical speech, with several features that are distinctive

---

8. The chiastic structure of these verses is noted by Heil, *Colossians: Encouragement to Walk in All Wisdom as Holy Ones in Christ*, 83. The structure offered here is similar but not identical to Heil's; the step parallelism of repeated words is a key structural feature of this prose speech, and v. 28, with its shift to first-person plural, stands out as the centre of the structure.

9. This is to be distinguished from Paul the letter writer. As set out in the introduction, this commentary takes the position that Paul is alive, located in Rome, and that Timothy drafts all but the opening and closing sections of the Letter.

in the Letter. The translation has been set out to highlight some of the structural aspects of the speech, which is a carefully structured prose exposition of the Gospel and of Paul's responsibility in making it known.

First, the use of the first-person 'I' stands out. The pronoun *egō*, I, opens the section, which begins in the last phrase of v. 22:

It is of this Gospel that I, Paul, became the servant.

This emphatic use of *egō* appears again in v. 25:

I (*egō*) became a servant of the church.

Most of the sentences in this section have the first-person singular as the subject: I am rejoicing, I am filling up, I became a servant, I labour, I want you to know, I am striving, I am saying, though I am absent in flesh, I am with you. Colossians 1.28 is an exception, where the first-person is plural: we proclaim, so that we may present. The effect of this concentration of the first-person 'I' (and the plural 'we') is to heighten the emotions of this section and intensify the urgency of the communication. Nowhere else in this Letter do we have this type of rhetoric. The first-person is not used again until ch. 4.3-4 and 18. However, when we meet the usage again at the close of the Letter, both short passages in ch. 4 echo the language of this section. In 4.3-4 some of the same words appear again: the word, the mystery of Christ and reveal. In the final sentence of the Letter, 4.18, we read the expression 'I Paul' again. Quintilian, a first-century rhetorician, recognized the effectiveness of the first-person in making an emotional connection:

When we pretend that the persons concerned themselves are speaking, the personal note adds to the emotional effect. (*Inst.* 6.1.25, LCL 125: 398–9)

Is this passage of Colossians best understood as a pretence of Paul's personal presence? I have set out in the Introduction why a theory of 'co-authorship' or 'partial pseudepigraphy' best suits the evidence. This is a carefully scripted rhetorical piece of prose that is different from Paul's undisputed writings, yet I think it likely that Paul is alive, giving his authority to this script. Prima facie this is Paul writing, crafting an epitome of his vocation and Gospel. If Timothy is indeed the script writer, as I think likely, he is distilling these key ideas and crafting a communication from Paul himself. Whatever is the case, the personal note has a strong emotional effect.

The passage opens and closes with a reference to Paul rejoicing, first in his sufferings for the Colossians' sake, and at the end, rejoicing again to see their good order and the stability of their faith in Christ. Inside this frame, in a pivotal section formed by vv. 1.29 and 2.1, we are told that Paul is striving – labouring not only for all people (1.28) but specifically for the recipients of the Letter. These recipients are specified as you (the Colossians), those in Laodicea, and all that have not seen Paul in the flesh (2.1). We will return to these verses shortly.

There are other notable structural features in addition to the ones set out above. At the opening and closing of this speech, the writer alludes to Paul's flesh. His flesh is the locus of filling up Christ's afflictions, and in 2.5, though Paul is absent in the flesh, he is with them in spirit.

The repeated use of filling full terminology (*pler-*) is striking. Paul and Timothy's prayer in Col. 1.9 was that the Colossians may be filled full, and this shaped the ensuing long section. In this section, the focus on filling full continues in 1.24, 25 and 2.2. There are no less than nine uses in various forms throughout the Letter (1.9, 19, 24, 25; 2.2, 9, 10; 4.12, 17). A discussion of this concept is given in Chapter 7 in relation to 2.9.

An acknowledgement of Christ opens and closes the speech, and there are three further references to Christ (1.27, 28; 2.2). These are closely associated with another key term – namely mystery (1.26, 27; 2.2), which is specified as 'Christ in you' (1.27). God is named in vv. 25 (twice), 27 and 2.2, as the One whose economy, mystery and choosing lie behind the grand plan of salvation. God is specified as the Father of Christ, in the unusual phrase in 2.2. A number of other terms are repeated (wisdom, 1.28; 2.3; knowledge, 2.2, 3). 'All people' is repeated three times in 1.28, again with strong rhetorical effect. Finally, there seems to be a contrast implied in the reference to filling full the word of God (1.25), which stands in opposition to the persuasive words (*pithanologia*) in 2.4

The overall effect of this 'I Paul' speech is striking. It evokes the presence of the apostle through the use of the first-person (who, though absent in the flesh, is with them in spirit). It urges the recipients to form a connection with the one who is suffering for their sake (1.24), labouring and striving on their behalf (1.29; 2.1) and who wants them to know how greatly he is concerned for them (2.1). It also seeks to give them an epitome – a very brief summary – of the Gospel, situating it in a universal context. This epitome is called the 'mystery of God' (Col. 2.2). It is to this concept of mystery that we now turn.

Mystery Mystery is a term with rich associations in various streams of ancient Judaism as well as in Hellenistic mystery cults. It mirrors a widespread sense of the hiddenness of God and the necessity of seeking divine revelation.[10] Such diverse Jewish sources as apocalyptic literature, the distinctive writings and exegesis at Qumran and also Wisdom literature show a keen interest in grasping divine mysteries.[11] We know that various mystery cults, including those honouring

---

10. 'Initiatory rites for Isis, Mithras, and Cybele all seem to have been developed during the late Hellenistic period, at a time when, for an ever-increasing proportion of the populace, bleak prospects on this earth made the promise of salvation in the hereafter look peculiarly attractive: it was a great age for demotic eschatology.' Peter Green, *Alexander to Actium: The Hellenistic Age* (London: Thames and Hudson 1993), 592.

11. See Markus N. A. Bockmuehl, *Revelation and Mystery in Ancient Judaism and Pauline Christianity*, WUNT 2/36 (Tübingen: Mohr and Siebeck, 1990).

Cybele and Dionysos, were practised in Asia Minor during the first century, and so the Colossians would have been aware of them.[12]

Mystery is a religious technical term in the cults of the Greco-Roman world, meaning a religious *secret* or *secret rite* confided only to the initiated.[13] Mystery is not a term much used in Hellenistic philosophy, in Stoic or other schools.[14] Philosophers recognized the need to find access to the hidden nature of things, but sought to do so via careful logic and inference.

In the New Testament the term 'mystery' is used in three main ways. First, it can refer to a revelation of something that was not known before, mediated from God (e.g. Mt. 13.11; 1 Cor. 15.51); second, it can be a supreme redemptive revelation of God through the gospel of Christ (e.g. Rom. 16.25; Eph. 3.9); and third, it can refer to the hidden meaning of a symbol with metaphorical significance (Eph. 5.32).[15]

The term 'mystery' is used three times in this passage (Col. 1.26, 27; 2.2) and once again in Col. 4.3, which echoes this passage. It is only used in the singular in Colossians, and only has the second of the meanings set out above, namely the supreme redemptive revelation of God through the gospel of Christ. Timothy and Paul are aware that the Colossian believers must be familiar with various things claiming the status of a mystery or practices that lead to such revelation ('mysteries'). But this passage affirms that there is only one true mystery of God, namely Christ in you, the hope of glory.

The word 'mystery' (or 'mysteries') is used quite frequently in the undisputed letters of Paul (1 Cor. 2.7 (2.1 has a significant variant); 13.2; 14.2; 15.51; Rom. 11.25; 16.25) and also in the wider Pauline corpus (2 Thess. 2.7; Eph. 1.9; 3.3, 9; 5.32; 6.19; 1 Tim. 3.9, 16). It is particularly prominent in the first Letter to the Corinthians and in the (later) Letter to the Ephesians, implying that it was a particularly useful term to be deployed both in continuity and discontinuity with its Hellenistic cultic overtones. In Paul's letters, it is closely associated with the revelation of God's secret wisdom, and twice the expansive vista of the ages is invoked:

> 1 Cor. 2.7 Instead we speak the wisdom of God, hidden in a mystery, that God determined before the ages for our glory. (NET BIBLE)

---

12. A. H. Cadwallader, *Fragments of Colossae: Sifting through the Traces* (Hindmarsh: ATF Press, 2015), 50–5.

13. Timothy Friberg, Barbara Friberg and Neva F. Miller, *Analytical Lexicon of the Greek New Testament*, Baker's Greek New Testament Library 4 (Grand Rapids, MI: Baker, 2000), 267.

14. See, however, Francesc Casadesús's paper 'The Transformation of the Initiation Language of Mystery Religions', in *Greek Philosophy and Mystery Cults*, ed. María José Martín-Velasco and María José García Blanco (Newcastle upon Tyne: Cambridge Scholars Publishing, 2016), 1–26. Casadesús argues that the language of both Plato and the early Stoic philosophers shows that they incorporated the characteristic language of mystery cults to underscore the notion that philosophical knowledge results from a process similar to a religious initiation, 1, 7, 23.

15. Friberg et al., *Analytical Lexicon*, 267.

Rom. 16.25 Now to God who is able to strengthen you according to my gospel and the proclamation of Jesus Christ, according to the revelation of the mystery that was kept secret for long ages. (NRSV)

In a similar way, Col. 1.26 refers to the way the mystery of God has been hidden from the ages and generations, and has now been revealed to the saints. However, there is a difference between these references to mystery in 1 Corinthians and Romans and the references in Colossians. What differs about the Colossians statement concerning God's mystery is that the context of the revelation is specified as 'among the Gentiles' in Col. 1.27: 'God chose to make known to the saints what the glorious abundance of this mystery *among the Gentiles* is.' This revelation is not limited to the select few, nor to the recipients of Jewish wisdom, but is intended by God to show the scope and magnitude of God's purposes outside the boundaries of Judaism, among the Gentiles. This is certainly good news for the Colossians, who are Gentile believers. Colossians 2.13 refers to the 'uncircumcision of their flesh' as the state in which God met them and 'made them alive'. We will shortly see that the scope of this mystery is in fact even broader than this.

Mysteries were normally thought to be for the initiated or the chosen few. Using this word anticipates the warnings that are the focus of Col. 2.8-23 and indicates that the Letter was making a contrasting claim about divine revelation. Just as the Letter to this point has emphasized how Christ is the source, goal and purpose of 'all things' (Col. 1.15-20), so too here the scope of the mystery of the Gospel is much more universal than anyone would have anticipated.[16]

The content of the mystery is distilled in two phrases: Christ in you, the hope of glory (1.27). We have considered the connection between hope, glory and the Good News in Chapter 2 as a triad which articulates the mystery of 'Christ in you'. Here we will explore this further.

Christ in you Christ, the embodiment of the unseen God, is revealed 'in' or 'among' those who receive the Letter. The preposition *en* has both a corporate and an individual sense, and the ambiguity does not require resolution.[17] If the one is true,

---

16. The parallels between, and influence of both, mystery cults and Pauline thought are a contested area of scholarship. Note particularly the work of Alfred Loisy, who argued that Pauline theology had transformed Jesus of Nazareth into a universal God of salvation, and had provided this deity with his own myth of death and rebirth, under the influence of the dying and resurrecting pagan mystery gods. See his 'The Christian Mystery', *Hibbert Journal* 10 (1911–12): 45–64.

17. There are many instances where Paul writes about the believers being 'in Christ' (*en Christō*) – no less than fifty-six instances in the undisputed Pauline letters alone. By contrast, there are very few instances of Paul using the phrase in this way, Christ in you (*Christos en umin*). We find it in Rom.8.10 and 2 Cor. 13.5, where 'you' is plural, and in Gal. 2.20 and Phil. 1.20, with Christ being in Paul. These instances show that both the corporate and the individual senses are in keeping with Paul's thinking.

the other is true as well. Nevertheless, given the cosmic scope of Christ in relation to all things in Col. 1.15-20, the corporate meaning stands out prominently. Christ, who is the reconciler of all things in heaven and on earth, and whose blood makes peace (1.20) is proclaimed to the Colossians as being among them and within them. Together they participate in and embody the divine fullness. Together they have become a salvific community. The significance of their participation in the divine fullness is that they also participate in Christ's reconciling of, and peace-making with, 'all things'. Their suffering is now more than 'indifferent'; it is for the sake of Christ's body.

Does being 'in Christ' mean the same thing as the statement 'Christ in you'? Paul and Timothy are of course familiar with both these expressions, as the Letter opened with the address 'to the saints and faithful brothers and sisters *in Christ in Colossae*' (Col. 1.2). To be 'in Christ' is to participate – through baptism – in the saving death and new life of Christ. When this fundamental shift has taken place, it is also possible to say that Christ is 'in' the believing community and each believer. The believers become so identified with Christ that it is also possible to identify Christ clearly in them.[18] So the two expressions are closely aligned, though not identical.

The expansive Christology of Colossians does not allow us to interpret the mystery of the Gospel as Christ *only* in the believing community, as though the hope of glory were *only* for them/us. It is to this phrase 'the hope of glory' that we now turn.

The hope of glory Glory (*doxa*), in the Greco-Roman world, meant good reputation. For many it was highly prized, as it reflected on both the honour of one's family and one's own character. However, as we have seen in the Stoic reading context above, glory was not deemed to be a virtue by the Stoics, but indifferent. Like strength, wealth and good health, it was preferred, but not in and of itself good. For the Stoic, both hope and glory are distractions from virtue.

The 'hope of glory' therefore runs counter to Stoic ideas. As we have seen in Chapter 2, hoping for a different and better future was a distraction for the Stoics, whereas for Paul, Timothy and their associates, it expressed God's gracious purposes for all creation. The 'hope of glory' is a concise way of saying that we and all creatures can participate in the life of God, now and into the future.

The 'hope of glory' evokes the eschatological vision of cosmic liberation and renewal set out in Rom. 8.18-25, and in particular vv. 19-21:

[19] For the creation waits with eager longing for the revealing of the children of God;

18. 'Christ in you' is an expression that has some scope for exhortation – calling the believer 'to themselves', as we see in 2 Cor. 13.5: 'Examine yourselves to see whether you are living in the faith. Test yourselves. Do you not realize that Jesus Christ is in you? – unless, indeed, you fail to meet the test!'

[20] for the creation was subjected to futility, not of its own will but by the will of the one who subjected it, in *hope*

[21] that the creation itself will be set free from its bondage to decay and will obtain the freedom of *the glory* of the children of God. (Emphasis mine)

The hope of glory is not simply about resolving finally the rift between God and humanity; the scale of this hope is even greater, namely that Christ will liberate creation itself to share the glory of God's children (Rom. 8.21). Through Christ, God is reconciling *all things*, whether on earth or in heaven (Col. 1.20).

In Rom. 1.18-23, Paul sets out the 'backstory' of how all have sinned and have come to lack God's glory (Rom. 3.23). He begins by stating that God's eternal power and divine nature, though invisible, could be seen and known through creation (Rom. 1.20). However, the human response was to distort this, culpably, by worshipping creation rather than the creator (Rom. 1.23). The distorted view of creation was in fact idolatry, whereby humans exchanged the glory of God for images resembling themselves or other creatures. Humans did so for their own interests, claiming to be wise (Rom. 1.22), but not acknowledging God (Rom. 1.28). In this way, humans arrogated to themselves the glory of God, but became futile in their thinking (Rom. 1.21). Creation was caught up in this futility, though not by its own will (Rom. 8.20). As Robert Jewett puts it, 'In this powerful symbolization, humans trying to play God ended up ruining not only their relations with each other but also their relation to the natural world.'[19]

It is this level of distortion and dysfunction that God is in the process of reconciling in Christ. The forfeiting of glory referred to in Rom. 3:23 alludes to the human distortion and abuse of the natural world, the human propensity to idolatry and the inability of humans to see the glory of God in creation and to reflect it truly in ourselves. Creation's subjection to futility and its slavery to perishability (Rom. 8.20-21) are the result of this complex network of dysfunction – the anthropogenic forfeiting of right relationship between God, humanity and all things.

The problem lies with humanity, and most of the solution set out in Romans traces salvation as it pertains to humanity. However in Romans 8, the eschatological horizon comes into focus, and the creation steps forward not simply as a passive object of human use and abuse but as an active subject. The glory about to be revealed to us (Rom. 8.18) shifts the gaze to creation, which is waiting with eager longing for the revelation – not in some disembodied or extraterrestrial way, but in the revealing of the children of God. Creation's freedom is directly connected with human freedom. This is the hope 'that the creation itself will be set free from its bondage to decay and will obtain the freedom of the glory of the children of God' (Rom. 8.21). The freedom that is brought about through the restoration of God's glory in the children of God will be the very same freedom that creation obtains.

19. Robert Jewett, *Romans: A Commentary on the Book of Romans*, Hermeneia (Minneapolis, MN: Fortress Press 2007), 513.

These freedoms are inextricably interconnected. The glory of one is the glory of the other – a restoration of glory to God and the visibility of God's glory in all things, including humanity.[20]

In this Pauline backstory, unredeemed humanity has lost its ability to reflect the glory of God. However, creation continues to communicate God's glory, as articulated in Rom. 1.20 even despite the human propensity to distort this communication. Psalm 19.1 also states this clearly:

> The heavens are telling the glory of God; and the firmament proclaims his handiwork.

This communication of God's glory is done effectively, though without words:

> [2] Day to day pours forth speech, and night to night declares knowledge.

> [3] There is no speech, nor are there words; their voice is not heard;

> [4] yet their voice goes out through all the earth, and their words to the end of the world. (Ps. 19.2-4)

We know from Rom.10.18 that Psalm 19 was important to Paul with regard to the proclamation of the word of Christ. Psalm 19.4 was the scriptural passage Paul chose to indicate that the word of Christ had gone out to all the earth, to the ends of the world. Just as we read in Col. 1.23 that the Gospel has been proclaimed in all creation under heaven, so in Romans, Paul states that the word of Christ has gone out, carried not only by the feet of those who bring the Good News (Rom. 10.15-18) but also through creation itself. Creation continues to communicate the glory of God, and the Logos of Christ makes this comprehensible.

The role of creation in communicating the glory of God through the Logos of Christ is difficult to grasp. In fact, because of our human propensity to distort things, it may seem to be an idolatrous claim. But according to the 'economy of God' (Col. 1.25), the hope of glory is not a hope that has implications for humanity alone. In the same way, we may expect that reference to the 'glorious abundance of this mystery among the Gentiles – Christ in you, the hope of glory' (Col. 1.27) means that *Christ in you* is not limited to humanity either. A restored, redeemed, reconciled humanity will be able to perceive the glory of God and perceive Christ not only in each other but in creation as well.

The knowledge of the mystery of God leads to being filled with assured understanding (Col. 2.2), and having access to all the hidden treasures of wisdom and knowledge (Col. 2.3). These things have been hidden, because God is unseen

---

20. For a longer exposition of this theology, see Vicky Balabanski, 'Pauline Epistles: Paul's Vision of Cosmic Liberation and Renewal', in *The Oxford Handbook on Bible and Ecology* (forthcoming).

(*aoratos*, Col. 1.15). Christ is the seen embodiment of God, and Christ in us restores our ability to comprehend these unseen things. This same word is found in Rom. 1.20, and I will conclude with a retranslation of this verse:

> For the unseen things (*aorata*) of [God], his eternal power and divinity,
> From the creation of the cosmos
> Were understood and clearly discerned by the creatures.

Humans and creation alike are these creatures. Christ 'in us' – humans and creation together – is restoring all things, including the capacity of all things to comprehend and mirror the glory of God. This is indeed the mystery of God.

Hermeneutical reflections

In the exposition of this passage, we have read 'Christ in you, the hope of glory', the mystery of God, as inclusive of creation. I have done so by reference to the backstory of creation and redemption set out in Romans, as Col. 1.24–2.5 shares a number of ideas with key passages in Romans concerning 'the hope of glory'. The 'I Paul speech' of Colossians sets out how much greater the mystery of God is than the recipients of the Letter may have thought. It bursts the boundaries of the Jewish apocalyptic and even wisdom traditions; it reaches beyond the secret rites of the mystery cults. It is a message to all people, leading all people to all wisdom and maturity (Col. 1.28). It is a mystery that fills the recipients full of the Logos of Christ, but it is also a mystery that reveals the fullness of Christ, through whom and for whom all things came into being and in whom all things hold together (Col. 1.16-17).

A key ecological challenge of this passage is to embrace 'all things' into the mystery of God. Mystery is a contested concept in the churches of today. In the Roman Catholic and Orthodox traditions, mystery is a highly valued term associated with the sacraments. By contrast, in Protestant churches one will rarely hear the term 'mystery' used, whether in relation to the sacraments or in other ways. This passage sets out the mystery of God as the overarching significance of the Gospel, not just for the initiated but for the sake of all people, and not just for the sake of people but for all things. The passage invites us to lift our gaze beyond what we can readily grasp, and see the purposes of God spanning all the ages and generations (Col. 1.26), leading to glorious abundance (Col. 1.27). To be deceived by persuasive arguments (Col. 2.4, 8) would be to reduce this expansive mystery to a small, tame, domesticated version, whereby Christ in you would mean 'Christ only as expansive as I am (or we are)'.

The expansive loving and comforting vision which unites rather than divides (Col. 2.2) is something worth striving for, recognizing that the striving is enabled by God's power at work in us (Col. 1.29). It matters that we speak of, as well as live out, this hope, exhorting all people and teaching all people; this is a process of helping them and ourselves towards maturity (Col. 1.28). Christ is mirrored in us both consciously and unconsciously as we participate in the mystery of God.

In terms of the ethical implications of this passage, the Stoic concept of distinguishing what is good from what is pleasurable matters. Contemporary views lean more closely to the hedonism of Epicurus, whereby what is pleasurable is the ultimate motivator. While Epicurus himself insisted that the pleasurable life entails and is entailed by living prudently, honourably and justly,[21] in practice today, the sort of hedonism promoted by the Western consumerist culture has few such categories. We and our children are shaped by a culture that believes more is better: more wealth, more pleasure, more clothing, food, travel and experiences. Some voices and subcultures call for moderation, but in practice, these voices are marginalized by the 'wisdom' of more. Virtue is only instrumental; I will be good to others, when it is in my interests.

For the sake of the Earth, recovering an ethic such as is reflected in this passage is vital. The willingness to forego pleasure and comfort for the sake of others is Christ-like. Paul can associate himself with Christ's afflictions for the sake of others, and we too can choose to self-limit, just as Christ did (Phil. 2.7). This may take the form of reducing or eliminating our meat intake. It will certainly take the form of assessing our carbon footprint and planning the steps involved in reducing it. It will take the form of befriending and advocating for at least one place or creature or person that does not benefit us, as a concrete association with the mystery of God in Christ, who emptied himself for our sake.

Nympha's notes

I have never met Paul. I hear that he is an old man now, though one would hardly think so to read his letters. Epaphras knows Paul well – he came to faith in Jesus Christ when he met Paul in Ephesus, and spent some months attending the lecture hall of Tyrannus every day, going deeper into the mystery of God with him. Epaphras said that he could see Christ himself at work in those meetings, not just in Paul, Timothy and the other leaders, but in the way the very gathering was filled with Christ's presence.

So it's very moving to know just how much our little community matters to Paul, and how the thought of us helps him to rejoice, even in his sufferings. I know he strives in prayer for us, just as Epaphras does. That really matters. Through God's grace we can also rejoice despite the suffering of recent months. Members of my household now attract the notice of other farming households in this part of the Valley by how kind they are to each other and to outsiders as well. They have come to recognize what is truly good and they live by it.

21. L&S 122.

Over the past week or so, the ewes have been lambing, and one of the newborns was weak. In times gone by, my shepherd folk would have delighted in dispatching it as soon as could be, so that they could have a tasty stew that evening. This time, though, I was amazed to see that they treated it gently and helped it to nurse. Within an hour it was as vigorous as the other lambs, and the shepherds' kindness meant that they will be waiting for their lamb stew until the Ides of March, when we celebrate the Most High God, not Jupiter, but Christ Risen from the dead!

We are all coming to recognize the presence of Christ – even and especially in the vulnerable creatures of Earth.

CHAPTER 7

Stoic reading context: Philosophies for sale

The love of wisdom is highly valued in Colossians. It is Paul and Timothy's prayer for the Colossians (1.9), it reflects their own method of teaching (1.28), all the treasures of wisdom are to be found in Christ (2.2-3), and the Colossians are to teach and admonish one another using wisdom (3.16). True love of wisdom permeates the Letter. But 'pseudo-wisdom' comes under fire in 2.8 and 2.22-23 – the sort of wisdom that claims to be something that it is not. Colossians 2.8 rejects *deceitful* philosophy that is a justification for human traditions and other worldly impulses; it is not a blanket rejection of philosophy. As Tor Vegge puts it:

> In the structure of reasoning, the author of Colossians seems to be meeting philosophy on its home ground, developing an argument that in certain respects may be considered to be wisdom, the proper subject of philosophy.[1]

Philosophers debated with one another about the nature of true wisdom. In a satirical work called *Philosophies for Sale*, the second-century comic rhetorician Lucian of Samosata depicts the merits and foibles of various philosophies. In one of his skits, a fictional Diogenes, a Cynic philosopher, claims to liberate people, and sets out his approach to a potential 'buyer'. It has something of the ring of the type of pseudo-philosophy condemned in Col. 2.8 and 2.20-23:

> DIOGENES: I am a liberator of people and a physician to their ills; in short I desire to be an interpreter of truth and free speech.
> BUYER: Very good, interpreter! But if I buy you, what course of training will you give me?
> DIOGENES: First, after taking you in charge, stripping you of your luxury and shackling you to want, I will put a short cloak on you. Next I will compel you to undergo pains and hardships, sleeping on the ground, drinking nothing but water and filling yourself with any food that comes your way. As for your money, in case you have any, if you follow my

---

1. Tor Vegge, 'Polemic in the Epistle to the Colossians', in *Polemik in der frühchristlichen Literatur: Texte und Kontexte*, ed. O. Wischmeyer und L. Scornaienchi, BZNW 170 (Berlin/New York: W. de Gruyter, 2011), 255–93, 289.

advice you will throw it into the sea forthwith. You will take no thought for marriage or children or native land: all that will be sheer nonsense to you, and you will leave the house of your fathers and make your home in a tomb or a deserted tower or even a jar. Your wallet will be full of lupines, and of papyrus rolls written on both sides. Leading this life you will say that you are happier than the Great King; and if anyone flogs you or twists you on the rack, you will think that there is nothing painful in it. (Lucian, *Philosophies for Sale* 8–9, LCL 54: 464–7)

In this amusing depiction of 'philosophy', Lucian offers a critique of the type of philosophy that requires severe self-abasement, including stripping down and shaming the philosophical adherent. Putting a short cloak on someone was a mark of shame, associated with slaves – or in this case, with a Cynic philosopher. Compelling someone to undergo pain and hardships, depriving them of a bed, narrowing their diet to scraps and water are all signs of humility – or humiliation. All the things that pertain to traditional morality – including care for one's estate, marriage, descendants, country – are brushed aside. The adherent would be homeless, penniless, with nothing but written words on papyrus rolls to accompany them. Flogging and even torture would be indifferent to them, for they have exchanged all the things valued by the world for philosophy. Lucian of course depicts anyone who would make this choice as an utter fool, but the picture must have had sufficient likeness to actual philosophical adherents for the humour to work.

Various aspects of this depiction are reminiscent of the empty philosophy condemned in the Letter to the Colossians. The focus on humility and self-abasement, on matters of food and drink and on severe treatment of the body all have their counterpart in Col. 2.8, 16, 21-23.

Lucian later puts Stoic philosophy under the spotlight, deftly satirizing the Stoics' most prolific early leader Chrysippus by means of a fictional Stoic slave called 'Chrysippos'. Hair-splitting and bandying of terminology come under fire, as does the focus on money:

BUYER: None but the scholar will get paid for his virtue?

CHRYSIPPOS: Your understanding of the matter is correct. You see, I do not take pay on my own account, but for the sake of the giver: for since there are two classes of people, the disbursive and the receptive, I train myself to be receptive and my pupil to be disbursive.

BUYER: On the contrary, the young student ought to be receptive and you, who alone are rich, disbursive!

CHRYSIPPOS: You are joking, friend. Look out that I don't shoot you with my indemonstrable syllogism.[2]

---

2. Indemonstrable in the sense that its propositions do not require demonstration, or indeed admit of it. (LCL 54: 499, n. 1). A syllogism is a form of reasoning in which a conclusion is drawn from two given or assumed propositions. Chrysippus was famous for this style of philosophical discourse.

BUYER: What have I to fear from that shaft?
CHRYSIPPOS: Perplexity and aphasia and a sprained intellect.[3]

These ideas have their serious counterpart in Colossians, too, where the recipients are warned against 'persuasive arguments' (Col. 2.4), against 'human traditions' (Col. 2.8), against 'human precepts and teaching' (Col. 2.23). When engaging in such philosophical debates, there was the danger of being captivated and led astray by losing the focus on, and confidence in, what God has achieved in Christ. The Letter does not reject 'secular' wisdom or advocate looking inward; it claims that every rule and authority is under the headship of Christ (Col. 2.11). This is a reassuring, confident, universal claim.

Before embarking on the exposition of this section, it is worthwhile to raise the question of what style of writing this is. In Hellenistic ethical discourse, there were various methods, including *protrepsis*, calling people to a new and different way of life, and *paraenesis*, for advice and exhortation.[4] There was also elenctic discourse, adopting the approach of Socrates, who in the early Platonic dialogues shows his interlocutors that they are living on the basis of beliefs that are inconsistent with each other.[5] Col. 2.16-23 fits this latter approach, as it questions the listener as to why they would live as though they are subject to the world, rather than as those in Christ, who are free with regard to the claims of human traditions and the elements of the world (Col. 2.20). Using elenctic discourse, the writers challenge the Lycus Valley recipients to live consistently with their faith in Christ. This style does not necessarily depict current practices, but rather warns against known dangers.

Eco-Stoic commentary on Col. 2.6-23

Translation of Col. 2.6-23

[6] Therefore, as you received Christ Jesus the Lord, continue to walk *in him*,

[7] having put down roots and being built up *in him*,
having become established in the faith just as you were taught,
overflowing with thanksgiving.

[8] Take care that no one takes you captive through the sort of empty, deceitful philosophy that is according to human traditions and the elements of the world, and not according to Christ.

---

3. Lucian, *Philosophies for Sale* 24, LCL 54: 496–9 (modified).

4. Neither is formally a genre, and both are part of the Pauline approach. See Diana M. Swancutt, 'Paraenesis in the Light of Protrepsis', in *Early Christian Paraenesis in Context*, ed. James Starr and Troels Engberg-Pedersen, BZNW 125 (Berlin/New York: Walter de Gruyter, 2004), 113–53.

5. Epictetus, *Discourses, Fragments, Handbook*, a new translation by Robin Hard, with an introduction and notes by Christopher Gill, Oxford World's Classics (Oxford: Oxford University Press, 2014), xix–xx.

[9] For *in Christ* the whole fullness of deity dwells bodily,

[10] and you have been filled full *in him*, [11] who is the head of every rule and authority.

In him you also were circumcised – not with a circumcision performed by human hands, but by the removal of the fleshly body, that is, through the circumcision of Christ.

[12] Having been buried *with him* in baptism, you also have been raised *with him* through faith in the power of God who raised him from the dead.

[13] And you – who were dead in your transgressions and in the uncircumcision of your flesh – he made you alive *with him*, having freely forgiven us all our transgressions. [14] He has obliterated the record of debt to the regulations which stood against us, and has lifted it right away from our midst, having nailed it to the cross. [15] Having stripped off the rulers and authorities, he made a public spectacle of them, leading them *in him* in a victory procession.

[16] Therefore, do not let anyone pass judgement on you with respect to food or drink, or in the matter of a feast, a new moon or Sabbath days – [17] these are only a shadow of the things to come; the real body is Christ!

[18] Do not let anyone claim that you are disqualified; such a person desires – by means of self-abasement and angelic reverence – the things he has seen when entering into worship, but is vainly puffed up with empty notions by his fleshly mind [19] and is not holding fast to the head. It is only from there that the whole body, supported and knit together through its ligaments and sinews, grows with a growth that is from God.

[20] If you have died with Christ to the elements of the world, why should you be subjected to regulations as though you were living in the world? [21] 'Do not handle, do not taste, do not touch.' [22] All of these things are in the process of perishing as they are used, according to human precepts and teaching. [23] They appear to offer a word of wisdom, in promoting self-made religious practices, self-abasement and unsparing treatment of the body, but are not of any value except in gratifying the flesh.

Structure

The structure can be set out as follows:

I. Introduction of theme: The believers are established in Christ (Col. 2.6-8)
II. Warning against empty philosophy, traditions and 'elements of the world' that are not in Christ (Col. 2.9)
III. Positive exposition of life in Christ initiated through baptism (spiritual circumcision) leading to fullness, life, freedom, victory (Col. 2.9-15)
IV. Polemical refutation of those who might pass judgement on them about religious practices, which are only a shadow of the things to come: the real body (v. 17, the body in, through and for whom all things came into being) is Christ (Col. 2.16-23)

Set out this way, it is apparent that both the positive and the polemical aspects of this passage seek to focus the attention of the recipients on Christ. The real interest is not in the aberrations, but in the fullness of life that they have through their baptism into the death and rising of Christ.

This central section of the Letter sets out the contrast between the confidence that the believers have *in* and *with Christ* and the pressures that they may be under to forfeit this confidence. It is an exposition of the full assurance that the believers have through their baptism, set in contrast with the sorts of pressures that could dislodge them from it. There is a great emphasis on the believers being *in Christ*, as indicated by the italics. This emphasis is in keeping with the Stoic cosmology of divine permeation, familiar to us in the saying 'In him we live and move and have our being' (Acts 17.28). Being *in Christ*, the believers are not subject to anyone, whether on intellectual or philosophical grounds, or on grounds of identity markers such as circumcision, diet or religious practices. Christ has subjected all rulers and authorities, so that those who lay claim to capture believers for their own agendas are in fact themselves captive to Christ.

Scholars tend to subordinate the affirmations of confidence in this Letter (e.g. Col. 2.6-7) to the verses that indicate some sort of conflict or problem. Colossians 2 looms large in our interpretation of Colossians, and overshadows the confident tone of Colossians 1 and, indeed, the rest of the Letter. The standard approach in Pauline research is to examine with great care the passages that indicate an issue/ set of issues that has/have prompted the writing of the Letter, and upon this basis, to interpret the Letter as a whole.

In seeking to find the most plausible context for this set of warnings, there is always the danger of circularity. If we reconstruct the Colossians' situation on the basis of Col. 2.8, 16-23, we will be inclined to read this back into Colossians 1, so that the confident Christological affirmations are viewed as anticipating the polemic to come. This line of research can lose sight of the overarching confidence of the Letter. In order to counter this tendency, I have chosen to retain these warnings in their epistolary context, framed and embedded in the positive affirmations and exhortations that surround them.

As set out in the Introduction, I understand the Letter to the Colossians to be a circular rather than an occasional letter. As such, it canvasses an array of possible issues: distraction by empty deceitful philosophy (Col. 2.8), attraction to Jewish practices like circumcision (Col. 2.10), certain feasts or Sabbath practices (Col. 2.16), or attraction to ascetic practices modelled on mystery cults (Col. 2.18). None of these is necessarily a current problem in the community, but provides opportunity for the letter bearers to customize their message to what they find in the Lycus Valley contexts.

Rather than providing the basis for reconstructing a particular 'Colossian heresy', this section urges the recipients to hold fast to their confidence and consider the grounds for it. These verses are punctuated in v. 9 by a warning about human traditions and the 'elements of the world', which flags the exposition that follows in vv. 16-23 about these things. Following this exposition, their gaze will be directed again to their future, which will be revealed in glory (Col. 3.1-4).

This commentary does not take the view that these warnings reflect an active heresy or specific false teachers among the believers in the Lycus Valley. Colossians is much less 'occasional' in nature than the undisputed Pauline letters. So while we have strong invective against false teachers or 'super apostles' in 2 Cor. 11.5, 13-15, and against those who mislead believers into the necessity of circumcision in Galatians (1.8-9, 5.3, 12), we do not have anything quite comparable in tone or urgency in Colossians. Philippians 3.2 – where the opponents are called 'dogs', 'evil workers' and 'those who mutilate the flesh' – shows that Paul and his co-workers are very ready to use passionate polemic against those who mislead the communities under their care. However, the warnings against false teachers or teachings in Colossians are, by contrast, relatively muted.

The Letter as a whole shows great confidence that the believers have put down roots and are being built up and established in the faith (Col. 2.7). The rhetoric of Colossians seems to be more about identity formation than about refuting false teachers.[6] The warnings are real, but prophylactic, as the letter writers seek to exercise pastoral oversight from a distance.

The series of warnings in Col. 2.8 and 2.16-23 names both Jewish and pagan practices. Circumcision, food regulations and observance of Sabbaths and festivals suggest Jewish practices, while the ascetic practices and rites alluded to in v. 18 are reminiscent of Hellenistic mystery cults. There is a tendency in protestant scholarship in particular to reconstruct an original purity in Pauline communities and to see everything later as a heretical deviation from this purity.[7] The problems envisaged in Col. 2.8, 16-23 were already inherent in the communities and their contexts from the beginning, and need not be seen as new developments. With the lapse of time and the distance from those well-versed in the Gospel, Paul and Timothy are concerned that these problems, known from various Pauline contexts, may have developed in the Lycus Valley communities.

The Letter warns that there are 'elements (*stoicheia*) of the world' that might be involved in seeking to captivate the believer using empty deceitful types of philosophy and human traditions (Col. 2.8). However, the believer has in fact died to these 'elements of the world', and is therefore free from their regulations (Col. 2.20). The fact that the phrase is flagged in the warning in v. 8, and then repeated in v. 20, makes it prominent. The range of other issues to be found in this section can be related to the distracting and misleading influence of these elements; they appear important, but the Letter stresses that they actually have no authority over believers and are of no lasting value.

---

6. See Vegge, 'Polemic in the Epistle to the Colossians', 258–62, 289–90.

7. Petter Spjut, 'The Protestant Historiographic Myth and the Discourse of Differentiation in Scholarly Studies of Colossians', *Svensk Exegetisk Årsbok* 80, ed. Göran Eidevall (Uppsala: Svenska exegetiska sällskapet, 2015), 169–85. 'The dichotomizing and simplistic taxonomy of one apostolic Christianity and several other Hellenized deviations (often referred to simply as "religion") is a modern scholarly construction, a "Protestant Historiographic Myth" … and it needs to be challenged'. 183.

What is meant by the 'elements (*stoicheia*) of the world'? Much scholarly attention has been given to the phrase, setting it in various interpretive contexts.[8] The term *stoicheia* refers to the basic elements in any field of knowledge, the rudiments or basic principles. The term also indicates the first in a series or list of things which follow one another in order.[9] By embarking with the *stoicheia*, there is a flow-on effect. The term here is specified by the phrase 'of the world', so the basic elements of the world (not universe[10]) are in view. These are further specified in the text as being in some sense parallel to human traditions, and from the context it is clear that they are being viewed negatively, as contrasted with things that are 'according to Christ'. The *stoicheia* appear to exercise some authority over people (Col. 2.20), and are linked with regulations about handling and eating food, and purity practices (Col. 2.21).

As set out in Chapter 4, Stoics distinguished between two principles of the cosmos: that which acts – the divine prime mover – and that which is acted upon – namely elements (*stoicheia*) which pass away.[11] The energy or power which moves or shapes matter is divine, while the elements are transitory. Against this background, to follow the misleading influence of the elements of the world would be to see oneself as controlled or determined by these transitory elements – inevitably embroiled in their flow-on effect. In a pagan context, this might mean being bound by the seasons to perform certain rituals for the fertility of the crops. In a context influenced by Orphic wisdom and magical practices, it might mean using magic to avert the harmful influences of spiritual forces. In a Jewish synagogue context it might mean being subject to the Law as though its requirements would lead to salvation. Whatever cosmological framework one came out of, the danger was real that one might cede the confidence one has in Christ to the demands of this framework. The elements of the world are thus very similar to spiritual forces, but do not necessarily require a spiritual reading.[12]

The phrase 'elements of the world' can reflect all or any of these influences. By choosing a term with wide associations, the writers are able to bundle together all

---

8. See, for example, Josef Blinzler, 'Lexikalisches zu dem Terminus τὰ στοιχεῖα τοῦ κόσμου bei Paulus', in *Studiorum Paulinorum Congressus Internationalis Catholicus 1961*, Vol. 2, AnBib 18 (Rome: Pontifical Biblical Institute, 1963), 429–43. C. E. Arnold, *The Colossian Syncretism: The Interface Between Christianity and Folk Belief at Colossae*, WUNT 2/77 (Tübingen: Mohr Siebeck, 1995), 158–94; George H. Van Kooten, *Cosmic Christology in Paul and the Pauline School*, WUNT 2/171 (Tübingen: Mohr Siebeck, 2003), 100–9. Neil Martin, 'Returning to the *stoicheia tou kosmou*: Enslavement to the Physical Elements in Galatians 4.3 and 9?' *JSNT* 40/4 (2018), 434–52.

9. Lohse, *Colossians and Philemon*, 96.

10. Note the differentiation between *kosmos* and *ta panta* set out in Chapter 4.

11. See Chapter 4, p. 70.

12. Unlike in Eph. 6.10-17, 'Elements/*stoicheia* of the world' could include 'humanistic teachings common to Jewish and pagan religions, involving binding traditions, taboos, prohibitions, ordinances, ceremonies, etc., teachings involving either supernatural elemental or animating spirits … or basic material elements', Friberg et al., *Analytical Lexicon*, 357.

the influences that lead away from confidence in Christ. The phrase '*stoicheia* of the world' connects with concepts that were familiar to these communities in Asia Minor, and reminds the recipients that they have died with Christ to these things, and in Christ are now free to live in confidence. This is a phrase that gives no undue weight to these elements. Rather, the believers are reminded that through baptism they have died to these elements, so they are no longer subject to their claims or regulations (Col. 2.20).

Another prominent phrase is repeated across vv. 18 and 23. Verse 18 includes the terms 'desiring', 'self-abasement' and 'angelic worship'; in v. 23 the terms are 'worship' and 'self-abasement', and 'desiring' is now a prefix for 'worship' (*ethelothrēskeia*). The repetition of these key terms is significant and suggests that any reconstruction of the problem must take its lead from these two warnings. The term that I have translated as 'self-abasement' (*tapeinophrosunē*, having a humble attitude) is generally a positive term in the Pauline writings.[13] Philippians 2.3 introduces the term as descriptive of the mind of Christ, who emptied himself. However, it is used twice in a negative sense in this section of Colossians. Then it appears again in 3.12, where it has returned to the positive sense we find elsewhere in the Pauline writings (Phil. 2.3, Eph. 4.2). Having a humble attitude may be Christ-like, but humility, when shaped by the 'elements of the world' to make it a source of pride, can become self-abasement.

The phrase in Col. 2.18 translated as 'angelic worship' is ambiguous and intriguing. It can mean worshipping angels, and many scholars hold that this is the sense here.[14] However, if the believers in the Lycus Valley were thought to be worshipping angels, one would expect more than a single passing reference to the practice.[15] Two issues arise: What is the sense of the term 'worship' (*thrēskeia*) and how is it connected with angels?

Thrēskeia is not found elsewhere in the Pauline writings. In Acts 26.5 and Jas 1.26 it refers to 'religion' as a system with which a person identifies. It is a term used quite often by Josephus to refer to the form of temple worship (e.g. *Ant.* 9.273, 12.253, 12.320). Philo uses the term positively of Jewish cultic worship (e.g. *Leg. Gai.* 298), but he also uses it in a negative sense, to mean ceremonious reverence and rituals, as opposed to true piety:

> People may submit to sprinklings with holy water and to purifications, befouling their understanding while cleansing their bodies. They may, having more money than they know what to do with, found a temple, providing all

---

13. *Tapeinos* can have the sense of lowly, as in Rom. 12.16; 2 Cor. 7.6; 10.1. The verb means humble or humiliate, as in 2 Cor. 11.7; 12.21; Phil. 2.8; 4.12 (passive = be brought low, humbled). However, when combined with *phrosunē*, this is a distinctive Christ-like quality.

14. Paul Foster opts for this reading (*Colossians*, 290) but acknowledges that 'the flexibility of the genitive construction in Greek often creates major interpretative debates, and this specific example is an extremely contested case'. 288.

15. This is not to deny that angel worship was not known or practised in the region. Compare also Heb. 1.5-14.

its furniture on a scale of lavish magnificence. They may offer up hecatombs [a great public sacrifice], and never cease sacrificing bullocks; they may adorn the sacred building with costly votive offerings, employing on them rich material in abundance, and skilled craftsmanship that is more priceless than silver and gold. Yet shall they not be inscribed on the roll of the pious. No, for such people ... have gone astray from the road that accords with piety, deeming it to be ritual (*thrēskeia*) instead of holiness, and offering gifts to the One who cannot be bribed and will not accept such things, and flattering the One who cannot be flattered, who welcomes genuine worship (*therapeia*) of every kind, but abhors all counterfeit approaches. Genuine worship is that of a soul bringing simple reality as its only sacrifice (*thusia*); all that is mere display, fed by lavish expenditure on externals, is counterfeit.[16]

Ritual or ceremonious worship seems to be the sense that we have in Col. 2.18 and 2.23. This would be a glimpse of a different style of worship in a Pauline community from the sort we see in 1 Cor. 14.26-40. It would be outward piety expressed in such things as bodily washing and public displays of reverence and sacrifice. This might be a model of worship that sat easily in the cultural context, but it would be surprising in a Pauline community that is deemed to have already put down secure roots and be walking in Christ (Col. 2.6-7).

The phrase 'angelic worship' (or 'worship of angels') is ambiguous. The genitive construction can be understood in two ways, either as an objective genitive, with the angels as objects of worship, or as a subjective genitive. If it is the latter, this would mean that the worship is the sort *modelled* by angels – of an angelic quality, superb and esoteric. Aspiring to angelic worship would be decried; this would fit well with the warnings about self-imposed rigour. Given the pastoral rather than polemical emphasis of this Letter, and the passing reference to this issue, I take this to be the more plausible meaning of the phrase in v. 18.[17] The reference to angels does not occur again in v. 23, where one might expect it; there the reference is to self-made or self-willed religious practices. Given these factors, the issue does not appear to be the angels, but the hubris of the worshippers themselves.

---

16. Philo, *That the Worse Is Wont to Attack the Better*, LCL 227: 214–7 (modified).

17. For a summary of scholarship on this issue which reaches a different conclusion, see Arnold, *The Colossian Syncretism*, 90–5. Arnold reaches his own decision by pointing out that although there are various examples of subjective genitives with *thrēskeia*, there is no example of *a divine being or a typical object of worship* related to *thrēskeia* in the genitive case that should be taken as a subjective genitive. This is a circular argument, as it assumes that angels are typical objects of worship. Angels are not objects of devotion in other Pauline settings – quite the opposite (cf. 1 Cor. 6.3). If we draw upon Heb. 1.6, 'let all the angels of God worship him', angels are envisaged as involved in worship, not the object of worship. The word for worship in Heb. 1.6 (and LXX Deut. 32.43) is *proskuneō*, (which refers to the act of worship) not *thrēskeuō*, (which refers to the cultic practice of worship).

Verses 18-23 therefore warn the recipients against self-imposed religious practices that might promise to extend their spiritual experiences and enhance their proximity to the divine. Such practices are shown to reflect a human way of thinking: 'the more self-imposed rigour, the more effective'. To aspire to such angelic worship is to depart from the confidence they already have in Christ.

The self-imposed nature of these practices is key to the section, and is reflected in the repeated use in vv. 18 and 23 of 'desiring' (*thelō*). The writers of the Letter are prophylactically concerned that the Colossians, under various pressures, may have been looking to find further religious observances to supplement their newly-won faith in Christ. They are concerned that these believers may look to more rigorous practices rather than looking deeper into the power of God, which they have accessed through baptism.

The religious practices that are mentioned include dietary regulations, observance of certain festivals, calendrical issues and Sabbath practices (Col. 2.16), as well as various purity regulations (Col. 2.21). Timothy and Paul are concerned that the believers in Colossae may be gravitating to Jewish practices, but they also use a term in Col. 2.18, *embateuō* (entering into the mystery), which has strong associations with mystery cults.[18] The use of the term 'mystery' in Col. 1.26, 27; 2.2 anticipates such an allusion, by specifying that the true divine mystery is Christ in you, the hope of glory (Col. 1.27).

It is not necessary to argue that all these various practices should cohere in a particular syncretism, whether it be a particular philosophy, or magic and folk religion. The breadth of the warning is in keeping with the general nature of the Letter, allowing the letter bearers to address the breadth of issues that they will meet. It is in keeping with the overall confidence of the Letter (in its bearers as colleagues as well as its recipients) to state that the warnings do not envisage that the Lycus Valley communities are succumbing to such a philosophy. Rather, the Letter acknowledges that the desire for ritual observances, public devotion and ascetic practices is a real danger, as it reflects the *stoicheia* of the world and is part of a human way of thinking – a 'fleshly mind' (Col. 2.18).

The 'flesh' is referred to in Col. 2.11, 13, 18 and 23. Up to this point in the Letter, 'flesh' (*sarx*) has been a neutral or positive term, referring to the physical body of Christ (Col. 1.22) and Paul's own physical body suffering for the sake of the church (Col. 1.24), as well as Paul's actual presence (Col. 2.1, 5). However, in this section of the Letter, the semantic field of *sarx* is negative.

Flesh (sarx)

This overview of the uses of the term 'flesh' shows that the Letter does not have a uniformly negative view of it. In using the word 'flesh' to refer to the 'body of Christ's flesh' (Col. 1.22), it shows that the corporeal reality of the flesh is the central means whereby Christ has reconciled those who were at one time strangers and enemies

18. Arnold, *The Colossian Syncretism*, 104–57.

Table 7.1 Semantic field of *sarx* (flesh)

Christ (and the church)	Neutral	Negative
1.22 he has reconciled you 'in the body of his flesh by his death'	1.24 Paul rejoices that he is filling up what is needful of Christ's suffering in his flesh	2.11 they put off the body of flesh in the circumcision of Christ
	2.1 Paul is striving for the Colossians, Laodiceans and all who have not seen him in the flesh	2.13 they were dead in their transgressions and the uncircumcision of their flesh
	2.5 Although Paul is absent in the flesh, he is present with them in the spirit	2.18 Do not let anyone claim that you are disqualified; such a person … is vainly puffed up with empty notions by his fleshly mind
	3.22 Slaves, obey your masters according to the flesh	2.23 Ascetic practices are not of any value except in gratifying the flesh

in their mindset towards each other and towards God. Flesh, as known in Christ and his crucifixion, is indispensable.

All other uses of the word 'flesh' outside the current passage are neutral. Paul is able to rejoice that in his own flesh he is able to fill up, in turn, what is needful of Christ's afflictions. Flesh is a way of connecting with Christ (1.24).

However in Col. 2.6–3.4, flesh is used in a way reminiscent of the flesh/spirit opposition of the undisputed Pauline letters (cf. Gal. 5.17; 1 Cor. 3.3; Rom. 8.1-13). The flesh is something that has been stripped off in Christ's circumcision (Col. 2.11). Formerly, the uncircumcision of their flesh was an indication that they were strangers and enemies towards God, and so 'dead in their trespasses' (Col. 2.13). But since their baptism, they are alive in Christ, and so such outward signs are irrelevant. Anyone who says otherwise is puffed up with the fleshly way of thinking (Col. 2.18). There are people who advocate observances that appear to reflect a word of wisdom, but by promoting self-made (or irrelevant) religious practices, self-abasement and unsparing treatment of the body, they are actually gratifying the flesh (2.23). Such advocates of the flesh are not to be followed – nor are they to be feared.

The word 'body' (*sōma*) is also prominent in this section. Various forms of it are found in Col. 2 at vv. 9, 11, 17, 19 and 23. Elsewhere in the Letter we find this word at 1.18, 22, 24 and 3.15. In its various forms, the word is used with reference to Christ, the believer and the church.

Body (sōma)

The references to the body of Christ reflect the idea that true reality is embodied: reconciliation of humanity with God has taken place in and through the fleshly body of Christ (Col. 1.22). The whole fullness of deity is continually present bodily in Christ (Col. 2.9). In contrast with the shadow of things to come – the

Table 7.2 Semantic field of *sōma* (body)

Christ	Church	Believers
1.22 body of his flesh	1.18 The body which is the church	2.11 removal of the body of flesh
2.9 whole fullness of deity dwells bodily	1.24 His body, which is the church	2.23 severe treatment of the body
2.17 the (real) body is Christ	2.19 from whom the whole body grows	
	3.15 called in one body	

eschatological future – the embodied reality of these things is Christ. This shows the highest possible view of corporeality or embodiment when associated with Christ.

Material reality is thus the means of the engagement of the unseen God with God's creation. This is the opposite of the matter/spirit dualism that we so often expect to find in the Hellenistic culture influenced by Plato. The Stoic notion of the bodily permeation of the divine, evident in Zeno's claim that the whole world and heaven are the substance (*ousian*) of God,[19] mirrors this profoundly panentheistic Christology we discover in Colossians. There seems to be no need to argue this at length or seek to establish it. It appears to be self-evident that the 'whole fullness of deity dwells bodily' in Christ (Col. 2.9).[20]

The statements about the church as Christ's body, of which Christ is the head (Col. 1.18, 24), and the fact that the head has become the source of the growth of the whole body (Col. 2.19), shift the imagery towards body as corporation or collective. This connects with the imagery of being 'in Christ', namely being part of the corporeal reality of Christ and participating in his peace (Col. 3.15).

Against these profoundly positive views of embodied life, the reference to Christ's 'circumcision' – baptism – as the removal of the fleshly body (Col. 2.11) is surprising. It seems to give a negative view of corporeal reality. However, what is being set out in vv. 9-13 is not a rejection of embodied life. Rather there is a complex analogy being constructed between death through the waters of baptism and physical circumcision on the one hand, and life through being raised from those waters as the 'removal of the fleshly body' on the other. The fleshly body is here analogous to the foreskin, which has been 'removed' through a circumcision not performed by human hands (baptism). Physical circumcision is therefore unnecessary, not because corporeal reality is of no importance, but because Christ's 'circumcision' (baptism) enables a full identification with Christ's salvific dying and rising. Rather than a flesh/spirit dualism, we have here a different contrasting pair.

The analogy shifts in vv. 14-15 to a triumphal victory, destroying the records of debts, nailing them to the cross, stripping off the finery of rulers and authorities, and leading them publicly in a victory procession. This not only targets the apparent victory of those who put Jesus to a shameful death on the cross. It also implies that those who claim the 'high moral ground' with regard to circumcision

19. Diogenes Laertius 7.148-9, L&S 266.
20. More will be said about this in the conclusion, under the heading of 'Panentheism'.

Table 7.3 Contrast of fleshly body of Christ and that of circumcision

Fleshly body of Christ (1.22, 2.9, 2.17)	Fleshly body of circumcision (2.11)
Salvific: those in Christ participate in his dying and rising	Performed by human hands
Free from debt to regulations (2.14)	Still indebted to regulations

and rigorous treatment of the body (Col. 2.23) are mistaken in thinking that they have triumphed.

These highly nuanced twists and turns in imagery and analogy assume an audience who readily think in symbols informed by Jewish and Hellenistic practices, and who will appreciate the irony of contrasting shadows with reality (Col. 2.17). The shadow of reality is the whole human construct of rituals, calendars and religious observances. These things are passing away, even as they are used (Col. 2.22). By contrast, when the true things to come are revealed, namely their life that is currently hidden with Christ in God (Col. 3.3), it will be clear that the body is Christ (Col. 2.17).

Various other images are at work in this section to convey the confidence of their assurance in Christ. The image of a mighty tree with deep roots is evoked in v. 7, reminiscent of other scriptural passages denoting assurance. One such passage is Ps. 1.3, though there is no direct allusion evident. Other passages which share the same verb are *Pss. Sol.* 14.4: 'Their planting is firmly rooted for ever; they shall not be uprooted as long as the heavens shall last',[21] and Sir. 24.12: 'I took root in an honoured people, in the portion of the Lord, his heritage' (NRSV).[22]

Putting down roots (Col. 2.7) and growing (Col. 2.19) are part of a set of images in this section that emphasize the spatial (and natural, Earthy) dimensions of faith. The baptismal imagery of being buried and being raised also has a downward and upward movement, particularly in v. 12: 'Having been buried with him in baptism, you also have been raised with him through faith in the power of God who raised him from the dead.' This is also at work in v. 20, 'if you have died with Christ', and in Col. 3.1, 'if you have been raised together with Christ'. These two contrasting movements will be discussed in the next chapter.

Fullness

There is one further theme that is crucial for an ecological reading of this passage, namely the theme of fullness.[23] We have already met the verb *plēroō* (fill full) in

21. *Psalms of Solomon* 14.4, in *The Old Testament Pseudepigrapha*, Vol. 2, ed. James H. Charlesworth (London: Darton, Longman & Todd, 1985), 663.

22. Trees, gardens and gardening were also familiar images in philosophy. See John Dillon, 'The Pleasures and Perils of Soul-Gardening', in *Wisdom and Logos: Studies in Jewish Thought in Honor of David Winston*, ed. David T. Runia and Gregory E. Sterling, SPhiloA: Studies in Hellenistic Judaism 9, BJS 312 (Atlanta, GA: Scholars Press, 1997), 190–7.

23. See also Suzanne Watts Henderson, 'God's Fullness in Bodily Form: Christ and Church in Colossians', *Expository Times* 118/4 (2007): 169–73.

Col. 1.9 and 1.25, and here we meet it in Col. 2.10. The related noun 'fullness' precedes this in Col. 2.9, and was prominent in Col. 1.19. It is part of a compound verb in Col. 1.24 (to take one's turn in filling up, *antanapléroō*) and also of the compound noun *plērophoria* (fullness) (Col. 2.2). The term is used again in 4.12 as a participle 'having been made full' (*plērophorēmenoi*), and the final instance is in Col. 4.17, where Archippus is tasked with fulfilling (*plēroō*) the service that he has in the Lord. There are no less than nine instances of this fullness language in the Letter – as many as the references to body (nine instances), and as many as are devoted to the 'Colossian problem' (nine verses, Col. 2.8, 16-23). Although such a comparison is a crude measuring stick, it reminds us of the pastoral nature of the Letter.

We can gain an overview of fullness terminology in this way:

Table 7.4 Fullness/filling full (*plēroō* and cognates)

Christ	Church	Believer
1.19 in him all the fullness was pleased to dwell	1.9 praying that you (plural) may be filled full with all knowledge of God's will and all wisdom and spiritual understanding	1.24 Paul is filling up in his turn what is needful in the sufferings of Christ for their sake
	2.2 that they may have all the riches of full understanding leading to knowledge of the mystery of God	1.25 Paul's service to fill full the word of God
2.9 in him all the fullness of deity dwells bodily	2.10 you (plural) have been filled full in him (perfect passive)	
	4.12 Epaphras' prayer is that they may be filled full in all the will of God (perfect passive)	4.17 Archippus is charged to fulfil the service he received in the Lord

There is clearly a close correlation between all the fullness of deity which resides in Christ, the fullness that the believers already share (Col. 2.10), and the state of fullness for which Paul, Timothy and Epaphras continually pray (Col. 1.9; 2.2; 4.12). The believing community, indicated by the first- and third-person plurals, already shares this fullness, as they are 'in Christ'. Nevertheless, it is also something to pray for when viewed against the eschatological horizon, prior to the complete revelation of Christ who is their life (Col. 3.4). In this interim period, fulfilling the service which one has received (Col. 1.25; 4.17), including suffering (Col. 1.24), is part of the same process whereby Christ's fullness will become manifest in us. When seen in overview, the future horizon is more than we might assume. The realized perspective evident in Col. 2.10 is only possible in light of the affirmation in Col. 2.9 that in Christ all the fullness of deity dwells bodily, so those who are in Christ now have access to this fullness.

The body of Christ as cosmos, community and communion

Embodied existence is where our spiritual life takes place. For the first recipients of this Letter, that was obvious. For them it was altogether uncontroversial that flesh, bodies and minds were connected. What was controversial was what they should do about ensuring that their fleshly bodies were behaving in ways that were appropriate to the divine reality within and all around them. Observance of religious regulations about food and drink, about certain festivals, seasons and cycles of the moon, rigorous practices – all such things acknowledged the way in which the spiritual and material worlds permeate one another.

The Letter to the Colossians does not refute the claim that our embodied existence is where our spiritual life takes place. Instead, it sees this truth through the perspective of being in Christ, who is the embodiment of God, and in whose body the whole fullness of deity, God's life, exists. The Letter seeks to articulate to the recipients that the real connection between material and spiritual reality is not to be found in any practices or religious observances that we perform, even though these may have the appearance of wisdom. The real connection between material and spiritual reality is established by God and made freely available in Christ. Christ is the one in whom all things in heaven and on earth were created and in whom all things hold together. In Christ, all God's fullness is constantly present, and that fullness is available to all. That bodily reality is in all creation, that bodily reality is the church, and that bodily reality is in the individual believer.

The 'body of Christ', according to Colossians, is a multivalent concept. On a macro-scale, Christ's body is equated with 'all things'. In Christ, all things in the heavens and on the earth were created (1.15), and all things hold together (1.17). In Christ all the fullness of deity dwells bodily (2.9). Christ's presence therefore permeates all things, though all things are not coextensive with Christ, who is both immanent in all things and transcends all things. In 2.17, Christ's body is the ultimate reality – not just co-terminous with reality as we know it, but embodying the fullness of God's presence across time as well. Christ is in all things, and indeed is all things (3.11).

As a subset of this reality, Christ's body is the community of those who are 'in Christ' and who practise Christ's sovereignty (1.18, 24; 2.19; 3.15). This Pauline concept (1 Cor. 12.12-20; Rom. 12.4-5) is clearly familiar to the recipients of the Letter, but in Colossians the metaphor has shifted away from community coherence and connection, and has gone in the direction of exhortation to remain connected to Christ. Christ, who is the head of every ruler and authority (2.10, recalling Christ's cosmic body), is the head of the church (1.18; 2.19), and so Christ's body must hold fast to the head. It is no longer quite the same metaphor as in the undisputed Pauline letters, but the difference between the metaphors can be overstated.

Christ's body also refers to Christ's own incarnate body in Col. 1.22. It is this fleshly body that died that has effected reconciliation, as is also stated in Col. 1.20, with reference to Christ's blood shed on the cross.

Our own bodies are incorporated into Christ's body, the church, through baptism, as is stated in Col. 2.11. As stated earlier, this is depicted as a spiritual circumcision, whereby we 'remove' the fleshly body. Clearly Christ-followers are still living an embodied life; baptism was the means of the believers' embodied existence connecting with the community of Christ's body.

Alongside all these ways of perceiving and participating in the Body of Christ, we might expect to find some reference to the sacrament of communion (cf. 1 Cor. 10.16-17; 11.23-28). But the primary imagery in this letter is of baptism, not Holy Communion. Nevertheless, there may be a tangential reference to Holy Communion in Col. 2.16-17. In v. 16 there is reference to ritual eating and drinking as a matter of dispute and condemnation. This is immediately followed in v. 17 with the affirmation 'the real body is Christ!' This suggests that the writers are aware of the tendency among their communities formed primarily of Gentile converts (such as at Corinth) to perceive the eating and drinking of Christ's body and blood as the primary efficacious connection with Christ. Gentile converts found it much easier to see Christ as the bread and wine to be eaten and drunk than to see Christ as the community of Christ-followers. The Lycus Valley believers may have been similar, and so Colossians does not emphasize Christ's body and blood as bread and wine. Nevertheless, the concept appears to be present in these verses.

In these ways, we have the Body of Christ as cosmic reality, with all things carrying something of Christ's life-giving and life-enhancing presence in them, visible to those who can perceive it. Christ's body is the community of believers, those who are 'in Christ' and who are known by their Christ-like behaviour (3.12). Christ's body is his incarnate body which died on the cross, reconciling all things (1.20). Christ's body is known and experienced through eating and drinking the bread and wine, not primarily through the ritual, but through the way it invites us to know the Body as connecting cosmos, community and our own bodily communion with Christ.

Following is a diagrammatic representation of these diverse affirmations concerning the Body of Christ. The various domains co-exist and interconnect (Figure 7.1).

The whole diagram, including the outer area, represents 'all things' as created through and sustained in Christ; they find their embodiment in him. All things can be called Christ's body, in the sense that in Christ, the whole fullness of deity dwells *bodily* (Col. 2.9). All things visible and invisible came into being through Christ and are sustained in Christ; all creatures and creation itself manifests God's presence and God's glory.

The Body of Christ is also the church (Col. 1.18, 24). This is a corporate body; in the diagram the diverse community of Christ-followers is connected with each other. All flow from the centre, the head or source of life. Creating a diagonal cross is a further community of people with linked hands, all peoples of the Earth. The Body of Christ can be seen in all as they practise the Christ-like virtues described in Col. 3.12 – then, indeed, Christ is all and in all (Col. 3.11).

Furthermore, the body of Christ is also the unique incarnate body of Jesus Christ, whose death on the cross and rising to new life reconciles all things and makes peace (Col. 1.20). This is not explicitly depicted in the diagram, but could be any one of the human forms.

The human forms float free of the Earth. This challenges us (who indeed do float above the earth via the internet and aeroplanes, but also in our attitudes to the rest of reality) to rethink what it is that grounds us.

Figure 7.1 Perceiving the interconnected domains of the Body of Christ; courtesy of Mark Hewitt © 2019.

At the centre of the sphere (the Earth) is bread and wine, grain and grapes, the sacramental Body and Blood of Christ.[24] The human figures connect in with biological reality at that point; we all require the sustenance of food and drink.

The cross, the symbol of grace and self-giving, looms large. It is a mosaic of animals and plants, as the hope of the Gospel is proclaimed to every creature under heaven (Col. 1.23). The space between the arms of the cross is filled with the oceans, reminiscent of the waters of baptism.

The various domains of the Body of Christ co-exist and interconnect. Christ's body is universal in scope, while at the same time specific to the corporate body of Christ, to the church, and also to the unique, historically specific act of Christ's death on the cross – and rising to new life. The sacramental Body of Christ invites

24. This aspect of the Body of Christ is not emphasized in Colossians, as it may have been a point of contention (Col. 2.16–17). The verbal form of Eucharist (thanksgiving) is found in Col. 3.15 and 17. We know that this verb was associated with the sacrament of Holy Communion in Pauline communities (1 Cor. 11.24), so there may be an allusion to the sacrament in Col. 3.15 and 17, or in the use of *eucharistia* in Col. 2.7 and 4.2.

us to connect ourselves, our own bodies, with all these domains. It would be virtually impossible to comprehend how all these aspects of Christ's body coalesce, if it were not for the Stoic concept that the embodied divine Logos permeates all things, is present among all who seek wisdom, and is fully embodied in the sage. With this pre-understanding, pagans could hear and receive the Gospel.

That is still true today. Christ's body is transcendent and immanent, present to us in nature, in the Christian gathering, in ourselves and in the sacrament of Holy Communion. The feast of Corpus Christi is one we could come to value again in an inclusive and ecological way.

The body of believers is part of the diagram as well, not only in the church, but as individuals. Those who are in Christ could also see Christ in themselves. This is, in fact, the mystery of God among the Gentiles: Christ in you, the hope of glory! (Col. 1.27). This interconnection links the believer through Christ with all things, because they too are embodied in Christ and for Christ (Col. 1.16); the material universe is not irrelevant to the Christian spiritual life.

Life is at the heart of spirituality. The Letter states that Christ has made us alive with him (Col. 2.13). The true extent of this life will be revealed eschatologically (Col. 3.4), but, for the time being, our life is hidden with Christ in God (Col. 3.3). To conceive of this life as narrowly human-focused is to ignore the Letter's emphasis on fullness; all the fullness is in Christ (Col 1.19; 2.9), and God intends that this same abundant fullness will characterize humanity, leading us to comprehend how much God delights in creating and sustaining the glorious abundance of life.

In order to move forward in our understanding of God, of Christ and of ourselves, we need to move away from viewing anything that affirms the spiritual importance of the material world as potentially idolatrous. As we will see in the next chapter, there is a danger of idolatry, but that is greed (Col. 3.5), that is, not valuing the rest of creation as also created and sustained by Christ, and therefore kin to us. Neo-pagans should not be the only ones who value the natural world, its cycles and seasons, and its precious fertility and symbiosis. Christians can and must do these things too. We need to do so recognizing that these cycles and seasons are part of all things that have come into being through Christ. We are not to regard them as having spiritual power over us; rather we can celebrate them without fearing that we are compromising our faith in Christ.

This section of Colossians can remind us that we are to continue to walk in Christ, which is a deeply appropriate image for the spiritual and ethical steps we need to take each day to live a simple yet richly connected existence. The first recipients, 'being built up and established in Christ', overflowed with thanksgiving (Col. 2.7). An attitude of thankfulness to God, to each other and to all things which sustain us is at the heart of continuing to walk in Christ.

Nympha's notes

There is a beautiful kithara in the dining hall of my villa that makes a loud, sweet, piercing sound when someone who knows the way of the strings plays it. It's bigger than my little lyre; far more complicated. I remember that one of the musicians visiting my parents could make it cry, and I wanted him to teach me how to do it. He said that I first had to learn how to transpose a piece of music from one key into another. Everything about the piece of music had to stay the same, so that it flowed with its internal logic unchanged. But everything about the piece changed if you transposed it to a different key – every note, the shape of how you had to pluck the strings– and its overall 'tenor' changed as well, because different pitches have a different 'feel'. He said that a kithara could only weep if a player knew how to transpose the heart up and down.

When I came to know Christ and to know Christ in me, my life was transposed. It's not that the music of my life altered so much – the seasons still follow their logical sequence, there are still setbacks and conflicts to manage. But I am no longer troubled by those who take delight in criticizing a woman and enjoy telling even the head of a household her duty. The Gospel has transposed my life – the same phrases sound different to me now, and the tenor of the whole is one of thanksgiving, lifting the heart in praise.

CHAPTER 8

Stoic reading context: Vices and virtues

Stoics are famous for their control of 'passion', *pathos*. Today we often use the word 'passion' in a positive sense for an abiding connection with someone or something, but in the ancient world it was mostly viewed negatively as referring to experiences that make a person physically or emotionally vulnerable.[1] The word 'craving' conveys this negative view of *pathos*.[2] For Stoics, *pathos* included not only the turbulent emotions of sexual desire, ambition and jealousy, but also such states of mind as hesitancy, malice and pity. They subdivided *pathos* into four primary passions: appetite, pleasure, fear and distress. *Pathos* for the Stoics is an unhealthy state of mind, not just synonymous with emotion.[3] The following Stoic list of passions quoted by the fifth-century compiler of Greek extracts, Stobaeus, categorizes those states of mind to reject:

> (1) The following are classified under appetite: anger and its species ... intense sexual desires, cravings and yearnings, love of pleasures and riches and honours, and the like. (2) Under pleasure: rejoicing at another's misfortunes, self-gratification, trickery, and the like. (3) Under fear: hesitancy, anguish, astonishment, shame, confusion, superstition, dread, and terror. (4) Under distress: malice, envy, jealousy, pity, grief, worry, sorrow, annoyance, mental pain, vexation. (Stobaeus 2.90, 19 – 91, 9 (*SVF* 3.394, part), L&S 412).

The Stoic alternative to all of these appetites is virtue. To understand what they meant by virtue, it is illuminating to begin with Seneca as he reflects on the difference between someone who does a single noteworthy deed, and someone who lives consistently according to virtue. What might appear an act of generosity may in fact be an act of extravagance, if it is not grounded in a consistent life. Seneca states that 'there is the greatest difference between one who knows how to

---

1. LSJ, 1285.
2. The term *pathos* is used in Col. 3.5 in a list of negative impulses and actions, and has been translated as 'craving'.
3. L&S 419–20.

give and one who does not know how to save'.[4] We see that a Stoic list of virtues has a strong focus on consistency, foresight and self-control:

> We divided virtue into parts: the obligation of curbing desires, checking fears, foreseeing what has to be done, dispensing what has to be given. We grasped moderation, courage, prudence, justice, and gave to each its due. From whom then did we perceive virtue? That person's orderliness revealed it to us, their seemliness, consistency, the mutual harmony of all their actions, and their great capacity to surmount everything. From this we perceived that happy life which flows on smoothly, complete in its own self-mastery.[5]

In between vice and virtue was a deep chasm, according to Stoic thinking. Either you were virtuous or you were not; there was no gradation. There is a comparable distinction in Colossians between the recipients' former life, their old self, and their new life, which has been clothed anew (Col. 3.9-10). Nevertheless, this was also a matter requiring exhortation (Col. 3.12-14). Not everyone in the ancient world agreed with the Stoic chasm, as we see in Plutarch's acerbic comment:

> 'Yes', they [the Stoics] say, 'but just as in the sea the person an arm's length from the surface is drowning no less than the one who has sunk five hundred fathoms, so even those who are getting close to virtue are no less in a state of vice than those who are far from it. And just as the blind are blind even if they are going to recover their sight a little later, so those progressing remain foolish and vicious right up to their attainment of virtue'. (Plutarch, *On common conceptions* 1063A-B (*SVF* 3.539, part), L&S 382, modified).

Plutarch would have us focus on the action itself, whereas the focus of Stoics is on the consistency of the action with the rest of one's life.

Homologia *(consistency)*

The term *homologia* was key to the Stoic concept of virtue. The linguistic form (*homo-logia*) is interpretable as 'harmony with reason', the commanding faculty and thus with Logos.[6]

The unlikelihood of anyone achieving true *homologia* was a topic of conversation (and humour!) between philosophers:

> If virtue and vice alone, in their [the Stoics'] opinion, are good and bad respectively, and no other creatures are capable of receiving either of them; and if the majority of people are bad, or rather, if there have been just one or two

---

4. Seneca, *Letters* 120.5, L&S 370.
5. Seneca, *Letters* 120.3–5, 8–11, L&S 370 (modified).
6. L&S 383.

good people, as their fables maintain, like some absurd and unnatural creature rarer than the Ethiopians' phoenix; and if all bad people are as bad as each other, without any differentiation, and all who are not wise are all alike mad, how could humans not be the most miserable of all creatures in having vice and madness ingrown and allotted?[7]

The rarity – indeed uniqueness – of true *homologia* lent itself to the proclamation of the Gospel of One who was truly Good, and in whom, through baptism, we are now able to live a Good Life.

Love

Love has a central and unifying role in Col. 3.14, and is characteristic not only of God (Col. 3.12) but of relationships between those whom God loves (cf. Col. 1.4, 8; 2.2; 3.19). Love does not take centre stage in Stoic ethics, because it makes the wise person vulnerable to passion:

> I think Panaetius gave a charming answer to the youth who asked whether the sage would fall in love: 'As to the sage, we shall see. What concerns you and me, who are still a great distance from being a sage, is to ensure that we do not fall into a state of affairs which is disturbed, powerless, subservient to another and worthless to oneself.' (Seneca, *Letters* 116.5 (Panaetius fragment 114, part) L&S 423).

Nevertheless, in the famous hymn by Cleanthes, quoted in full in Chapter 2, we read: 'You love things unloved.' By implication, to do so is to be like God. (Cleanthes, *Hymn to Zeus* (SVF 1.537) L&S 327).

Singing and thanksgiving

Thanksgiving is a theme that is prominent throughout Colossians (see Col. 1.3, 12; 2.7; 3.15, 16, 17; 4.2). The close connection between singing hymns of praise and the practice of thanksgiving and gratitude is found not only in Col. 3.16-17 but in Stoic writings as well. Epictetus' student Arrian recorded his teacher's words quite vividly:

> [15] For if we had any sense, what else should we do, both in public and in private, than sing hymns and praise the deity, and recount all the favours that he has conferred! [16] As we dig and plough and sow, ought not we to sing this hymn of praise to God: [17] 'Great is God, for having provided us with these implements with which we till the earth; great is God for having given us hands, and the power to swallow, and a stomach, and enabling us to grow without being

---

7. Alexander of Aphrodisias, *On fate* 199.14–22, L&S 381 (modified).

conscious of it, and to breathe while we're asleep.' [18] This is what we should sing on every occasion, and also the most solemn and divine hymn to thank God for having given us the power to understand these things, and to make methodical use of them.

[19] Well then, since most of you have become blind, isn't it necessary that there should be somebody to take your place, and sing the hymn of praise to God on behalf of one and all?

[20] And what else can I do, lame old man that I am, than sing the praise of God? If I were a nightingale, I would perform the work of a nightingale, and if I were a swan, that of a swan. But as it is, I am a rational being, and I must sing the praise of God. [21] This is my work, and I accomplish it, and I will never abandon my post for as long as it is granted to me to remain in it; and I invite all of you to join me in this same song.[8]

Thanksgiving is a way of life, connecting every mundane action with the wider horizon of God's providence. To give thanks to God is to be truly rational and to perform one's life's work, just as the nightingale or the swan perform their work by being who they are. Living from a place of gratitude, both publicly and privately, represents this truth to others, and invites them to be attentive to God's providence as well.

Stoic thinking on one's duties in relation to others

Stoic thinkers valued the idea that all people should be regarded as kin to each other. This ideal is noted by Plutarch (who is generally critical of Stoic philosophy), and suggests that Col. 3.11 (there is no longer Greek and Jew...) would have had wide resonance at that time:

> The much admired Republic of Zeno ... is aimed at this one main point, that our household arrangements should not be based on cities or parishes, each one marked out by its own legal system, but we should regard all people as our fellow-citizens and local residents, and there should be one way of life and order, like that of a herd grazing together and nurtured by a common law. Zeno wrote this, picturing as it were a dream or image of a philosopher's well-regulated society.[9]

Stoic thinkers pondered how to conceptualize the transition between viewing ourselves as only responsible for ourselves and our immediate family, to a wider concept of kinship. In Chapter 5 we met the Stoic concept of *oikeiōsis* – making

---

8. Epictetus (Arrian) *Discourses*, 1.16, in Hard, tr., *Epictetus*, 38. The capitalization of *God* is Hard's.

9. Plutarch, *On the fortune of Alexander* 329 A-B (*SVF* 1.262, part), L&S 429 (modified).

someone or something to be of the same household, family or kin as oneself. In the following excerpt from Hierocles, he reflects on how to make a wider and wider circle 'one's own'. The concentric circles of relationship should draw us closer to those who are our wider 'kin':

> Each one of us is as it were entirely encompassed by many circles, some smaller, others larger, the latter enclosing the former on the basis of their different and unequal dispositions relative to each other. The first and closest circle is the one which a person has drawn as though around a centre, one's own mind. This circle encloses the body and anything taken for the sake of the body. For it is virtually the smallest circle, and almost touches the centre itself. Next, the second one further removed from the centre but enclosing the first circle; this contains parents, siblings, spouse, and children. The third one has in it uncles and aunts, grandparents, nephews, nieces, and cousins. The next circle includes the other relatives, and this is followed by the circle of local residents, then the circle of fellow-tribesmen and women, next that of fellow citizens, and then in the same way the circle of people from neighbouring towns, and the circle of fellow-countrymen and women. The outermost and largest circle, which encompasses all the rest, is that of the whole of humanity. Once these have all been surveyed, it is the task of a well-tempered person, in properly treating each group, to draw the circles together somehow towards the centre, and to keep zealously transferring those from the enclosing circles into the enclosed ones. ... But we should do more, in the terms of address we use, calling cousins brothers, and uncles and aunts, fathers and mothers. ... For this mode of address would be no slight mark of our affection for them all, and it would also stimulate and intensify the indicated contraction of the circles.[10]

This idea views all of humanity as a 'household'. However, the concept is not limited to humanity, as plants and animals are regulated by nature towards *oikeiōsis*, to care for their own well-being (Diogenes Laertius 7.85). *Oikeiōsis*, in widening one's sphere of kinship and concern, has great ecological potential, and we will explore this later.

Stoic philosophy has a strong practical and ethical focus in the first century CE. One of the topics of philosophy was what each of our proper functions is, given the various roles that we have in life. Epictetus asks how he should maintain his natural and acquired relationships, 'as a religious man, as a son, a brother, a father and a citizen'(*Discourses*, 3.2.4, cf. *Discourses* 2.10.1-11). The Household Code in Col. 3.18–4.1, which sets out behaviour and attitudes for wives and husbands, children and parents/fathers, slaves and masters, raises similar questions, as many of the recipients of the Letter would fall into more than one category – a husband would also be a child, possibly a father and a master of slaves. How should one conduct oneself? We may find it hard to think of the Household Code in

---

10. Hierocles (Stobaeus) 4.671,7 – 673,11, L&S 349–50 (modified).

Col. 3.18-22 as anything other than inscribing a hierarchical blueprint into family life, but it is embedded in ethical discourse, and would have been seen to contribute to ethical reflection on the household. The longest attention in this code is given to slaves (Col. 3.22-25).

Slavery

The Stoic philosopher Epictetus had been a slave in Rome to Epaphroditus, a powerful freedman of Nero. As a slave, Epictetus studied philosophy under Musonius Rufus and, after being freed by Epaphroditus, set up as a philosophy teacher himself. Epictetus does not hesitate to address his elite pupils as 'slave', to remind them of their kinship with slaves, within a common family:

> [3] Slave, can't you put up with your own brother or sister, who have Zeus for their father and are, so to speak, born of the same seed as you, and are of the same heavenly descent? [4] Or because you've been stationed in a somewhat more eminent position, will you set yourself up all at once as a tyrant? Won't you keep in mind who you are, and who these people are whom you are ruling over? That they belong to the same family, that they are by nature brothers and sisters of yours, that they are offspring of Zeus?

> [5] 'But I have right of purchase over them, and they don't have any such right over me.'

> But don't you see to where it is that you're directing your view? That it is to the earth, to the pit, to these miserable laws of ours, the laws of the dead, so that you fail to have any regard for the laws of the gods?'[11]

It is striking that not only the ethical point is very similar to the Household Code in Colossians 3 but also the philosophical underpinning and even the language of descent and ascent are similar. Both are examples of *oikeiōsis* in practice. This Stoic kinship/*oikeiōsis* perspective can offer a significant opportunity for an ecological re-reading of Colossians. For too long, a misreading of the Letter, which sees it presenting a dualistic perspective, has shaped the common heritage of Western Christianity. The Neo-Platonism of Plotinus from the third century CE onwards, which assumes and advocates the superior quality of immaterial reality, is the filter through which we interpret scripture in general, and a passage such as Col. 3.1-8 in particular. We have read Col. 3.1-8 as a value statement, execrating the 'lower' physical life as gross and inferior and only valuing the 'higher' spiritual, non-material realm. It is easy to do this, as the references to downward focus in this passage are uniformly negative. However, what these references challenge are aberrant human behaviours and attitudes. They are *not* saying there is anything intrinsically inferior about Earth. The Stoic view of all things being permeated by the divine – physical matter included – is far more true to this Letter's world view.

---

11. Epictetus *Discourses* 1.13.3-5, in R. Hard, tr., Epictetus, 34, (modified).

The implications of the Neo-Platonic assumptions for our historical and present care for Earth and indeed for our relations with each other are tragically apparent. If, as we read in 3.11, Christ is all things and is in all things, then a re-valuing of the physical world is a Gospel imperative.

Eco-Stoic commentary on Col. 3.1–4.1

Translation of Col. 3.1–4.1

3.1 Therefore, if you have been raised together with Christ, keep seeking the things that are focussed upwards, where Christ is, seated at the right hand of God. 2 Set your minds on the upward focussed things, not on the things that are downward focussed. 3 For you died, and your life is hidden with Christ in God. 4 When Christ – our life! – is revealed, then you also will be revealed with him in glory.[12]

5 Therefore put to death those parts of yourself that are downward focussed: sexual wrongdoing, impurity, craving (*pathos*), evil desire and greed, which is idolatry. 6 On account of these things, the wrath of God is coming [on those who follow disobedience][13]. 7 These are the ways you also once walked, when you were living among those things. 8 But now you also must lay aside all these things: anger, rage, malice, blasphemy, abusive language from your mouths.

9 Do not deal falsely with each other; since you have stripped off your old self with its habits 10 and have clothed yourself with the new self that is being renewed in knowledge according the visual embodiment (*eikon*) of its Creator. 11 In that, there is no longer Greek and Jew, circumcised and uncircumcised, barbarian, Scythian, slave and free; but Christ is all things and is in all things!

12 Therefore clothe yourselves as God's chosen ones, holy and loved, with compassion, mercy, kindness, humility, gentleness and patience, 13 accepting one another and freely forgiving one another, if anyone has a complaint against you. Just as the Lord has also freely forgiven you, so you must do the same. 14 Over all these things put on love, which binds them all together perfectly.

15 And let the peace of Christ rule in your hearts; it is into this peace that you were also called in the one body, and practise thankfulness.

16 Let the Logos of Christ continually dwell in you richly, teaching and exhorting one another in all wisdom, singing psalms, hymns and spiritual songs with gratitude in your hearts to God.

---

12. Many ancient manuscripts read 'your life'. I have favoured 'our life'. It is the more difficult reading, but one which is in keeping with other pithy and memorable phrases in Colossians such as Col. 2.17 'The body is Christ!', and 3.11 'Christ is all things and in all things!'.

13. This phrase is not present in some significant ancient manuscripts, including Sinaiticus and Alexandrinus, hence the square brackets. The phrase is reminiscent of Eph. 5.6, and literally refers to 'sons of disobedience', evoking long-term allegiances and habits.

[17] And all things – whatever you do in word or deed – do all things in the name of the Lord Jesus, giving thanks to God the Father through him.

[18] Wives, be subject to your husbands in a way that is fitting in the Lord.

[19] Husbands, love your wives and do not be embittered against them.

[20] Children, obey your parents in all things, for this, in the Lord, is acceptable.

[21] Fathers, do not provoke your children to anger, so that they may not be disheartened.

[22] Slaves, obey your lords according to the flesh in all things, not only when you are under their eye, as if you had only to please human beings, but wholeheartedly, out of reverence for the Lord. [23] Whatever you are doing, put your whole self into the work, as serving the Lord and not as serving human beings, [24] knowing that you will receive the reward of an inheritance from the Lord; it is the Lord Christ that you are serving.

[25] Anyone who does wrong will be repaid accordingly. For there is no favouritism.

[4.1] Masters, provide what is just and fair for your slaves, knowing that you also have a Master in heaven.

Structure

The structure of this passage can be set out as follows:

I Baptismal life in Christ:
    a. Having been raised, direct the gaze upwards towards Christ – our life 3.1-4
       Having died, put to death the death-dealing practices that direct the gaze downwards 3.5-8
    b. Having stripped off the old self, the image of Christ is in all things 3.9-11
       Clothe yourself as God's chosen, forgiven and forgiving, with a waistband of love 3.12-14

II Three marks of being in Christ, leading to thankfulness:
    a. Let the peace of Christ rule in your hearts, be thankful (*eucharistoi*) 3.15
    b. Let the Logos of Christ dwell, (*enoikeitō*), with thanks (*chariti*) in your hearts 3.16
    c. Do all things in the name of the Lord Jesus, giving thanks (*eucharistountes*) to God 3.17

III Three pairs of relationships, in the Lord:
    a. Wives and husbands 3.18-19
    b. Children and parents/fathers 3.20-21
    c. Slaves and masters 3.22–4.1

I. Baptismal life in Christ

a. The ethical dimensions of having been raised, and having died (3.1-8) From
the spatial imagery associated with the dying and rising of baptism, this section
develops a contrast between downward-focused and upward-focused things.
In the Greek, these are literally 'things on the earth' and 'the things above'.
By choosing to use spatial imagery this way, Col. 3.1-5 moves away from a
cosmology of Christ permeating all things (Col. 2.9), and instead invokes a
dualistic cosmology familiar from Plato, where the lower realm is associated with
mortal things and tainted with passion, fear and evil. (Timaeus 69 B-D, LCL 234:
178–81) Colossians 3.1-5 exhorts the recipients to turn their attention upwards to
the elevated horizon, which is here associated with Christ.

These verses are problematic for an ecological reading, as they seem to associate
Earth with all the practices that we are called to leave behind: sexual wrongdoing,
impurity, craving, evil desire and greed, which is idolatry. In dismissing the
'things on the earth' in favour of the things above, these verses seem to commit
the believers to a view that sees our true life and values as unconnected with
Earth, even opposed to Earth. It seems to reinscribe the idea that concern for and
connection with Earth is tantamount to idolatry.

This way of reading is not in keeping with the other key themes of Colossians,
which emphasize the fact that all things have come into being and are sustained in
Christ (Col. 1.16-17). All things 'in earth and on heaven' have been reconciled to
God through Christ, who 'made peace through the blood of his cross' (Col. 1.20).
Bodily reality is validated in Christ, in whom 'the whole fullness of deity dwells
bodily' (Col. 2.9). The Letter proclaims the profound vision of Christ's reconciling
work in his fleshly body (Col. 1.21), and this is where the theological emphasis lies.
Christ is all things and is in all things! (Col. 3.11).

Earth is not culpable for the human vices listed in Col. 3.5. Rather, it is used
here as a spatial depiction of contrasting human behaviours, with the things below
as evil and the things above as good. I have therefore translated *ta anō* (Col. 3.1, 2)
as 'upward focussed things', which is a literal translation (cf. Phil. 3.14), and *ta epi
tēs gēs* as 'downward focussed things', retaining the spatial imagery associated with
dying and rising in Christ through baptism, but omitting the term 'earth'. This is a
functional rather than formal equivalence.

'Things on the earth' is in fact an idiom, as we have already seen from its use in
Epictetus' Discourse 1.13.5:

> But don't you see to where it is that you're directing your view? That it is to the
> earth (*eis tēn gēn*), to the pit (*eis ton barathron*), to these miserable laws of ours,
> the laws of the dead (*nomous tous tōn nekrōn*).[14]

14. Hard, tr., *Epictetus*, 34.

Epictetus, writing in the late first century, uses the image of directing one's gaze to the earth as equivalent to staring into a pit into which criminals were thrown.[15] He also compares directing one's gaze to the earth with the 'laws of the dead', which were formal laws relating to the body, or the corpse (Epictetus 1.19.9), not the mind or reason.[16] We see from this example that directing one's view 'downwards' this way was an idiomatic expression meaning giving one's attention to those things that are evil, futile or associated with death. I will call these vices 'death-dealing' practices.

What is being conveyed in Col. 3.1-5 by these contrasting images of downward and upward gaze are the ethical implications of dying and rising with Christ through baptism. The baptismal imagery of dying and rising was established in the previous section (Col. 2.20 'If you have died with Christ') and is picked up in Col. 3.1 'if you have been raised together with Christ'. Christ our life is the goal, as we put to death those things that lead away from Christ.

Baptism as dying and rising is a characteristically Pauline way of conceptualizing what is taking place in the waters of baptism (cf. Rom. 6.3-5). The old life – the old self – dies and is stripped away. The new life, the new self, has been raised with Christ (Col. 3.1) and is in the process of being renewed (Col. 3.10), though the full completion of that process is still anticipated (Col. 3.4).

The eschatological framework associated with baptism, when compared to Rom. 6.3-5, differs in Colossians.[17] In Romans, the believer has been baptized into Christ's death and has been buried with him, but there is no statement that the believer has been raised. Instead, Rom. 6.4 frames it as a subjunctive of purpose (so that we might walk), and then in Rom. 6.5 as a future hope of resurrection. The analogy between the dying and rising of Christ and the dying and rising of the believer is also framed differently in Colossians from Romans. In Colossians both the dying and the rising are named as the believers' current reality. Nevertheless, the point of both passages is very similar: the believer is now actually free to live in Christ, liberated from those behaviours that once marked their old life, and is able to live accordingly (Col. 3.5, 8, 12; Rom. 6.11-14). The chronological difference between the current reality and the future reality – which is clearly maintained in Rom. 6 – recedes in language of Colossians, and the spatial idiom of directing the gaze upwards, not downwards, takes precedence. By moving away from the chronological depiction of eschatology to a spatial one, it is possible to emphasize that life in God is already a reality, though not fully accessible. The future is being associated with the 'things above'. Just as in Col. 1.5 the Colossians were told that

15. A gulf, pit: – at Athens a cleft behind the Acropolis, into which criminals were thrown. LSJ, 306.

16. Hard, tr., *Epictetus*, 311–12.

17. Lohse for example argues that in contrast to Romans, Colossians implies that the believers' resurrection to new life had already taken place in their baptism, *Colossians and Philemon*, 180. Todd D. Still nuances this in 'Eschatology in Colossians: How Realized Is It?' *NTS* 50/1 (2004):125–38.

their hope was laid up for them in heaven, so here, their life is hidden (Col. 3.3), and yet to be fully revealed (Col. 3.4).

This contrasting imagery – hidden/revealed; below/above – is chosen for the purpose of exhortation. The images are a reminder that baptismal life is not 'business as usual'. They are also a call not to be so invested in the practices of religious observance and ritual (Col. 2.20-23) that they lose sight of those things to which they actually point – life in Christ. It reminds the recipients that they are to invest themselves in the big picture of reality. The downward-focused gaze, set on their former lives and the evils of the world, is a distraction to this perspective, as they await the shared future, shared between Christ, humanity and all things. Christ's epiphany will be their own epiphany (Col. 3.4).

Death-dealing practices The list of behaviours associated with death is divided into two parts (vv. 5-7, and vv. 8-9). The first part emphasizes behaviours particularly associated with the pagan world and their life prior to being in Christ, as is indicated in v. 7: 'These are the ways you also once walked, when you were living among those things.' In v. 5 there are three pairs of negative practices: sexual wrongdoing and impurity, craving and evil desire, and greed (which is) idolatry. The last of these pairs makes it clear that the meaning of the former term is clarified and specified by the latter term; greed is known as a death-dealing practice, as it leads to idolatry, making an idol of wealth and leading a person astray from Christ, who makes visible the invisible God (Col. 1.15). If the other pairs are similarly epexegetical or explanatory, the second pair indicates that craving (*pathos*) is desiring that which is evil. This is important, because it is not condemning all desire, as though the Christian life were to be lived out without emotional attachment. It is the dysfunctional desire for things that lead away from life and goodness that is condemned.

The first pair – sexual wrongdoing (*porneia*) and impurity (*akatharsia*) – can also be understood as reciprocally clarifying and explanatory. This pair of terms is also found in Gal. 5.19; 2 Cor. 12.21 and Eph. 5.3 (see also 1 Thess. 4:3-7, where both terms are present, but not juxtaposed). *Porneia* is a term often used without further specification,[18] referring to various acts such as adultery, prostitution or other sexual practices outside marriage.[19] Here and elsewhere in the Pauline letters, *porneia* is associated with impurity, the opposite of sanctity or holiness. Drawing on imagery associated with the Temple Cult, Paul and his associates could specify sexual wrongdoing as making one's body 'impure'. For example, in 1 Cor. 6.12-20, Paul makes this analogy explicit: 'Do you not know that your body is a temple of the Holy Spirit within you, which you have from God, and that you are not your own?' (v. 19). Similarly, in 1 Thess. 4.3, abstaining from sexual wrongdoing

18. William Loader, *Sexuality in the New Testament: Understanding the Key Texts* (Louisville, KY: Westminster/John Knox, 2010), 76.

19. For a comprehensive discussion of sexuality and the New Testament, see William Loader, *The New Testament on Sexuality* (Grand Rapids, MI: Eerdmans, 2012).

is equated with being sanctified or made holy. Across the Pauline letters, the recipients' bodily life is the locus either of sanctification or of impurity, expressed in sexual wrongdoing (*porneia*). More will be said about the interpretation of *porneia* later.

Four of the terms in Col. 3.5 are also found in Rom. 1.24-29 ('impurity' and 'evil desires', Rom. 1.24; 'cravings', Rom. 1.28; and 'greed' Rom. 1.29),[20] and three of them in Gal. 5.19-20 ('sexual wrongdoing', 'impurity' and 'idolatry'). Such lists have been interpreted as a condemnation of the body and its desires, particularly sexuality. However, we have seen that Colossians views bodily life positively, as set out in Chapter 7 in the discussion of *sarx* (flesh) and *soma* (body). Bodily existence is affirmed, as in Christ 'the whole fullness of deity dwells bodily' (Col. 2.9). Therefore, to view this list in Col. 3.5 as condemning bodily existence, including sexuality, would be to misread it.

Embodied life, as we have seen in Chapter 7, is central to a Stoic world view and crucial to an ecological reading of Scripture. The Judaeo-Christian tradition in the past has been careful to reject idolatry primarily in the form of rejecting pagan ways of 'worshipping' the natural world. But there is another idolatry that is much more subtle and pernicious, namely the idolatry of the self. Col. 3.5 names idolatry as 'evil desire and greed', which is a description of the worship of self. The worship of self sets no limits on perceived entitlement, so that there is no boundary between consumption and addiction. This fundamental type of idolatry perceives Earth only instrumentally, viewing it as *other* or *lower* than oneself. This idolatry of evil desire and greed is working itself out in the devastation humans are inflicting upon Earth. This is a death-dealing practice that is suicidal – for all the species of Earth, including humanity. We need to move away from understanding idolatry as honouring the divine presence in nature, and move towards comprehending the basis of idolatry as selfish desire and greed.

Sexuality is part of embodiment, as is food, and both these vital areas require healthy attitudes and practices to be whole. However, when sex is connected with commercial exploitation (greed), addictive behaviours (cravings) and practices that make an idol of it (idolatry), the result is sexual wrongdoing (*porneia*). *Porneia* is the shadow side of the good and gracious gift of bodily intimacy, where one is diminished or diminishes others through exploitation, addiction or idolatry.

Revisiting what *porneia* means is perhaps more urgent, and more difficult, than in former times, when there was a general consensus in the church and in society about what sexual wrongdoing is. In particular, the marriage of two persons, irrespective of gender, has been a particularly challenging issue for Christians in Western countries where the civil marriage laws have changed. There is not scope in this context to give a full treatment of this topic.[21] The concept of the

---

20. The Romans parallel is even stronger, when one considers Col. 3.6, which refers to the wrath of God coming on all those who are disobedient.

21. For an online copy of a report resourcing the Uniting Church in Australia on this issue, see https://uniting.church/b23-standing-committee-report-on-marriage-and-same-gender-relationships/ (accessed 22 May 2019).

human body as set apart for God's purposes can perhaps help us to distil what is abiding in sexual ethics, and what is transitory or simply culturally defined. If sexual wrongdoing is (or leads to) impurity, and sexual well-being is (or leads to) sanctity, how do we discern which is which? A life characterized by the qualities described in Col. 3.12-17 is a sanctified life. A later Pauline writing (Titus 1.15) states that our minds and consciences are crucial on this issue of discerning what is sanctified and pure. In a Pauline ethical framework, there is room for differences of practice, as long as each is fully convinced and follows through consistently in honour of God (Rom. 14:1-23).

There is a common thread between the various death-dealing practices in Col. 3.5. The list evokes one of the definitions of *pathos* from the Stoic list cited earlier – *pathos* as 'appetite' – referring not to healthy appetite, but to compulsion or obsession that leads to addiction and loss of self-control. This destructive *pathos* can be a personal matter, or as we see today, it can happen on a societal scale.

The second list of death-dealing practices, set out in Col. 3.8, focuses on other relational behaviours, particularly verbal ones. If the earlier list was associated with their life prior to being in Christ, this list indicates behaviours that may be current challenges: 'anger, rage, malice, slander, abusive language from your mouths'. If the earlier list focused on the integrity of one's own body, this list focuses on the integrity of the community as the Body of Christ.

The first practice is *orgē*, translated as 'anger'. It is the same term used in 3.6 for the *orgē* (wrath) of God. Anger can therefore be righteous (3.6), or death-dealing (3.8). Just as vengeance is God's, not ours (Rom. 12.19; Deut. 32.35), so too is anger – in the context of community life – something to be laid aside.[22] Learning to lay aside rage, malice, slander and abusive language is reminiscent of the Stoic list of passions under the other subheadings: pleasure (at another's misfortunes), fear and distress. All of these practices undermine the fabric of the community, sow division between people and lead to behaviours that exploit Earth. The common thread is self-gratification and self-aggrandizement. The Logos of Christ, who reconciles and makes peace (Col. 1.20) is absent in these ways of speaking and behaving.

All of these things (*ta panta*) need to be laid aside. In Col. 1.15-20 we had a striking number of positive references to *ta panta* (all things) in relation to Christ, through whom all things came into being. In Col. 3.8, they are to lay aside *ta panta*, which here refers to all the many behaviours that no longer have a place in Christ's body, the church (Col. 1.18). This serves as a reminder that while all things came into being through him, this does not justify 'all things' – any action or behaviour which is not in keeping with Christ. Christ is all things and is in all things! But some things ultimately have no place in Christ, and must be discarded – stripped away and replaced.

---

22. This is not to suggest that there is no such thing as righteous anger among human beings, particularly in the face of injustice and exploitation.

The opening of v. 9 – 'Do not deal falsely with each other' – functions as a summary of all the death-dealing practices of v. 8. To deal authentically with each other is to reflect Christ, who is their life; to deal falsely with each other is to negate their own life. The phrase provides a bridge to the next section, which focuses on making visible the image of Christ, by stripping off the old self, and clothing themselves as God's chosen ones, forgiven and forgiving, with a waistband of love (3.12-14).

b. Stripping off the old self and putting on Christ-like clothing (3.9-14) The dominant image in this section is of stripping off the old and putting on the new. This is a vivid evocation of baptism, with the laying aside of garments prior to baptism and putting on a baptismal garment after baptism.[23] Having ceased the practices associated with their old self – summarized as dealing falsely with one another, they have clothed themselves with a new set of behaviours. Their identity – their new 'self' – is in the process of being renewed in the direction (*eis*) of true knowledge, *epignosis*. This term we have already encountered in Col. 1.10, where it refers explicitly to the knowledge of God, and is a way of recalling the recipients of the Letter to consistency between outward and inward reality (see Chapter 3). Similarly here, the exhortation is to become who they truly are: shaped according to the image of the one through whom and for whom all things came into being (Col. 1.16). The renewal has begun, but is not yet fully complete. In verse 10, the terms 'knowledge' (*epignosis*), 'visual embodiment' (*eikon*) and the verb 'create' (*ktidsō*) together recall the Colossian hymn in Col. 1.15-20, and remind the recipients that this renewal is set against the background of cosmic renewal, cosmic salvation. The transformation may be personal, as it applies to each person, but it does not remain private.

The image of stripping off and putting on clothing is not limited to baptismal garments. Verse 11 refers to a great variety of people: Jews and Greeks, barbarians, Scythians, slaves and free persons. These contrasting groups of people defined their identity over against the 'other', and their affiliation and status were on display in their clothing. In the Lycus Valley cities, there were Greeks wearing the linen *chiton* and the heavier *himation* as a cloak; Roman men with their toga communicating their power and prestige, and a few with the distinctive stripes on Roman tunics denoting senatorial rank.[24] There were Roman women draped with a *stola* as a

---

23. There is considerable evidence of this as an established practice in early church documents – both Ante- and Post-Nicene. See E. C. Whitaker, *Documents of the Baptismal Liturgy* (London: SPCK, 1960), 5, 19, 26, 32-3, 36. See also Tor Vegge, 'Baptismal Phrases in the Deuteropauline Epistles', in *Ablution, Initiation, and Baptism: Late Antiquity, early Judaism, and early Christianity*, vol. 1, ed., David Hellholm, Tor Vegge, Øyvind Norderval and Christer Hellholm, BZNW 176/1 (Berlin/New York: W. de Gruyter, 2011), 497–556, at 512-3.

24. Rosemary Canavan, *Clothing the Body of Christ at Colossae: A Visual Construction of Identity*, WUNT, 2/334 (Tübingen: Mohr Siebeck, 2012), 3.

sign of respectability and tradition[25]. There were barbarians with their pointed beards and trousers[26], Scythian horsemen and women in their padded leggings, indigenous Phrygians with their pointed caps and Jews with fringed garments. Alongside all these were slaves of various ethnicities with short garments and exposed legs. All these items of clothing were visual displays of identity, showing peoples' ethnic origins, their political status, rank and office, their social standing and their gender, as well as their religious and philosophical affiliation. Their clothes proclaimed their identity.[27]

One might assume that stripping off the old self and putting on the new self means ridding oneself of the old identity markers, indicated by distinctive clothing. However, the metaphor does not require this. To put on Christ-like clothing was *not* to strip off their identity – as reflected in their clothing – and join a different subgroup with particular clothing as its identity marker. Rather than stripping off their ethnic and other identities as Christ-followers, they are to put on the Christ-like virtues described in vv. 12-17. Because of these virtues, people of any ethnicity, status or gender – wearing any garment! – can be known as being in Christ. That is at least one implication of the twofold exclamation 'Christ is all things, and is in all things!' Christ is not only in the Jew, but in the Greek, the barbarian and the Scythian. Christ is not only in the free person, but in the slave. Without shedding their cultural identities, Christ-followers are able to recognize and celebrate Christ's presence in each other – Christ is all things, and in all things! (Col. 3.11). But as we saw in Chapter 2, *all things* means much more than all these categories of people; it is literally *all things* – Earth and beyond.

The kind of 'clothing' that is their identity marker in Christ is described in Col 3.12-14: compassion, mercy, kindness, humility, gentleness and patience, accepting one another and freely forgiving one another. Love is the 'waistband' that binds all of these things together. The analogy of Christ-like clothing as their new identity marker is striking, as it cuts across the visual culture of displaying one's distinctiveness and implied superiority, and instead advocates an identity that is profoundly inclusive. Christ-like clothing is not specific to any ethnicity, status or indeed religion or gender.[28] It follows that Christ-like clothing is not so much *visual*, as *visible* in their behaviour towards one another.

This issue of fostering an inclusive vision of ourselves in relation to those *unlike us* – including other species and forms of life – is ecologically significant. We live in a time when the rifts in society are being turned into major fissures by violent people who use death-dealing acts of terror to seize attention and instil fear into

---

25. Canavan, *Clothing the Body of Christ*, 130.

26. Canavan, *Clothing the Body of Christ*, 123.

27. Vicky Balabanski, 'Neither Greek nor Jew ... for Christ Is All and In All' (Col 3:11-17), A Bible Study', in *Receptive Ecumenism: Listening, Learning and Loving in the Way of Christ*, ed. Vicky Balabanski and Geraldine Hawkes (Adelaide: ATF Press, 2018), 5–14.

28. This is implicit, though gender is not mentioned in this list of contrasting identities. See the further discussion of gender later.

societies. These acts steal the attention and resources that should be given to the real threats that face Earth – climate change, habitat loss, species extinction and the accompanying pressure on the poor and the displaced.[29] Christ-like clothing can be recognized and valued in all peoples, not just Christians, and this way of relating gives space for cooperating with one another in serving and protecting Earth (Gen. 2.15).

'Christ is all things, and is in all things!' Col. 3.11 In the Greek, this phrase is even more striking than it is in English. It is a pithy distillation of the panentheistic theology that we met in the Colossians' hymn (Col. 1.15-20), and in Col. 2.9. It assumes – without the need to argue the case – that Christ is in the closest possible relationship with the whole creation and that Christ's presence permeates all things – the world, and indeed, the universe. Stoic cosmology enabled the recipients of the Letter both to grasp the concept of Christ as the individual embodied being and seamlessly and coherently to recognize Christ as the cosmic body in whom, through whom and for whom all things exist (Col. 1.16). This was possible through the concept of Logos, which is the same whether present in an individual or throughout the cosmos.[30] If Christ was the only human being in whom the divine Logos was fully present, it follows that the Logos which permeates the universe is Christ's Logos, Christ's presence.

Christians have often perceived their allegiance to Christ in a sectarian way, as though Christ's reign was something precarious that relied on the efforts of Christ's followers to bring it about. However, if Christ is all things, and is in all things, this cannot be the case. There is no great gulf between Christ and creation – only a gulf in humanity's knowledge of God, who is made known in Christ (Col. 1.15). The aim of proclaiming the Gospel is to bless all things with the knowledge and experience of God's love, which is forgiveness and reconciliation in and through Christ. The Gospel does bring about a change of identity – as we are being renewed in knowledge according to the image of our Creator (v. 10) – but the identity is not a sectarian one.

Forgiveness There is a particular emphasis on forgiveness in v. 13. Just as our forgiving others and God's forgiving us are connected in the Lord's Prayer, so here, our forgiving others is grounded in the forgiveness that we have in Christ. Even so, forgiveness is a difficult aspect of the new identity that the believer has in Christ. To *require* a survivor of a serious wrong to forgive the perpetrator of that wrong is not in keeping with the compassion, kindness and patience of the Christ-like clothing described in v. 12. The verb translated as 'forgive' means to give or grant graciously and generously, with the implication of good will on the part of the

---

29. See for example *Ecological Aspects of War: Engagements with Biblical Texts*, ed. Anne F. Elvey, Keith Dyer and Deborah Guess (London: Bloomsbury/T & T Clark, 2017).

30. Balabanski, 'Critiquing Anthropocentric Cosmology', 151–9.

giver.[31] Perhaps it is legitimate to describe the behaviour implied here as active and positive nonviolence, which declines to retaliate, and so breaks the cycle of revenge and payback.[32] Gracious behaviour towards the other is the key; not the suppressing or dismissing of emotional or affective pain/trauma.

II. Three marks of being in Christ, leading to thankfulness

a) Let the peace of Christ rule in your hearts, be thankful (*eucharistoi*) 3.15
b) Let the Logos of Christ dwell (*enoikeitō*) with thanks (*chariti*) in your hearts 3.16
c) Do all things in the name of the Lord Jesus, giving thanks (*eucharistountes*) to God 3.17

Following the call to forgive as we have been forgiven, there are three positive exhortations concerning the believers' inner disposition and outward behaviour. The peace of Christ, the Logos of Christ and the choice to do all things in the name of the Lord Jesus are the marks of all believers. They are not three separate ideas, but connect with each other both in their reference point (the Lord Jesus Christ) and in the resulting attitude of thanksgiving.

Thanksgiving to God was already named in Col. 1.12, where it was set against the big picture of salvation, and connected with endurance, patience and joy. Similarly, peace was named in Col. 1.2 and 1.20 as coming from God, and having been enabled by Christ's blood. In using these terms, the writers are recapitulating and emphasizing these things as characteristic of a Christ-like life.

There is contemporary research that demonstrates that gratitude – thanksgiving – and happiness are connected.[33] The practice of calling to mind and being attentive to the good things one has is valuable for well-being, and an antidote to consumerism. The emphasis on thankfulness in each of these verses has a further spiritual dimension; it calls to mind that we are part of one body. In Chapter 7 we considered the interrelated nature of the body of Christ as cosmos, community and communion, and here we are reminded of the one body – in all these senses. Christ is all things and is in all things! (Col. 3.11) The peace of Christ into which we are called is relevant not only at the individual or the communion level but at the community level and the worldwide level as well. It is our choice and calling to let peace rule – a just and

31. J. P. Louw and Eugene Nida, *Greek-English Lexicon of the New Testament: Based on Semantic Domains* (New York: United Bible Societies, 1988), 57.102.

32. See Christopher Hrynkow, 'No to War and Yes to So Much More: Pope Francis, Principled Nonviolence, and Positive Peace', in *Advancing Nonviolence and Social Transformation: New Perspectives on Nonviolent Theories*, ed. Heather Eaton and Lauren Michelle Levesque (Sheffield: Equinox, 2016), 135–52.

33. Nathaniel M. Lambert, Frank D. Fincham, Tyler F. Stillman and Lukas R. Dean, 'More Gratitude, Less Materialism: The Mediating Role of Life Satisfaction', *The Journal of Positive Psychology* 4/1 (2009), 32–42.

ecologically sustainable peace, not just the absence of war. The ecological significance of this is obvious; such a perspective is the logical enabler for a worldwide move to communities who live in harmony with each other and with Earth.

The second of the three exhortations refers to the Logos of Christ. As set out in Chapter 2, the true Logos, the Gospel, is the 'Speech Act' of God, into which we are drawn, and by whose logic we live. In Col. 3.16, believers are called to allow this Logos to dwell in them richly and continually.

The word 'dwell' is significant. While the noun *oikeiōsis* is not found in Paul's writings, in the word 'dwell', we do have a verb that is part of this word group: 'Let the Logos of Christ dwell (*enoikeō*) in you richly.' This is reminiscent of Col. 1.19, which states that all the divine fullness was pleased to dwell/live (*katoikeō*) in Christ. The word group has connotations not just of indwelling, but of affiliation, making something one's own, as we have seen in Chapter 5. Against the background of *oikeiōsis*, the Logos of Christ is the word about not just Christ but the logic of Christ, particularly as it affects relationships. The Logos of Christ affiliates even those who are very different from each other. If the Logos of Christ takes up residence in or among them, Christ is indeed in them all (Col. 3.11).

They are to teach and exhort one another; there is no gender distinction in this exhortation (compare 1 Tim. 2.12-14). The Logos of Christ is associated not with male leadership but with the wisdom of all believers. This is important to note, particularly in the context of the following injunctions in Col. 3.18–4.1.

Psalms, hymns and spiritual songs are a key way of inviting the Logos of Christ to dwell richly in and among the community of believers. It is likely that the three terms are distinct, referring to biblical Psalms, composed hymns (such as we meet in Col. 1.15-20), and songs improvised in the Spirit. All of them are valid means for allowing the continual indwelling of Christ's Logos, and for fostering the 'upward' focus set out in Col. 3.1-4.

The third injunction refers to all things, this time in relation to everything that a believer says or does. All things came into being through and for Christ (Col. 1.16), and those who are in Christ should do all things in his name. This draws the circle of creation and new creation together, calling to mind the reconciliation and peace that have been made in him. The outworking of this harmony is thanksgiving to the Father through the Lord Jesus. As we saw in the Stoic reading context, thanksgiving can be a way of life, connecting every mundane action with the wider horizon of God's providence. To give thanks to God is to be truly infused with Christ's Logos and to perform one's life's work.

III. Three pairs of relationships, in the Lord

  a. Wives and husbands 3.18-19
  b. Children and parents/fathers 3.20-21
  c. Slaves and masters 3.22–4.1

Marriage in the ancient world was a much-debated topic, particularly between the Stoics and the Cynics. Entering a marriage meant accepting the responsibilities of a household, of parenthood and citizenship, as a household was the equivalent of a small business. This committed its head, and the other members of the household, to the social, political and economic life of the home town.[34] Stoics held that marriage was designed by nature, and part of the structure of the cosmos, which consisted of city-states, and these in turn consisted of households. Households, through the union of husband and wife and the raising of children, ensured the future of the whole. Stoics drew on the first book of Aristotle's *Politics* for these ideas, but took them a step further. As nature for the Stoics is the divine principle, it was in accordance with nature for the sage to marry and have children.[35] Households and their functioning were, from a Stoic's point of view, connected with God.

Cynics, by contrast, prioritized freedom for the pursuit of philosophy, which meant freedom from marriage and all that it implied.[36] Epictetus described the Cynic's calling to a student considering adopting it in this way:

> Isn't it necessary that the Cynic should remain free from all distraction, to dedicate himself wholly to the service of God, and be able to walk about among people without being tied down by private duties, or being involved in social relationships that he cannot violate if he is to preserve his character as a virtuous and good person, and which he cannot maintain, on the other hand, without destroying his nature as a messenger, spy and herald of the gods? (Discourses 3.22.69, Hard, tr., *Epictetus*, 188–9).

Cynics viewed their role as allegiance to a higher order or calling.[37]

This debate played itself out in the early church too. In the most general terms, there were streams of thought that supported the Cynic approach to marriage, advocating freedom from the ties of marriage for the sake of the Lord. We find such echoes already in 1 Cor. 7.1, which drew strength from Paul's own celibacy (1 Cor. 7.7; 1 Cor. 9). These impulses are seen more fully in traditions such as the Acts of Paul and Thecla, which later claimed Paul and his followers for the side of celibacy.[38] By contrast, there were also those who later claimed Paul and his legacy for the cause of marriage, such as we find in 1 Tim. 5.14. Each side of the debate could draw strength from aspects of Paul's life and teaching, but it is clear that in Corinth, Paul adopted a Stoic mode of argumentation to address the various issues

---

34. Will Deming, *Paul on Marriage and Celibacy: The Hellenistic Background of 1 Corinthians 7*, 2nd edn (Grand Rapids, MI: Eerdmans, 2004), 49.

35. Diogenes Laertius (7.121) states that Zeno held this view. Deming, *Paul on Marriage and Celibacy*, 52–3, 65.

36. Deming, *Paul on Marriage and Celibacy*, 57.

37. Deming, *Paul on Marriage and Celibacy*, 72–3. The debate is set out more fully by Deming, 50–107.

38. Elizabeth A. Clark, 'Antifamilial Tendencies in Ancient Christianity', *Journal of the History of Sexuality* 3 (1995), 356–80.

there.[39] The very fact that a household is addressed here identifies these injunctions with the Stoic rather than the Cynic attitude to marriage and household.

In Col. 3.18–4.1, we have the first extant biblical example of a codified address to members of households.[40] There are three pairs of injunctions, and an individual would most likely have found herself or himself addressed by more than one of them. In each pair, the first-person to be addressed is the one with less power in the household structure. Given the profoundly different cultural context in which we seek to read and interpret this code from that of first-century Asia Minor, certain observations are in order.

First, suspicion about such a code is in order. It has been understood as 'sanctifying' the power imbalance and subservience of the subordinate or disadvantaged member in a relationship. It has been used this way and continues to be used this way in many parts of the world. It has legitimated abusive relationships, and continues to do so.[41] This is not acceptable, before God or in any context. Violence is incompatible with the love of God and neighbour. There is no context in which the Household Code legitimates abuse or violence. Contemporary Christians are called to educate themselves on the dynamics of domestic and family violence and repudiate all forms of it.

Second, these injunctions have a context.[42] The whole of the ethical section, with its focus on the baptismal life and its ethical implications, is the interpretive context of the Household Code. The 'stripping off of the old self and the clothing oneself as God's chosen people' is addressed to all, and the garment that is implied is the baptismal robe, common to all. This is a 'unisex' garment. There is no distinction drawn between people along the lines of gender, age or status in Col. 3.1-17; all who are in Christ are to be characterized by Christ-like qualities. Further, the three marks of being in Christ – Christ's peace, Christ's Logos, and doing all in the name of the Lord Jesus – are not compatible with an abusive reading of the Household Code.

Third, each pair of injunctions is specified as being 'in the Lord'. This means that in knowing the love and the humility which shaped the way in which the Lord lived and exercised power and authority, none of these injunctions can be a justification for abuse or violence. For those who seek to take them literally, the statement to wives has its own inbuilt limitation: 'Wives, be subject to your husbands in a way that is fitting in the Lord.' Only a way that corresponds to the Lord's way is fitting in the Lord.

---

39. Deming, *Paul on Marriage and Celibacy*, 212–14.

40. In 1 Cor. 7.16, wives and husbands are addressed directly, as are slaves or freed slaves in 1 Cor. 7.21-24. However, the injunctions are not (yet) codified.

41. See the report by Julia Baird and Hayley Gleeson, "'Submit to Your Husbands": Women Told to Endure Domestic Violence in the Name of God'. Available online: http://www.abc.net.au/news/2017-07-18/domestic-violence-church-submit-to-husbands/8652028 (accessed 20 May 2019).

42. That is also why, in this discussion, the Household Code is situated in the context of this chapter, rather than being set apart as is often done in commentaries.

Fourth, the eschatological horizon is visible in the last of the three pairs. The service that slaves render is to the Lord, not to human beings, and the inheritance that they will receive is from the Lord. This has already been named in Col. 1.12 as a cause of thanksgiving, and it is reiterated in Col. 3.24. This eschatological focus is clear at the close of the Household Code: 'You also have a Master in heaven.' This horizon does not permit even the most powerful of these roles in the Household Code to take their power for granted. Not they, but the Master in heaven will apportion the inheritance.

Each of these observations emphasizes that an abusive use of the Household Code goes against the code itself, and must be rejected – publicly and vocally. But the question remains: Why introduce such a code, given that the undisputed letters of Paul did not do so? Is it simply the rise (or recurrence) of patriarchy that accounts for it?

We can trace something of the developments in the Pauline communities in the light of the inclusive gospel. The earliest trace we have of Paul's attitude to issues of ethnicity, status and gender in the light of the Gospel is Gal. 3.28, 'There is neither Jew nor Greek, there is neither slave nor free, there is neither male nor female – for all of you are one in Christ Jesus.' Being 'in Christ' meant that the dividing lines across ethnicity, status and gender were radically redrawn. What Stoic philosophers had imagined and dreamt of had come to pass in Christ – *oikeiōsis*, drawing a wide circle into our sphere of kinship. Paul proclaimed this, and it is likely that the statement in Gal. 3.28 reflects words that were used at the baptism of new believers, not just in Galatia but in other Pauline communities as well.[43]

In the context of the community of Christ-followers at Corinth, which was founded by Paul and his associates, people were living out their new life in Christ by taking the Pauline baptismal words to heart. They had started downplaying any difference between the genders, dressing androgynously and rejecting the need for marriage.[44] They were embracing some ascetic practices, framed in the light of devotion to the Lord; these tended to mirror the Cynic view of marriage. It seems that Paul had not anticipated the Corinthians taking his original baptismal proclamation quite so literally! When he subsequently wrote a baptismal saying to the Corinthians, it was framed somewhat differently. It no longer included the male and female categories: 'For in the one Spirit we were all baptised into one body—Jews or Greeks, slaves or free—and were all made to drink of one Spirit' (1 Cor. 12.13). The Corinthian experiences were already making Paul and his co-workers more cautious about how to express the boundary-breaking reality of Christ.

When we come to the Letter to the Colossians, we have another saying that is framed like a baptismal formula: 'There is no longer Greek and Jew, circumcised and uncircumcised, barbarian, Scythian, slave and free; but Christ is all things and is in all things!' (Col. 3.11). There were perhaps only ten or twelve intervening

43. Richard N. Longenecker, *Galatians*, WBC 41 (Dallas, TX: Word Books, 1990), 154–5.

44. Margaret Y. MacDonald, *Colossians and Ephesians*, SP 17 (Collegeville, MI: Michael Glazier/Liturgical Press, 2000), 145–8.

years between the radically inclusive baptismal saying in Gal. 3.28, and the similarly radical (though not quite as inclusive) formula in Col. 3.11. Whereas in the earlier one, being in Christ flagged the irrelevance of gender divisions, in the later one, ethical and religious differences are done away with, along with divisions between slave and free, but gender differences are no longer mentioned. Instead, we have the inclusion of a gendered Household Code, with a formulaic distillation of key relationships in the Lord. It seems the Corinthian experience had made the Pauline leadership team yet more cautious in how they articulated the new life in Christ, particularly in relation to women.

Against the background of the Stoic/Cynic debate about whether marriage, or rejection of marriage, constituted a higher calling and a more fervent love of God, it seems that the Pauline position required further articulation. While Paul himself remained celibate (1 Cor. 9.5), and expressed the wish that others be like himself (1 Cor. 7.7), he argued in favour of the Stoic side of the debate (pro-marriage) rather than the Cynic side (remaining unencumbered by commitments).[45] The Household Code is such an articulation. It validates the household and gives significance to all who are part of the household. Together with the inclusive formula in Col. 3.11, the Household Code grounds the social and ethical teaching of this section in community life.

Colossians 3.11 affirms, and even enhances, the inclusive, universal valuing of different groups across ethnic lines, vis-à-vis the earlier baptismal articulations (Gal. 3.28; 1 Cor. 12.13). In doing so it offers an ethical outlook that is directly comparable to Stoicism: 'Nature begot me loving all people' (Seneca, *Ep.* 102.18).[46] However, issues concerning gender are addressed differently in Colossians 3, by addressing them in a *Household* Code.

Households were central to Stoic ethical reflection. Musonius Rufus wrote on marriage (13A.88, 13.B.90, 14.90–6), on having children (15.96–100) and on one's duty to parents (16.100–6, 'Must one obey one's parents under all circumstances?'). The characteristic Stoic term for affinity is *oikeiōsis*, 'making something one's own', as we have seen in Chapter 5 and already in this chapter. This has as its basis the concept of the *oikia*, the household. The connection between *oikeiōsis* and *oikia* is not just one of superficial etymology. There is a direct connection between the concepts of *oikia*, a house or household, *oikeios*, 'in or of the house', *oikeiotēs*, 'living together as a married couple', marriage, and *oikeiōsis*, affinity.

Prior to vv. 3.18–4.1, all the exhortations in Colossians have been 'unisex' – aimed at all believers, irrespective of gender or status. The Christ-like clothing

---

45. Deming, in *Paul on Marriage and Celibacy*, demonstrates that 'Paul's audience in 1 Corinthians 7 held a theological outlook that combined Stoic philosophy with apocalyptic and sapiential traditions' (207), and also shows Paul's own facility and willingness to work with Stoic systems of thought (210).

46. See Runar M. Thorsteinsson, *Roman Christianity and Roman Stoicism: A Comparative Study of Ancient Morality* (Oxford: Oxford University Press, 2010), 190–8.

(3.12-14) is same for all. Verses 15-17 distil all that has gone before, emphasizing the Christological foundation of our living, and the outworking of our living in thanksgiving to God. When seen this way, Col. 3.18–4.1 is a subordinate section, customizing the Christ-like clothing for service in the household. It is presumably meant to facilitate the peace, naming and circumventing pressure points that undermine peace in households. By viewing the following household section not so much as a prescriptive code (and certainly not a civil code) but as an example of exhortation aimed at facilitating peace in the first-century household, we may be more ready to customize the garment appropriately in the twenty-first century. Given the often oppressive reception history of Col. 3.18–4.1 even today, we may regret that Pauline ethical teachings moved in this direction, and that the chapter did not end at v. 17. Nevertheless, it is possible that the injunctions to masters may at times have relieved the lot of slaves. One might hope that vv. 3.22–4.1 were presented to the Lycus Valley communities by Onesimus, the former slave, and that other slaves benefitted from his story and his role in the Pauline mission (Col. 4.9; Phlm. 1-25).

In many parts of the world, the Household Code continues to justify male domination of women and intimate partner violence.[47] Climate change is adding a further layer of pressure on women, particularly in the Pacific, where rising sea levels are disrupting food production, and traditional women's roles in providing adequate food for their family is consequently increasingly difficult. Under this sort of pressure, domestic violence is not uncommon. In damaging Earth's ecology, we are damaging human ecology, and in particular, the lives of women and children.

Nympha's notes

I have been not just a daughter, but a wife and a mother. Indeed I *am still* all those things, though now without parents, husband or child. Those identities live on in me.

When I reached the age of eighteen, my parents arranged for a prominent military family who had retired into the Lycus Valley to visit, bringing their younger son Callipho with them. Callipho was well educated and I found his company pleasing. He got on well with my father, and they discussed philosophical ideas at length, as well as plans for the lands and business. My mother and I were included in all the important discussions, as was consistent with our Stoic values, and we had great times together. After the marriage took place, I gave birth to a son, our young Timon, and we thought that our happiness was complete.

---

47. Catherine Holtmann, 'Women Seeking Safety: Nonviolent Responses to Intimate Partner Violence', in *Advancing Nonviolence and Social Transformation: New Perspectives on Nonviolent Theories*, ed. Heather Eaton and Lauren Michelle Levesque (Sheffield: Equinox, 2016), 188–200.

But then our fortune changed. In the third year of Gaius Caligula's reign, my mother took ill and began to waste away. If that were not evil fortune enough, a virulent sickness took my beloved father and our son as well. You might say that it took my husband too, in that he changed. His grieving was overbearing and he became bitter against the gods. His philosophy did not help him. He could not find the indifference to fate that he had talked about so long. I took over the running of the household and business single-handed, and carried my grief as my companion. From time to time Callipho would come by and issue orders about how to manage things differently, and then ride away again to Laodicea or Colossae to drink with his companions. I did not comply – how could I, when I had just enough strength to manage things as they had always been? When he would return, he was not only bitter against the gods, but bitter against me too. One day he did not return. I heard that he had joined his father's old legion in the war against the Parthians, where his anger and his courage had an honoured place. He was killed in a border skirmish, and his fellow soldiers buried him there without procession or cremation. They sent me only his armband, and I have laid it on the little grave of Timon. Each year I commemorate them both here in this place.

If I had known then what I know now, I could have spoken some words of hope and comfort to him. Perhaps I could have found the strength to put his wishes into practice; perhaps that may have helped. Since Epaphras brought us the Word of the Gospel, I have been able to forgive Callipho for leaving me to bear my grief alone. As it is, I have been baptized for my parents, for my son and also for Callipho. They are all part of the treasure laid up for me in heaven, I believe, as they shared so many of the values of the Gospel, though without knowing the Lord himself. As I sing, I also sing to their memory – sometimes with the words of the psalms, sometimes with the great songs to the Lord, and sometimes with no words at all. The Logos of Christ connects me with them and teaches me to trust that they are all now safe.

I am still a daughter, a wife, a mother and a householder, and now a sister to many in Christ. My life is hidden with Christ in God. My household is now my immediate family, as we bear with one another and clothe ourselves with love.

CHAPTER 9

Stoic reading context: Concord (homonoia) *– the value of harmony*

Just as today when you ask a public figure about their hopes for the future, you might not be surprised to receive the answer 'world peace', so in the ancient world, 'concord' was a widely held value and aspiration. Rival cities entered into concord negotiations, concord games took place, and concord coins were minted to proclaim good will and harmony between cities.[1]

Concord is a divine attribute which makes possible all the best things about community, according to Dio Chrysostom:

> All the greatest things are preserved [through] concord, while that through which everything is destroyed is its opposite. ... The only respect in which we fall short of the blessedness of the gods and of their indestructible permanence is this – that we are not all sensitive to concord. On the contrary, there are those who actually love its opposite, strife, of which wars and battles constitute departments and subsidiary activities, and these things are continually at work in communities and in nations, just like the diseases in our bodies.[2]

Human affairs are often characterized by the 'disease' of strife, whether that be on the civic stage, or between individuals.

Discord within a household is one such 'disease' of strife. By contrast, Plutarch likened 'the concord of brothers both family and household' (*oikos*) to a 'harmonious choir'.[3] The Psalms, hymns and spiritual songs of Col. 3.16 are similarly an outward expression of the inner harmony of the community.

1. Alan H. Cadwallader, 'The Historical Sweep of the Life of Kolossai', in *Epigraphical Evidence Illustrating Paul's Letter to the Colossians*, ed. Joseph Verheyden, Markus Öhler and Thomas Corsten WUNT 1/411 (Tübingen: Mohr Siebeck, 2018), 25–67.

2. Dio Chrysostom, *Discourses 38, On Concord with the Nicaeans*, LCL 376: 60–1 (modified).

3. Plutarch, *Moralia. On Brotherly Love*, LCL 337: 250–3.

Heeding advice was also a sign of harmony within the household.[4] This demonstrated respect between members of a household. Similarly, gratitude was a mark of respect for others. According to Seneca, ingratitude was a sure way of disrupting harmony:

> Ingratitude is something to be avoided in itself because there is nothing that so effectually disrupts and destroys the harmony (*concordiam*) of the human race as this vice.[5]

It seems that ingratitude was viewed as a foundational 'disease'.

Gossip is another 'disease' that disturbs harmony. Timon of Phlius in his *Silloi* (lampoons) criticized the 'disease of gossip' within the history of philosophy.[6] When it came to a group of philosophers known as the Academics, Timon denounced their gossip as 'the prolixity of Academics unseasoned by salt'.[7] Clearly Timon thought that these people were long-winded and wordy, but there was an added problem – their speech about one another was not 'seasoned with salt'.

One of the functions of salt is to make food savoury, and conversely, a lack of salt makes food bland. By extension, when speech is 'seasoned with salt', this idiom is sometimes taken to mean that the speech is savoury or witty.[8] However, it is unlikely that Timon's point was that the Academic philosophers were lacking in wit. Rather, it is more likely that he meant they were lacking in attention to the effect of their speech on their relationships with other people. That is what made this speech 'gossip'. The most important function of salt in the ancient world was in fact as a preservative of food – keeping food good that might otherwise go bad. So, by extension, salt refers to that which preserves what is good.[9] To be seasoned with salt is to preserve good relations and enhance concord. This idiom lies behind the saying of Jesus to the disciples in Mk 9.50: 'Have salt in yourselves and be at peace with one another.' To be seasoned with salt preserves good will, by building concord between different people. We meet the saying in Col. 4.6 in this sense: 'Always make your conversation gracious, seasoned with salt.' So for clarity, I have translated the phrase as 'seasoned with the salt [of good will]'.

---

4. Trevor J. Burke, 'Paul's New Family in Thessalonica', *NovT* 54/3 (2012) 269–87, 286.

5. Seneca, *De Beneficiis*, 4.18.1, LCL 310: 240–1.

6. Stéphane Marchand, 'Sextus Empiricus' Style of Writing', in *New Essays on Ancient Pyrronism*, ed. Diego E. Machuca, PhA 126 (Leiden/Boston: Brill, 2011), 113–41, 115.

7. Diogenes Laertius, *Lives of Eminent Philosophers* 4.10, 'Clitomachus', LCL 184: 442–3.

8. See The New Jerusalem Bible translation of Col. 4.6: 'Always talk pleasantly and with a flavour of wit'.

9. Compare this saying attributed by Diogenes Laertius to Pythagoras: 'Of salt he [Pythagoras] said it should be brought to table to remind us of what is right; for salt preserves whatever it finds, and it arises from the purest sources, sun and sea.' Diogenes Laertius, *Lives of Eminent Philosophers* 8.1. 'Pythagoras', LCL 185: 350–1.

Another aspect of community life that could undermine concord was resentment about one's status. Chrysippus, the early Stoic leader renowned not only for his razor sharp mind, but for his many books, wrote a multi-volume work called *On Concord*. It is no longer extant, but we do have a quotation from it by Athenaeus, in which Chrysippus reflects rather cryptically on the distinction between different categories of service in a household:

> Writing in his *On Concord* book 2, Chrysippus says that there is a difference between a slave (*doulos*) and a house servant (*oiketēs*): those who have been freed (*apeleutherous*) are [effectively] still slaves, but those who have not been released from ownership are house servants (*oiketai*). 'A house servant', he says, 'is a slave who belongs to someone.'[10]

Chrysippus implies that the difference is moot, as not only slaves and house servants but also freed persons are still connected with and serve the household, though their legal status differs.[11] A slave can choose to see himself or herself as a house servant, because of his or her connection to the household. From a Stoic perspective, those who are wise perform their duties not from external compulsion but from their decision to do so, making status irrelevant.[12] So, the concord of a household should not be undermined by simmering resentments over status.

In the final chapter of Colossians, we have several references to 'fellow-slaves in the Lord': Tychicus is called a fellow-slave in v. 7, and in v. 12, Epaphras is called 'a slave of Christ Jesus', echoing the same word used to describe him in Col. 1.7. In Pauline usage, to be a 'slave of Christ' is an honorific title, and it is used sparingly. In the light of Col. 3.11, through our baptism, there is no longer any distinction between slave and free – Christ is all and in all! Nevertheless, it is interesting that the title 'slave of Christ' is not given to Onesimus, the former slave. This is perhaps a delicate acknowledgement that Onesimus has quite recently been freed.

The final chapter of Colossians gives us a glimpse of Paul and Timothy seeking to reinforce concord between the missionary team in Rome and the Lycus Valley communities of Christ-followers, between the Lycus Valley believers and 'outsiders' (their neighbours), between people of different status within the believing communities, and between the different communities 'in Christ' at Colossae and Laodicea. The letter writers are not giving a formal discourse about concord – the

---

10. Athenaeus 267 B (*SVF* 3.353) L&S 432 (modified); cf. Athenaeus. *The Learned Banqueters*, LCL 224: 228–9.

11. Freed persons generally stayed connected with the household from which they had been manumitted. Chrysippus's point indicates that such externals are indifferent. It is likely that the early Stoics rejected any natural basis to slavery. See L&S Vol. 2, 427, citing Miriam T. Griffin, *Seneca: A philosopher in politics* (Oxford: Clarendon Press, 1976) 459–60.

12. Serving a household is reminiscent of the concept of *oikeiosis*, which we met in Chapter 5. This concept emphasizes kinship with ever-widening circles.

word *homonoia* does not appear[13] – but the function of these final instructions and greetings is to reinforce harmony within and across communities.

Concord is a concept that can describe relations in the natural world as well. Cicero, in his *De Natura Deorum*, depicts a discussion between Balbus (a Stoic) and Cotta (a Sceptic), where they agree about the remarkable concord in nature, but Cotta questions whether a single divine breath accounts for it:

> Nature by its own motions and mutations impart[s] motion and activity to all things. And so I fully agreed with the part of your discourse that dealt with nature's punctual regularity, and what you termed its concordant interconnexion and correlation; but I could not accept your assertion that this could not have come about were it not held together by a single divine breath. On the contrary, the system's coherence and persistence is due to nature's forces and not to divine power; she does possess that 'concord' (the Greek term is *sympatheia*) of which you spoke, but the greater this is as a spontaneous growth, the less possible is it to suppose that it was created by divine reason.[14]

The Stoic, Balbus, in this dialogue sees the concord in nature as reflecting the divine breath, divine reason. In a similar way, the small communities of Christ-believers in the Lycus Valley are exhorted to see all things holding together in Christ (Col. 1.17), who embodies divine reason/Logos. The concord in nature – the cosmic sympathy we explored in Chapter 5 – and the concord between human beings are all part of the mystery of Christ, which is at the heart of the Pauline vocation and mission (Col. 4.3).

Eco-Stoic commentary on Col. 4.2-18

Translation of Col. 4.2-18

> [2] Continue in prayer, being alert as you do so to thanksgiving. [3] At the same time, pray also for us, that God may open a door for us to speak the Logos, the mystery of Christ – for which I have also been put in prison – [4] so that I may make it clear, to utter it in the way I should.

> [5] Walk in wisdom towards those who are outside, taking advantage of the time. [6] Always make your conversation gracious, seasoned with the salt [of good will], and giving attention to how best to answer each person.

> [7] Tychicus, the beloved brother, faithful servant and fellow slave in the Lord, will let you know all things concerning me. [8] I have sent him to you particularly

---

13. There were temples to the goddess Concord in the ancient world (e.g. Plutarch, *Lives, Vol. 2: Themistocles and Camillus* LCL 47: 204–5), which may have been a reason to avoid the term.

14. Cicero, *On the Nature of the Gods. Academics,* LCL 268: 312–13.

so that I may know what is going on for you,[15] and that your hearts may be encouraged. [9] Onesimus, the faithful and beloved brother, who is one of you, is accompanying him. They will let you know all the things going on here.

[10] Aristarchus, my fellow prisoner, sends his greetings to you, as does Mark, Barnabas' cousin. He is the one about whom you have received instructions – if he comes to you, make him welcome. [11] Also Jesus, the one known as Justus, sends greetings. They are my only fellow-workers for the kingdom of God from the circumcision, and have become a real encouragement to me.

[12] Epaphras, who is one of you, and a slave of Christ Jesus, sends his greetings to you. He is always striving in prayer on your behalf, that you may stand mature and fully assured in the will of God. [13] I can testify that he is working very hard for you, and for those in Laodicea and in Hierapolis.

[14] Luke the beloved doctor sends his greetings to you, as does Demas.

[15] Give greetings to the brothers and sisters in Laodicea, as well as to Nympha and the congregation in her house. [16] And when the letter has been read in your gathering, see to it that it is also read in the Laodicean assembly and that you also read the one from Laodicea. [17] And say to Archippus, 'Give attention to the service which you took on in the Lord, that you fulfil it.'

[18] The greeting in my own hand – PAUL. Remember my imprisonment. Grace be with you.

Structure

The structure of this final chapter can be set out as follows:

I. Recapitulating key themes 4.2-4
II. Behaviour towards outsiders 4.5-6
III. The letter bearers Tychicus and Onesimus are introduced and commended 4.7-9
IV. Greetings from:
- Paul's fellow workers of the circumcision (Aristarchus, Mark, Jesus Justus) 4.10-11
- Epaphras, and testimonial to him 4.12-13
- Luke and Demas 4.14

15. There is divergence in the ancient manuscripts as to whether this should read 'that you may know what is going on for us', which is the reading favoured by Metzger et al., *Textual Commentary*, 626, or whether the reading *gnō* of P46 should be given priority. I favour the latter reading, for reasons set out in the main text later.

V. Greetings to:
- The brothers and sisters in Laodicea 4.15a
- Nympha and the congregation in her house 4.15b

VI. Instructions:
- After the letter has been read in Colossae, have it read in Laodicea 4.16a
- Read the letter from Laodicea 4.16b
- Admonishment to Archippus 4.17

VII. Final greeting and blessing 4.18

Paul's own 'voice' can be heard again in Col. 4.2-18, as depicted by the use of the first-person singular ('I'/'me'/'my'), used eleven times in these verses.[16] Timothy's authorship recedes at this point to foreground Paul, the authoritative leader. This is a rhetorical move, to allow the 'head of the household' to speak. The first-person singular was also prominent in 1.23–2.5 (used fourteen times in various forms). In these two sections, Paul's persona is emphasized.

This is in contrast to the opening of the Letter, Col. 1.1-14, where Paul and Timothy's co-authorship was emphasized by the cluster of 'we', 'our' and 'us'.[17] At the close of the Letter, Timothy's presence is much more muted.[18] From Col. 2.6 through to 4.1 – the central section of the Letter – no first-person singular pronoun ('I'/'my') is used, and the first-person plural ('our'/'us') only occurs as a general statement in 2.13 – 'God made us/you alive together with him, when he forgave us all our trespasses.' I take it as likely that Timothy's distinctive style and theological emphases are more clearly visible in the main body of the Letter (2.6–4.1), though his rhetorical presence is muted. The overall impression given by these different rhetorical sections is that this is a collaborative letter, but one that seeks to place Paul's interest in, and concern for the recipients in the foreground at two strategic points in the Letter: an exordium, commending Paul as trustworthy to the recipients (1.23 – 2.5), and a peroration, concluding the Letter and recapitulating key ideas (4.2 – 18).

I. Recapitulating key themes 4.2-4

The Letter opened with reference to prayer and thanksgiving. There, Paul and Timothy assured the recipients that they were praying constantly for them

---

16. Vv. 3, 4 (twice), 7, 8 (twice), 10, 11, 13, 18 twice). As set out in the Introduction, I consider it likely that this is not pseudepigraphy.

17. See Col. 1.1, 2, 3, 4, 7, 8, 9, 13, 14, then again only in 1.28; 2.13-14 and 4.3. By naming Paul and Timothy's co-authorship, I do not mean to suggest that other co-workers such as Epaphras were unimportant in the writing process. See Michael Trainor, *Epaphras: Paul's Educator at Colossae. Paul's Social Network: Brothers and Sisters in Faith* (Collegeville, MN: Liturgical Press, 2008).

18. Note the two first-person plurals in v. 2.

(Col. 1.3, 9) and giving thanks for them (Col. 1.3). In Col. 1.11-12, we read that the prayer was for the recipients to be strengthened, so that they could give thanks joyfully, even while enduring 'everything'. Col. 4.2 now reminds them to imitate the constant prayer and thanksgiving of Paul and his associates.

The main verb in 4.2 is *proskartereō*, which means to continue to do something with intense effort.[19] The verb is also used in Rom. 12.12, where it is linked with persevering in tribulation. Ephesians 6.18 also has this term in a similar constellation of concerns. We are given a hint here that the writers are concerned that something may be causing the recipients to slacken in their attention to prayer. The nature of that constant prayer is further specified with the following clause, which urges them to 'keep alert' (*grēgoreō*) in prayer. The combination of keeping alert and praying is reminiscent of the sort of watching and prayer that Jesus asked of his disciples in the Garden of Gethsemane (Mk 14.38). One might have expected a reference to supplication or intercession at this point, as we meet in Eph. 6.18 (*deēsis*), but instead the admonition is specified as giving attention 'in thanksgiving'. As we saw in Seneca's quotation earlier, gratitude/thanksgiving is foundational to community life, and the exhortation in 4.2 gives particular emphasis to this. So the community's prayers are to be constant, alert, and characterized by thanksgiving.

Verse 3 continues this thought, and asks that the recipients may pray that a door or opportunity may open to speak the Logos, the mystery of Christ, clearly. Such a door of opportunity is mentioned in 1 Cor. 16.9 and 2 Cor. 2.12, but in these references, it is acknowledging that this has taken place, rather than asking for it to be enabled, as it is here. This request recapitulates the close connection between Logos and the mystery of Christ, discussed in Col. 1.25-29, where Paul's commission is described as making this Logos fully known. In Col. 4.3, this commission is reiterated, and the words emphasize that the communication of the mystery should not be private or esoteric, but clear and open. There is no hint here that some may be unable to hear or comprehend it. The verb *dei* (it is necessary = I should) in Col. 4.4 implies that God has placed the onus on Paul to communicate the mystery clearly. The same verb is used again in Col. 4.6, and there the necessity is placed on the recipients to know, before God, how best to answer each person.

Paul's imprisonment is mentioned in Col. 4.3 and also in the final verse of the Letter, 4.18. Both references imply that the Colossians already understand the significance of Paul's imprisonment; his suffering is associated with sharing Christ's afflictions (Col. 1.24). By remembering Paul's imprisonment, and its connection with the sufferings of Christ, the recipients are also incorporated into this ongoing story. There is an underlying cruciformity apparent in this logic/Logos, which directs their gaze back to the cross of Christ (Col. 1.20).

The ecological significance of these verses is to be seen in the meaning of the 'mystery of Christ', which is the focus of Col. 1.26-27, and is discussed in Chapter 6. The mystery of Christ is not just for the Gentiles, though they are put in the

---

19. Louw–Nida Lexicon, 68.68.

foreground in Col. 1.27, nor is it just for humanity more broadly; the mystery of Christ is the hope of glory to be shared with all creation. The well-being and future of creation is not a footnote to human salvation, but an essential part of the mystery of Christ.

The ecological impact of disharmony between different groups or factions in our world today is profound. The priority that we should give to preserving the natural world has been characterized as a contentious political issue, so political parties in many parts of the world can use wedge politics to capitalize on voters' fear or self-interest. When it comes to such a crucial issue as climate change, turning it into an opportunity for wedge politics is a completely inadequate approach. We need policies that benefit all species and future generations of humanity. Politicians must find ways to cultivate concord across groups with different values, so that with bipartisan or multi-partisan support, there can be real progress towards caring for Earth.

II. Behaviour towards outsiders 4.5-6

Verse 5 acknowledges that there is a difference between the community of Christ-followers and those on the 'outside'. It is important to reflect on the tone of this difference. The translation given here is literal, and the preposition 'towards' (*pros*) indicates that the way of life being enjoined on believers is not a sectarian one, which turns away from those who are unlike ourselves. Instead, we are, in wisdom, to walk towards them. How one does so with integrity is the subject of the field of Receptive Ecumenism, an approach pioneered by Paul Murray of Durham University, and taken up in many parts of the world, that asks, 'What do we need to learn from the other?'[20] Read in such a receptive framework, it becomes clear that the phrase 'taking advantage of the time' does not refer to a chronological shortness of time to make them like ourselves, but rather to the *kairos* time of opportunity to engage with these people for mutual benefit. Every interaction with those outside our own community can be, by God's grace, an opportunity for God's wisdom to be discovered afresh through the encounter with the other. Through this encounter, Christ – who is already present – becomes known in and through the believing person and community.

Verse 6 makes this gracious stance towards the outsider explicit: 'Always make your conversation gracious, seasoned with the salt of good will, and giving attention how best to answer each person.' This verse is of particular importance in an era in which the name of Christ is being co-opted in some quarters in the interests of sectarianism and violence. Christ-like behaviour is gracious, and this is the appropriate way of speaking with all people, not just those within our own communities. As set out earlier, the reference to salt is to preserving and fostering good relationships. When we give attention to how best to answer each person, we turn away from generic or stereotypical interactions, which can give Christians

20. See for example the collection by Balabanski and Hawkes, *Receptive Ecumenism*, viii.

today a reputation of 'scalp-hunting' for converts rather than genuinely befriending others. In a world hungry for genuine, respectful and trustworthy relationships, v. 6 is a gem of wisdom.

The impact of climate change and ecological degradation is already putting further stress on vulnerable communities and families across the world, and will increasingly do so in the years to come. In public and political life, it is also becoming increasingly countercultural to be gracious towards one another when we strongly disagree with each other, and in various societies, aggression is at times being confused with strength. All these developments indicate the need for Christian leadership to model gracious speech seasoned with the salt of good will, and for careful and appropriate engagement with those who disagree with our own views.

III. The letter bearers Tychicus and Onesimus are introduced and commended 4.7-9

Letter bearers played an important role in the Pauline mission. They had the task not only of travelling with the letters but also of reading them out and explaining them to the various communities. Those entrusted with these tasks had a high level of responsibility invested in them.

We meet the figure of Tychicus in various other NT writings. In Eph. 6.21, Tychicus is performing a similar task, and is described as 'beloved brother' and 'trustworthy' (faithful) servant in the Lord. In Acts 20.4, we learn that Tychicus was from Asia, meaning the province of Asia Minor. In 2 Tim. 4.12, we are told that Tychicus was sent to Ephesus,[21] and in Tit. 3.12, the possibility of him being sent is mentioned. The difficulty of harmonizing the chronology of all these writings with Colossians is well known, but it does suggest that Tychicus had become a significant leader in the Pauline churches of Western Asia Minor.

Verses 10 and 11 name those with Paul who were 'of the circumcision', which indicates that Tychicus, not named among them, was a Gentile convert. He may have been a relatively late addition to the Pauline ministry team, perhaps arriving on the scene at the time of Paul's stay in Ephesus (Acts 19.10).[22] Having joined Paul's mission, he is entrusted with tasks primarily in Asia Minor, his home territory, as it is likely that his local knowledge and connections were viewed as being of benefit to the mission.

Verse 8 is generally translated differently from the translation given here ('that I may know what is going on for you'), due to variations between the ancient manuscripts.[23] I favour the reading based on the earliest manuscript P46 and other

---

21. Various people mentioned in Colossians 4 are also mentioned in 2 Timothy 4, including Tychicus, Demas, Luke and Mark.

22. James D. G. Dunn sets this out as a possibility; *The Epistles to the Colossians and to Philemon*, 272.

23. The three main possibilities are: 'That you may know how we are', 'That he (Tychicus) may know how you are', and 'That I may know how you are.' In favour of the first reading, see Metzger, *Textual Commentary*, 626. For the second, see Peter M. Head, 'Tychicus and

important manuscripts[24] for three reasons. First, the flow of information from Rome to the Lycus Valley is named in both vv. 7 and 9, so that the standard view ('that you may know how we are') makes this very repetitive. Second, the persona of Paul is very prominent rhetorically in this section, as set out earlier. Third, this indicates that the concern for the Lycus Valley communities is reciprocal, with information flowing both ways, and this is in keeping with the purpose of the Letter and the sending on of a letter from Laodicea. My contention is that Paul, Timothy and their associates do not have very recent information about the Lycus Valley (see the Introduction), and are keen to learn what is going on. All of this is in keeping with the emphasis on concord, which can never be simply a 'one-way' relationship.

Onesimus is to accompany Tychicus, and is described – like Tychicus – as faithful and beloved. In addition, he is also originally 'one of them'. Onesimus' fate as a runaway slave had not yet been sealed when the Letter to Philemon was written, but here, Onesimus is an integral part of the Pauline mission, entrusted with a vital task. From this we can deduce that Philemon is an earlier letter than Colossians.[25] Onesimus was a slave who originated from the Lycus Valley area, and so this journey to Colossae would be a return to his place of origin. The standard commendation given to Onesimus does not give any indication that the Lycus Valley churches were informed about the earlier tensions between Onesimus and Philemon.

The issue of slavery – the lived experience of those who do not have jurisdiction over their own bodies and the Stoic downplaying of servitude as one of the 'indifferents' – is a vexed one. Freedom from coercion and abuse, and freedom to make decisions about oneself and one's future are foundational to human flourishing, yet are sadly still aspirational for many in the world today.[26] What is true for humans is true for all species – the right of all creatures to live and flourish freely needs to be recognized. Those who are raising the need for recognizing nature as a legal entity with rights[27] have grasped the need to enshrine this into our

---

the Colossian Christians: A Reconsideration of the Text of Colossians 4:8', in *Texts and Traditions: Essays in Honour of J. Keith Elliott*, ed. Peter Doble and Jeffrey Kloha, NTTSD 47 (Leiden/Boston: Brill, 2014), 303–15. The third, supported by the Tyndale House *Greek New Testament*, takes *gnō* as the first-person subjunctive. The various points made in Head's article also support this third reading, as the form is identical in the ancient manuscripts, with only later additions of accents making a difference.

24. Head, 'Tychicus and the Colossian Christians', 304.

25. I have argued elsewhere that we have made a mistake in assuming that overlapping information in both the Letter to Philemon and the Letter to the Colossians means that Philemon, Apphia and the house church were located in Colossae; it is much more likely that they were in or near Rome. Balabanski, 'Where Is Philemon?' 131–50.

26. See for example http://stopthetraffik.com.au/

27. Guillaume Chapron, Yaffa Epstein and José Vicente López-Bao, 'A Rights Revolution for Nature', *Science*, 29 March 2019: Vol. 363, Issue 6434, 1392–3. Available online: https://science.sciencemag.org/content/363/6434/1392?rss=1 (accessed 21 May 2019).

legal systems. Rights cannot simply be economic or utilitarian. There is an urgent need for humanity to codify in law the intrinsic value of all ecosystems.

The Pauline usage of 'slave of Christ' must not be understood as reinscribing slavery. The meaning of this designation can only be understood as a paradox (cf. 1 Cor. 7.22), meaning that a slave of Christ is indeed free from the power of sin (Rom. 6.16), and so freely willing to serve others (1 Cor. 9.19). It is a privilege to serve Christ, but that privilege must never become a means of manipulating others into servitude.

IV. Greetings from Paul's fellow workers 4.10-14

Colossians 4.10 indicates that this is not the first communication that the Lycus Valley communities have received from Paul and his associates – they have already 'received instructions' about a possible visit of Mark, Barnabas's cousin. This is an interesting fragment of information, because Colossians reads as an initial introductory letter rather than a subsequent communication. As we shall consider later with regard to v. 17, Archippus may have been entrusted with an earlier verbal communication. Philemon 24 names a certain Mark as one of Paul's fellow workers, and if this is the same Mark, it seems that he is currently visiting the Pauline missionary team, as he sends greetings. However, he is not under their 'instruction', as Paul and Timothy cannot say whether or not he will visit.[28] That gives an interesting glimpse into relationships between different missionary groups in the early church.

The positive mention of those 'of the circumcision' (Aristarchus, Mark and Jesus Justus) in 4.10-11 suggests that Paul's inclusive theology (Gal. 3.28) was still at work, but that the number of Judaic believers associated with the Pauline mission was no longer large.[29]

The important figure of Epaphras has already been discussed in Chapter 2. The testimonial given to him here in 4.12-13 is that he is 'striving in prayer' for the Lycus Valley believers. It is possible that this prayer is the 'hard work' (*ponos*) described in v. 13, but the expression refers to hard, exhausting work producing great stress (especially battle), and is not normally a way of describing prayer. Epaphras, who brought them the Gospel, now continues to be engaged very actively for the well-being of those in Colossae, Laodicea and Hierapolis.

This suggests that the Pauline mission was not just offering spiritual leadership, but also working for the practical well-being of Pauline communities. As suggested in the introduction, the earthquakes of the period may have necessitated some disaster relief, and as Epaphras was not free to travel (Phlm. 23), Archippus may have been sent to offer support – perhaps even material support that Epaphras

---

28. See the discussion of possible implications in Dunn, *The Epistles to the Colossians and to Philemon*, 276–8.

29. This would be in keeping with the trend indicated in Rom. 9–11.

had worked to accumulate. Luke and Demas are named as being with Paul both in Philemon 24 and in Col. 4.14, but as they are not directly associated with the Lycus Valley, their greetings form a brief conclusion to the list of those with Paul.

The diverse 'human ecology' set out here (including those of differing religious backgrounds, origins and social standing) reminds us that with trusted colleagues, the impact of one's work for change can increase exponentially. A clear vision, and concord between colleagues, is vital for widespread change. Today, clear vision and concord can help humanity move towards the necessary changes in lifestyle needed for the Earth community to survive and flourish.

V. Greetings to those in Laodicea and to Nympha and the congregation in her house 4.15

These instructions to greet specific groups of people on behalf of Paul involves the Colossian recipients in a necessary process of contacting neighbouring communities of faith. It could have been left to Tychicus and Onesimus to carry the greetings of Paul and his associates forward, but as it is, all of the recipients are entrusted with this charge. The promotion of concord between these communities seems to be a priority, suggesting that the letter writers suspect there has been a lack of contact or a lessening of concord between the communities.

Distinguishing those in Laodicea, on the one hand, and Nympha and the believing community in her household on the other, implies that Nympha's household is not in Laodicea. By way of comparison, the Letter to the Romans is addressed to 'all God's beloved in Rome' (Rom. 1.7); this appears to be addressed to an individual community, but it is probable that there were multiple communities – at least eight – across the metropolis.[30] If Nympha's household had been in Laodicea, we might have expected the general greeting to have sufficed. I take this to imply that Nympha and her household lived in the broad, fertile Lycus Valley, but not in one of the cities.

We have noted some clues about Nympha in the introduction. Nympha is the head of a household, and a gathering of believers meets there. This gathering of believers is presumably not coterminous with the household – others from the area may join them, and not all the household is necessarily part of the gathering. The ancient manuscripts are divided over the gender of Nympha (Nympha = female, Nymphas = male). Given the tendency in the scribal tradition to interpret female names as male, it is remarkable that some early and diverse witnesses retain the key phrase 'the church in *her* house', confirming the reading of Nympha as a woman.[31] The greeting is addressed both to Nympha herself and to the gathering in her household, which suggests that she is a woman of some importance in the region, and someone known personally to Epaphras. The wealth of the region derived

---

30. Peter Lampe, *From Paul to Valentinus: Christians at Rome in the First Two Centuries* (Minneapolis, MN: Fortress Press, 2003), 359.

31. Metzger, *Textual Commentary*, 627. Compare Junia/Junias in Rom. 16.7.

from textiles and allied trades, and there was a long history of respect for women working with wool.[32] No other leader from Colossae, Laodicea or Hierapolis is singled out in this way by name. Like many women, her achievements are not recorded in history; her story, as imagined at the close of each chapter of this book, is a piece of historical fiction, or an imaginative biography.

VI. Instructions: After the letter has been read in Colossae, have it read in Laodicea 4.16a; read the letter from Laodicea 4.16b; admonishment to Archippus 4.17

These verses position Colossians as a 'circular' or 'encyclical' letter. Rather than being addressed to one community and mirroring the specific issues facing that community, the Letter to the Colossians is to be circulated to various contexts.[33] As a circular letter, one aim of Colossians would be to confirm the reliability and the personal concern of the Pauline leadership for their community. This would include confirming Epaphras' leadership, and reconnecting Pauline communities with each other. Tychicus and Onesimus were instructed to take the same letter to both places and to customize it verbally. The Colossians were first on the itinerary, and the Laodiceans second. This means that not all the problems envisaged in the Letter need necessarily apply to one community.

Notably, the Colossians are charged with seeing to it that the circular reading actually happens: 'See to it that it is read ...' (Col. 4.16). This involves the Colossians in carrying through this request. This seems to be both respectful of the Colossian community, and also a good strategy to involve them in the implementation of the networking.

The Colossians are then instructed to read the letter *from* the Laodiceans, not *to* the Laodiceans.[34] Verse 16 indicates that the believers at Laodicea had sent a letter to the Pauline leadership that predates the writing of Colossians. The Pauline leadership then responded with this Letter to believers at Colossae, in the first

32. Cadwallader, *Fragments of Colossae*, 122–6.

33. Not all the undisputed letters of Paul are strictly occasional. 1 Thessalonians is addressed to an individual community; however, Galatians and the Corinthian correspondence as a whole are not in this category, as 2 Cor. 1.1 is addressed not only to Corinth but to 'all the saints in Achaia', and Galatians is addressed to the churches of Galatia (Gal 1.2).

34. This is obscured in some translations, which supply extra words to indicate that it was Paul's letter to the Laodiceans. See, for example, the NAS translation: 'And when this letter is read among you, have it also read in the church of the Laodiceans; and you, for your part read my letter that is coming from Laodicea.'

There is a ninth-century miniscule that reads *en* instead of *ek*, but this is not a textual issue. The NAS translators appear to be unable to conceive of a community being instructed to read a letter from another believing community rather than from Paul himself. There are of course various scholars who hold that Ephesians is that very letter, so they also need to read this verse accordingly.

instance, and then also to Laodicea, to be carried and customized by Tychicus and Onesimus. After the Colossian believers had heard the reading of the Letter addressed to them, then the earlier letter from Laodicea was to be read out at Colossae.

It is intriguing to ponder the fact that v. 16 is referring to a letter from a Pauline community that is of significance to another Pauline community, arriving not directly from one community to another but forwarded via the Pauline network of communication. This otherwise unknown letter from the Laodiceans to Paul and his associates started as an occasional letter that has subsequently been circulated, and has been sent on to enhance the Pauline network and its leadership and authority structure.[35]

Was this a letter from believers at Laodicea setting out concerns about the believers at Colossae? Perhaps the issues raised in Colossians 2 may have been prompted by this letter from Laodicea. However, as stated in the introduction, Colossians does not read as though it is a reply to specific concerns. Moreover, if the letter from Laodicea were one setting out complaints against the Colossians, it would hardly be something they would have wanted the Colossians to read. I will propose later that the letter from Laodicea is one that describes their struggles due to the earthquakes. Whether or not that is the case, the Colossian believers are to hear the letter from Paul and Timothy before they hear the earlier letter from Laodicea; the encouraging communication from Paul and Timothy would have ameliorated tensions. Tychicus and Onesimus would be the witnesses of their response, and this would put a certain obligation on the believers to respond generously. If this were a strategy to encourage the Colossians to foster greater concord with Laodicea, it would be a similar strategy to the one Paul took with Philemon concerning Onesimus.

All of this paints a picture of a network that does not function as a centralized hierarchy, but seeks to enhance concord between the different sectors and groups.

By noting the interconnectedness of the Pauline communities, we are reminded of the value of maintaining open channels of dialogue with others and cultivating good relations with all. When these break down, it is easy for attitudes towards others to deteriorate and for groups to descend into sectarianism. If the Logos of Christ is universal, we are universal citizens, and our good will extends beyond our own territory and indeed beyond our own species.

Archippus receives a particular and specific message as the Letter concludes: he is to complete a service which he took on. In the context of so many greetings and words of positive affirmation, it is striking that there is no greeting to Archippus

---

35. The distinction between public and private letters is less clear than we might suppose. Carlos Noreña observes 'there is a significant overlap between what we would call 'official' and 'personal', 'public' and 'private' in Pliny's correspondence with Trajan.' Carlos F. Noreña, 'The Social Economy of Pliny's Correspondence with Trajan', *AJP* 128 (2007): 239–77, 245. This is applied to Pauline Letters by Lyn Kidson, '1 Timothy: An Administrative Letter', *Early Christianity* 1/5 (2014), 97–116, 104.

prior to this message. The message appears to be an admonition, as it reminds Archippus of a specific task that he chose to take on, and that this service was undertaken for the Lord, not simply for any human being. The verb *blepe* can function as a warning or 'watchword', giving a tone of solemnity to this reminder.[36]

Archippus had been described in Phlm 2 as a 'fellow-soldier', named together with Philemon, Apphia and the church in Philemon's house. As argued elsewhere, this house was in or near Rome; Archippus has since been deployed to the Lycus Valley, and an interval of one to two years has elapsed.[37] Archippus has not completed the service he undertook, or the Pauline missionary team has not heard that he has done so. In enlisting the communities of Colossae, Laodicea and Nympha's household to convey this message to Archippus, it implies that the Rome-based team think that Archippus is in contact with them. This strengthens the impression that there has not been recent direct news from Colossae.

The nature of the service (*diakonia*) that Archippus is to complete is not specified. There are some instances in Pauline writings where *diakonia* is associated with money (Rom. 15.31; 2 Cor. 8.4; 9.1, 12-13, and possibly 11.8).[38] It may be that the trusted fellow-soldier was to have distributed some funds to the saints in greatest need.[39]

36. Compare Timothy Geddert, *Watchwords: Mark 13 in Markan Eschatology*, JSNTSup 26 (Sheffield: JSOT Press, 1989).

37. Balabanski 'Where Is Philemon?' 145-6.

38. While the collection for the poor in Jerusalem undoubtedly occupied Paul in the fifties prior to visiting Jerusalem (Rom. 15.25-29), it is clear that Paul advocated Christian benefaction more generally (e.g. Gal. 6.10). This was connected with Paul's theology of the body of Christ and with establishing interpersonal networks, among other motivations. See Bruce W. Longenecker, *Remember the Poor: Paul, Poverty and the Greco-Roman World* (Grand Rapids, MI: Eerdmans, 2010), 281-94.

39. By the fourth century, Archippus was remembered as having become bishop of Laodicea. See 'Apostolic Teaching and Constitutions' 7.76, in *Ante-Nicene Fathers. Volume 7: Lactantius, Venantius, Asterius, Victorinus, Dionysius, Apostolic Teaching and Constitutions, 2 Clement, Early Liturgies*, ed. A. Cleveland Coxe (New York: Christian Literature Publishing Co., 1886). So perhaps he did complete the task. My own hypothesis is set out in Nympha's notes later: Archippus brought some funds for relief of the communities in the Lycus Valley, but became embroiled in a dispute about the fair distribution of them. Laodicea was harder hit by the earthquakes, but was also a wealthier community, and the Colossians may have thought it diminished their honour not to receive a fair share. By having the Letter (Colossians) addressed to them, and by being visited first, the Colossians have been honoured by Paul, Timothy and Epaphras over the Laodiceans. However, the letter from the Laodiceans may have described the needs of their community. By instructing the Colossians to read this letter from Laodicea, it may have given the Colossian believers the opportunity to be compassionate (Col. 3.12-13).

VII. Final greeting and blessing 4.18

The last sentence of the original Letter, or autograph, would have been written in large letters, as this practice of adding Paul's imprimatur had been developing since the Letter to the Galatians (Gal. 6.11). There, however, it was not his name, but his closing remarks that were written by him personally.[40] The longest autograph is in Phlm. 19-25, urging Philemon to benefit Paul by benefitting Onesimus.[41] Here in Col. 4.18, it is brief and relatively impersonal; one might even say terse. Perhaps the apparent failure of Archippus to complete his task was a substantial disappointment to Paul.

The reference to imprisonment is literally 'chains' (*desmoi*), and in the Pauline writings, this term is used twice in Philemon (10, 13), and four times in Philippians (1.7, 13, 14, 17). It is also used in 2 Tim. 2.9, where its significance is developing as a symbol of the freedom of the Gospel. While the epistolary persona of Paul rejoices in his sufferings (Col. 1.24),[42] the reality of imprisonment must have required substantial courage and perseverance in the face of hardship.

Nevertheless, the final phrase returns to grace. This central term, which opened the Letter (Col. 1.2 and 1.6), points to the Gospel as growing and bearing fruit, so the final word is one of hope.

For all who face the reality of the ecological destruction underway in our world today, and for all those who try to tackle the causes, feelings of discouragement and hopelessness can seem inevitable. The Letter to the Colossians affirms that there is hope, because the Gospel is proclaimed to every creature under heaven (Col. 1.23), not just to a few, nor to one species only. Just as the Colossian believers came to embrace hope rather than fatalism, so we, who believe in a God who created all things and sustains all things in Christ, can trust that God is at work. Christ is in us, and we are in Christ; this is the hope of glory (1.27) – a glory to be shared with all things (Rom. 8.21).

Nympha's notes

It is wonderful to be greeted by name in Paul and Timothy's letter. We have Epaphras to thank for that, who is our champion, striving in prayer for us, and raising funds for our relief. To have people we can trust makes all the difference!

---

40. Compare 1 Cor. 16.21-23, which includes Paul's name and closing remarks.

41. In 2 Thess. 3.17, Paul's final greeting in his own hand is named as a mark of authenticity in every letter he writes, yet it is not found in any of the other disputed letters.

42. According to Patricia Rosenmeyer, 'The letter writer … is free to present himself in whatever light he wishes (within the limits of probability or believability), and he is most likely to offer a picture which will have a specific targeted effect, whether negative or positive on his reader. … Letter writing is inherently "fictional" in that the writer can create himself anew every time he writes.' Patricia A. Rosenmeyer, *Ancient Epistolary Fictions: The Letter in Greek Literature* (Cambridge: Cambridge University Press, 2001), 10–11.

It was nearly three years ago that Epaphras set out for Rome. He heard the news that Paul was in prison and felt the strong need to join him and care for him. The first of the earthquakes shook us not many weeks after his departure. I am glad that Epaphras was spared the distress of those days and months. I heard from Archippus when he arrived almost a year later that Epaphras had arrived in Rome safely, but with his bold proclamation of the Logos of the Gospel in the market places, he was soon under arrest himself. When the news of the earthquakes and aftershocks had reached Rome, it seems that Paul, Timothy and their fellow workers in the Gospel took counsel with Epaphras, and they decided to send Archippus to encourage the believers in the Lycus Valley and bring some funds for the relief of the poor. Those at Laodicea were the worst affected by the earthquakes, but they were also the ones with the means to care for the homeless. The communities of Christ at Laodicea and Colossae argued about the distribution of the funds, and as an outsider, Archippus found it difficult to mediate between them. Thanks be to Christ, our low buildings could be repaired from the limestone on the property. But poor Archippus' task has dragged on and on. In the meantime, those in Laodicea have sent a letter to Paul describing their sufferings, and asking him to intervene with the believers in Colossae.

It is an encouragement that Tychicus and Onesimus have arrived, bringing news of all that is happening with our beloved brothers in Rome. I think that Tychicus will return to Rome in the next few weeks, taking Archippus with him. Onesimus may stay – he grew up as one of us, and he knows our ways.

As a slave owner, I am glad for the words in the letter reminding my slaves of their duty. The example of Onesimus' manumission as such a young man had disquieted our household peace and made the young house servants restless. The letter reminds us that Tychicus and Epaphras himself are 'slaves in the Lord'. Paul shows us with his bonds that each of us in our suffering participates in Christ's suffering for one another. We are all part of the household of God, constantly in our heavenly Master's presence, serving each other in our daily work.

We are preparing a gift for each brother in Rome, a special cloak from our glossy black wool. The whole household is involved in making them – shearing, carding, spinning, weaving and sewing, so that the feel and fragrance of our valley can encourage them. We are indeed with them in Spirit, as they are with us in Christ Jesus. Thanksgiving shapes our life together – thanksgiving for our freedom, for the wide valley and fertile fields, for our sheep and their renowned black wool, for the special waters of the Lycus, and for the mystery of Christ revealed to us and in whom we now live. All is connected in Christ.

CONCLUSION

We live at a time in history when there are deep divisions, even contradictions, as to what the values of our society should be, and what the Christian faith should stand for. On the one hand, the United Nations' IPBES Global Assessment Report on Biodiversity and Ecosystem Services has warned that over one million species face the threat of extinction because of human actions.[1] At the very same time, Western countries are electing or returning governments whose policies are winding back the protection of the environment and speeding the burning of fossil fuels. Human self-interest is the priority, and Christian eschatology – the promise of a new heaven and a new earth – has been harnessed in the interests of greed. The Christian faith is also invoked to restore 'family values', with the Household Codes a key to that agenda. More generally, faith is held to be a private, individualized option.[2]

The vision of the Letter to the Colossian stands in contrast to any individualized version of the Christian faith. The Letter proclaims Christ both as the One who redeems and forgives the sins of each person (Col. 1.13-14) and as the One through whom the whole universe was created and for whom it exists (Col. 1.16). The fate of the million and more species at risk of extinction matters to Christ, and it must therefore be a matter of urgent concern for every one of Christ's human community. This is the context in which Christians must decide what it is that their faith in Christ is demanding of them. Solidarity with Christ is solidarity with the Earth community, and that requires of us a new level of altruism for ecosystems that we have not yet recognized as being 'part of us'.

This Eco-Stoic reading of the Letter to the Colossians offers something that has long been needed – an extended exegetical exploration of the Letter that brings contemporary ecological questions into dialogue with the distinctive Christology

---

1. United Nations' IPBES Global Assessment Report on Biodiversity and Ecosystem Services. Available online: https://www.un.org/sustainabledevelopment/blog/2019/05/nature-decline-unprecedented-report/ (accessed 22 May 2019).

2. 'I don't mix my religion with politics or my faith with politics…' Australian Prime Minister Scott Morrison, quoted by Eryk Bagshaw in, '"I support the law of the country": Debate over sexuality and religion creeps into election campaign', *The Sydney Morning Herald*, 13 May 2019. Available online: https://www.smh.com.au/federal-election-2019/i-support-the-law-of-the-country-debate-over-sexuality-and-religion-creeps-into-elect ion-campaign-20190513-p51mxm.html (accessed 21 February 2019).

and cosmology of the Letter. The conceptual framework of Stoic thought makes it possible to see how Christ is understood to transcend and have primacy over all things and yet to be embodied and present, permeating all things.

We meet Christ as the One *in*, *through* and *for* whom all things were created (Col. 1.16) and who currently, continually and bodily manifests the whole fullness of God (Col. 2.9). As such, Christ is the divine presence in Earth who animates and directs all things towards life and wholeness, and sustains all things (Col. 1.17). At the same time, Christ is also the One whose particular bodily human life, and his actual death on the cross, reconciles all things to God (Col. 1.20, 22). In Stoic thought there is no necessary disjuncture between the cosmic and the particular; both are embodied, and the same Logos animates both. The logic of the Gospel is the same: there is no disjuncture between the Christ of the universe and the Christ of Earth – the human person – who actually suffered and shed his blood on the cross. The Colossian hymn depicts this in two movements: the universal Christ as the firstborn of all creation (Col. 1.15) and the particular Christ as the firstborn from the dead (Col. 1.18). The Logos permeating both the universal and the particular is one and the same, creating all things, reconciling all things and so manifesting visibly the invisible God (Col. 1.15). The two movements – creation and reconciliation – are inclusive of and efficacious for all things, not just for humanity.

The Letter does not depict this as a surprise to the recipients, but presents it as the very same Gospel that they have already received through the teaching of Epaphras (Col. 1.5-7). Nevertheless, the Letter does emphasize aspects of the teaching. First, it assures the believers that they can continue to have confidence in the effectiveness of the reconciliation (Col. 1.21-23). Second, it confirms that this is the very same Gospel that Paul proclaims (Col. 1.23, 4.3-4). And third, it reminds them that the Gospel proclaims peace to all things (Col. 1.20), all creation under heaven (Col. 1.23). This is an expansive vision, and the recipients are assured that they are already well established in it (Col. 2.6–7).

The Letter develops the implications of the teaching to reflect on the connectedness of Christ's body and our bodies. In the economy of God, Christ's affliction, borne in his body of flesh, is connected with Paul's bodily sufferings on behalf of the church, Christ's body (Col. 1.24). Embodiment becomes a connecting point, not only to reveal God's glory but also to reflect on the reality, even necessity, of suffering.

The body of Christ has a shifting meaning in this Letter. It is the bodily manifestation of the divine presence (Col. 2.9), and so is seen in Earth and the impulse towards life. The body of Christ is also the community of Christ, the gathering of those who seek to live in concord with God, with each other and with Earth (Col. 1.18, 24; 3.15). The body of Christ is also the Eucharistic body, though this may have become a point of tension (Col. 2.16-17). The real body is not dependent on the particular days (Col. 2.16) or on particular practices, but on the connection with the head and the growth that comes from God (Col. 2.18-19).

Clothing the body does not require uniformity, as 'Christ is all things and is in all things' (Col. 3.11). Instead, Christ is manifest in the quality of the relationships and the ethical and loving behaviour of each person (Col. 3.12-14). This also holds true for the body of the household, where the general instructions are customized to address particular pressure points.

The Letter concludes with extended greetings. They are shaped in a way that seeks to enhance the concord between and within the communities in the Lycus Valley and secure the connection between those communities and the letter writers.

This Eco-Stoic reading examines the Letter in dialogue with some key concepts:

- Happiness, Heaven and Hope (Ch. 2)
- Living consistently and with integrity; the rhetoric of plerophory (Ch. 3)
- Embodiment and Cosmos (Ch. 4)
- Cognition, Cosmic Sympathy and *Oikeiōsis* (restoring kinship) (Ch. 5)
- Suffering as 'indifferent'; Mystery (Ch. 6)
- The pitfalls of philosophy and religious practices (Ch. 7)
- Vices and Virtues; Baptismal life (Ch. 8)
- Concord (*homonoia*) – the value of harmony (Ch. 9)

Many of the concepts in the Letter have resonances with Stoic ideas. At times, however, the Pauline Gospel diverges substantially from the Stoic framework, such as we see in relation to the theme of hope (Ch. 2). Hope for a different and better future was a distraction for the Stoics, whereas for Paul and his associates, it was a quintessential expression of God's gracious purposes for all creation. By introducing philosophical reading contexts prior to the exegetical sections in each chapter, we can hear more clearly the ideas that the Gospel could build upon, or at times refute.

Each chapter concludes with Nympha's notes, a piece of historical imagination intended to bring us closer to the first reading of the Letter by one of the Earth community. This conclusion will also give Nympha the last word. However, prior to her concluding reflection, I will set out two scholarly trajectories of this work, which have significance for those engaged with theology and ecology: first, Panentheism, and second, Deep Incarnation.

1. Panentheism

Panentheism is the concept that 'the Being of God includes and penetrates the whole universe, so that every part exists in God, but God's Being is more than, and not exhausted by, the universe'.[3] It is a conceptual framework that is held – in various forms – by many of the great theologians of the twentieth and twenty-first centuries, as well as by great thinkers of the past (particularly Hegel and Schelling). The list includes Martin Heidegger, Paul Tillich, Hans-Georg Gadamer, William Temple, John Robinson, John Macquarrie, Karl Rahner, Hans Küng, Jürgen Moltmann, James Cone, Gustavo Gutierrez, Juan Luis Segundo, Leonardo Boff,

---

3. F. L. Cross and E. A. Livingstone, ed., *The Oxford Dictionary of the Christian Church*, 2nd edn (Oxford: Oxford University Press, 1983), 1027 (modified).

Rosemary Ruether and Sally McFague, as well as some who work on the interface of science and theology: Arthur Peacocke, Ian Barbour, Paul Davies, Philip Clayton and Steve Knapp.[4] With such an eminent array of theologians and scientists who conceptualize God's transcendence and immanence in this way, it is surprising that biblical scholarship has not begun to explore how this framework may contribute to the reading of biblical texts. Theologians draw on biblical passages such as Acts 17.28 (For 'In him we live and move and have our being') and Ps. 139. 5-10 to show that panentheism has biblical warrant, but there has been no explicit endeavour among biblical scholars to see how the reading of biblical texts may be refreshed or reshaped if one reads biblical texts with an ontology of divine permeation.

One may say that this is beyond the scope of biblical studies, as it is imposing a philosophical or ontological framework that is foreign to the original readers or auditors. There are several reasons why this is no longer a convincing position. First, it implies that biblical scholars who work within a framework of classical philosophical theism – the traditional Aristotelian ontology of Western theology, which holds that God is fully distinct from the world, though present to it – have no philosophical or ontological framework. In an era of post-colonial studies, we can no longer assume that because a framework seems self-evident, there are no philosophical and cultural roots to it. Second, people might claim that the reading lens of classical philosophical theism is the appropriate one because in using

---

4. The list is derived from John W. Cooper *Panentheism. The Other God of the Philosophers. From Plato to the Present* (Nottingham: Apollos, Intervarsity Press, 2007). Cooper raises the question as to whether the Stoics might be the original proto-Christian panentheists, but considers that they are best categorized as 'naturalistic pantheists', 38–9. This is a position with which I disagree. The key issue for Cooper seems to be whether there is a metaphysical distinction between the world and God. The Stoic account of reality brings physics and metaphysics together in a highly nuanced way. Their methodology and divisions of topics reflect that they were conscious of the distinction between physics and metaphysics, but also that they gave an account of reality by taking the present world-order as the starting point. Cooper himself recognizes that there are various distinctions between types of panentheism (explicit and implicit panentheism; personal and non-personal panentheism; part-whole and relational panentheism; voluntary and/or natural panentheism; and classical (divine determinist) or modern (cooperative) panentheism). Within this wide range of variations, it is not convincing to claim that the metaphysical distinction of classical philosophical theism is requisite in panentheism. The Stoic emphasis on the universe as a living, rational body would only exclude Stoics from the category of panentheists if the universe and God were identical. However, this is not the case. The fact that the Highest God, 'amid the dissolution of the world, when the gods are confounded together and nature rests for a space from her work, can retire into himself and give himself over to his own thoughts'. (Seneca *Letters* 9.16, LCL 75: 50–3) means that God and the world are not identical and that God's being is not exhausted by the universe. Therefore the primary reality must be God (known to the Stoics as Zeus or Jupiter), not the universe. In this way, the Stoics fit better into the category of panentheists than pantheists.

it we share the framework of the original audience. However, that is also a risky assumption. Ancient audiences did not necessarily understand God's presence as primarily transcendent; in fact, it is likely that they were more ready to perceive God's (or the gods') presence in the natural world. Particularly among readers/ auditors who were recently pagan, God's immanence in the tangible material world would not have been surprising or controversial. It is part of the biblical scholar's task to consider what sort of ontological framework the original audience would have had. And third, it presupposes that the ancient framework for all audiences was something akin to the Platonic or Neo-Platonic ones that have shaped the interpretative tradition of which we are a part. A claim that this commentary makes is that Platonism (and its descendants) was not the only – or most influential – philosophical school in the Hellenistic and Roman eras. Stoic thinking was widespread as education and entertainment, not just sporadically and among certain elite thinkers, but among all classes, slaves as well as free, men and women, Jews and Christians as well as pagans. It was the philosophical Koine of the day.

This commentary brings Stoic thought to the reading of Colossians. This helps us to look again at what the original recipients of Colossians, steeped in the thought world of their day, may have known and assumed. The Gospel of Jesus Christ was not preached in a theological, philosophical vacuum to the people at Colossae, but addressed, affirmed and critiqued concepts that were known to those people.

Panentheism is encapsulated in an axiom, expressed in the *Shepherd of Hermas*, and quoted by Irenaeus in the second century: 'First of all, believe that there is one God, who has established all things, and completed them, and having caused that from what had no being, all things should come into existence: *He who contains all things and is himself contained by no one*.' [italics mine].[5]

By reading Colossians with a Stoic ontological framework in mind, we find evidence of a type of panentheism which left an important legacy in some canonical and patristic writings. If this is so, then contemporary panentheistic ideas are not just hermeneutical thought experiments, but are the ontological framework in which we need to progress our dialogue between the Bible and ecology.

2. *Deep incarnation*

The Letter to the Colossians shows how a high Christology – the highest of all in the New Testament writings[6] – can also be a Christology that emphasizes embodiment

---

5. Irenaeus, *Against Heresies* 4.20.2. Available online: http://www.newadvent.org/ fathers/0103420.htm (accessed 20 May 2019). Irenaeus cites *Shepherd of Hermas* Mandate 1[26]:1 'First of all, believe that God is one, who created and completed all things, and made everything that exists out of that which did not, who contains all things but is himself, alone, uncontained.' LCL 25: 236–7.

6. Only in Colossians are all things created not only *in* and *through* Christ, but *for* Christ (Col. 1.16). Sterling, 'Prepositional Metaphysics', 232.

and values 'all things'. Colossians is a foundational source for a theology that recognizes that the universe is permeated and sustained by the presence of Christ. This theology is known as 'deep incarnation', a concept coined by Niels Henrik Gregersen in 2001:[7]

> 'Deep Incarnation' is the view that God's own Logos (Wisdom and Word) was made flesh in Jesus the Christ in such a comprehensive manner that God, by assuming the particular life story of Jesus the Jew from Nazareth, also conjoined the material conditions of creaturely existence ('all flesh'), shared and ennobled the fate of all biological life forms ('grass' and 'lilies'), and experienced the pain of sensitive creatures ('sparrows' and 'foxes') from within. Deep incarnation thus presupposes a radical embodiment that reaches into the roots (radices) of material and biological existence as well as into the darker sides of creation: the *tenebrae creationis*.[8]

Colossians is a key biblical source for 'radical embodiment' in material and biological existence, and all the more so when the Stoic background is taken into account. Some fine theological minds have been engaging with deep incarnation, including Denis Edwards,[9] Ernst Conradie,[10] Elizabeth Johnson,[11]

---

7. Niels Henrik Gregersen, 'The Cross of Christ in an Evolutionary World', *Dialog: A Journal of Theology* 40/3 (2001): 192–207.

8. Niels Henrik Gregersen, 'The Extended Body of Christ: Three Dimensions of Deep Incarnation', in *Incarnation: On the Scope and depth of Christology*, ed. Niels Henrik Gregersen (Minneapolis, MN: Fortress Press, 2015), 225–6.

9. Denis Edwards, *Ecology at the Heart of Faith* (Maryknoll, NY: Orbis Books, 2006), 52–64; '"Every Sparrow that Falls to the Ground": The Cost of Evolution and the Christ-Event', *Ecotheology* 11/1 (2007):103–23; *Partaking of God: Trinity, Evolution and Ecology* (Collegeville, MN: Liturgical Press, 2014), 54–67; 'Incarnation and the Natural World: Explorations in the Tradition of Athanasius', in *Incarnation: On the Scope and Depth of Christology*, ed. N. H. Gregersen (Minneapolis, MN: Fortress Press, 2015), 157–76; 'Sublime Communion: The Theology of the Natural World in Laudato Si', *Theological Studies* 77 (2016): 377–91; 'Key Issues in Ecological Theology: Incarnation, Evolution, Communion', in *Theology and Ecology Across the Disciplines: On Care for Our Common Home*, ed. Celia Deane-Drummond and Rebecca Artinian-Kaiser (London: Bloomsbury, 2018), 65–78.

10. Ernst M. Conradie, ed., *Creation and Salvation, Volume 1, A Mosaic of Selected Classic Christian Theologies* (Zurich: LIT, 2012), and *Creation and Salvation, Volume 2, A Companion on Recent Theological Movements* (Zurich: LIT, 2012).

11. Elizabeth A. Johnson, 'An Earthy Christology', *America: The National Catholic Review* 200/12 (2009): 27–30; 'Deep Christology', in *From Logos to Christos: Essays in Christology in Honour of Joanne McWilliam*, ed. Ellen M. Leonard and Kate Merriman (Waterloo, ON: Winifred Laurier University Press, 2009), 163–80; *Ask the Beasts: Darwin and the God of Love* (New York: Bloomsbury, 2014); 'Jesus and the Cosmos: Soundings in Deep Ecology', in *Incarnation: On the Scope and Depth of Christology*, ed. N. H. Gregersen

Celia Deane-Drummond,[12] Christopher Southgate[13] and Richard Bauckham.[14] They are reflecting on the relationship between the presence of Christ and the necessary, indeed inbuilt, suffering and hardship of the world. As Gregersen states: 'The ruthless hardship of natural selection is part of God's creativity, but does not reveal the nature of God.'[15] Colossians 1.24 teases this out further: it is part of the nature of God to be present with those who suffer, and in the economy of God, we can bear one another's suffering for Christ's sake.

Most Westerners, whether Christians or not, are functionally Epicurean. Epicureans saw pleasure and pain as primary motivators and viewed them as the standard for all choice and avoidance respectively: all creatures maximize pleasure and avoid pain. The Gospel as set out in the Letter to the Colossians is much closer to Stoic thought on the issue of suffering than to Epicurean thought; neither pleasure nor suffering is ultimately good or evil. Pleasure is preferred, but not ultimately good, and pain is not preferred, but not ultimately evil. The Cross of Christ reveals God as the divine Presence who draws close to us, in our weakness, vulnerability and suffering, surrounds us with that Presence, and assures us that even in the depth, we are not alone. For Stoics, the ultimate Good is virtue. For those in Christ, the ultimate Good is Christ, in whom all virtue is found, and through whom all virtue is possible. It is nothing less than this Presence of Christ, who was crucified, that accompanies us and all creatures in our suffering and even death.

(Minneapolis, MN: Fortress Press, 2015),133–56; *Creation and the Cross: The Mercy of God for a Planet in Peril* (Maryknoll, NY: Orbis Books, 2018).

12. Celia Deane-Drummond, *Christ and Evolution: Wonder and Wisdom* (Minneapolis, MN: Fortress, 2009). See her 'Deep Incarnation and Eco-justice as Theodrama', in *Ecological Awareness: Exploring Religion, Ethics and Aesthetics*, ed. Sigurd Bergmann and Heather Eaton (Berlin: LIT, 2011), 193–206; 'Who on Earth Is Jesus Christ? Plumbing the Depths of Deep Incarnation', in *Christian Faith and the Earth: Current Paths and Emerging Horizons in Ecotheology*, ed. E. M. Conradie, Sigurd Bergmann, Celia Deane-Drummond and Denis Edwards (London: Bloomsbury/T & T Clark, 2014), 31–50; 'The Wisdom of Fools? A Theo-Dramatic Interpretation of Deep Incarnation', in *Incarnation: On the Scope and Depth of Christology*, ed. N. H. Gregersen (Minneapolis, MN: Fortress Press, 2015), 177–202; *A Primer in Ecotheology: Theology for a Fragile Earth* (Eugene, OR: Cascade Books, 2017).

13. Christopher Southgate, *The Groaning of Creation: God, Evolution and the Problem of Evil* (Louisville, KY: Westminster/John Knox Press, 2008); 'Does God's Care Make Any Difference? Theological Reflections on the Suffering of God's Creatures', in *Christian Faith and the Earth: Current Paths and Emerging Horizons in Ecotheology*, eds. E. M. Conradie, Sigurd Bergmann, Celia Deane-Drummond and Denis Edwards (London: Bloomsbury/T & T Clark, 2014), 97–114.

14. Richard Bauckham, *God Crucified: Monotheism & Christology in the New Testament* (Grand Rapids MI: William B. Eerdmans, 1998); 'The Incarnation and the Cosmic Christ', in *Incarnation: On the Scope and Depth of Christology*, ed. N. H. Gregersen (Minneapolis, MN: Fortress Press, 2015), 25–56.

15. N. H. Gregersen, 'Cur deus caro: Jesus and the Cosmic Story', *Theology and Science* 11/4 (2013): 370–93, 386.

The Stoic concepts of Cosmic Sympathy and *oikeiōsis* also offer rich resources for further reflection on the deep incarnation of Christ.

3. Trinitarian theology

Pursuing a theology of deep incarnation, in which Christ's presence is perceived as radically present in material and biological existence, raises the question: where, then is the Holy Spirit? Is the divine presence throughout creation not the presence of the Holy Spirit? If so, is this Cosmic Christology really a Trinitarian theology, or does it risk collapsing the second and third persons of the Trinity into one person? While there may be those who answer that this is an anachronistic question, I think it is an important one, particularly for those of us shaped in Western Christian traditions, for whom Jesus Christ is Lord and Saviour, but not obviously the One permeating all things.

I have previously explored the muted portrayal of the Holy Spirit in Colossians in an article entitled 'The Holy Spirit and the Cosmic Christ: A Comparison of their Roles in Colossians and Ephesians, or "Where has the Holy Spirit gone?"'[16] While there is a rich theology of Spirit in the undisputed letters of Paul, there are, by contrast, only two references to s/Spirit in Colossians.[17] I argue that this indicates something other than simply a 'decline in the Church's apprehension of the meaning of the dispensation of the Spirit from the time of the Pauline letters to the last decade of the first century'.[18] Against a Stoic background, it was uncontroversial that the universe was permeated by Logos, or *pneuma* (spirit) as these were used interchangeably.[19]

> The distinctive claim of Colossians is that the divine Spirit which is at work throughout the cosmos is none other than the Spirit of Christ. ... The Colossians appear to be well attuned to a Stoic cosmological outlook. ... But in their very openness to this, they may fail to see the divine Spirit *Christologically*. It is Christ who gives the deepest and most complete vision of the divine Spirit.[20]

16. Balabanski, 'The Holy Spirit and the Cosmic Christ', 173–87.

17. Colossians 1.7-8 and 2.5; the latter refers to Paul's spirit. I also examine the adjective 'spiritual' in Col. 1.9 and 3.16.

18. Stanley M. Burgess, *The Holy Spirit: Ancient Christian Traditions* (Peabody, MA: Hendrickson, 1984), 18.

19. Baltzly discusses *pneuma* as one of the ways the Stoics referred to God. He further specifies *pneuma* in this way: 'Recall that *pneuma* in its various gradations is tenor (*hexis*), the sustaining and unifying cause of inanimate objects; nature (*physis*) the internal source of growth and change in animate objects; soul (*psychē*) in virtue of which living things are sentient; and the ruling principle (*hēgemonikon*) of rational creatures. Baltzly, 'Stoic Pantheism', 24.

20. Balabanski, 'The Holy Spirit and the Cosmic Christ', 181–2.

The Letter to the Colossians does not reject a Stoic cosmology, with the Logos/Spirit permeating all things, but rather ties this presence to the risen Christ. The divine Logos, who is none other than Christ, is manifest in three ways in this Letter:

1. The Logos/Spirit of Christ is the primordial force that designed and created the universe;
2. The Logos/Spirit of Christ is the permeating power that governs and sustains the universe;
3. The Logos/Spirit of Christ is the reconciling presence that empathizes with and heals the universe.

In these ways, Christ visibly and tangibly reveals the unseen God, and does so by creating, sustaining and reconciling the universe, as the permeating Logos/Spirit. We have in the distinctive theology of Colossians the makings of a Trinitarian vision.

Experiencing the majesty of the natural world, in all its diversity and strangeness, its symbiosis and complexity, is becoming a rare and precious thing – the stuff of eco-tourism and World Heritage sites. Wild places are now packaged and marketed, to manage the tourist footprint. The velvety depths of the night sky unencumbered by artificial lights is now, for very many, a memory.

As I conclude this book, news of the death of the last male Sumatran rhinoceros has been announced.[21] If Christ embodies and reveals the invisible God in and through the natural world, this means of revelation is also becoming increasingly rare and precious. How are future generations going to glimpse the numinous, except artificially, in pre-packaged portions? As we allow the diminishment of species and ecosystems, we diminish our ability – and the ability of future generations – to perceive the glory of God. This can no longer be peripheral to those who love Christ.

Nympha's notes

This evening as the cicadas' song was quietening, the children of the household came running to me. 'Despoina, Despoina', they panted, 'Come and see the green sparks!' I hurried with them to the olive grove, and there we saw a magnificent sight – a glittering stream of *purigonoi*, fireflies, flicking through the trees, alighting on the trunks, crawling on the grass at our feet. Some even landed on our hair and shoulders, as we stood in awe. We were among the stars – a green night sky winking and dancing – entranced. One.

---

21. https://www.nationalgeographic.com/animals/2019/05/last-sumatran-rhino-malaysia-dies/

Time passed – it's hard to say how long – and the luminous constellations of *purigonoi* then arose, almost as one, and darted on to bless another hillside. The children and I breathed thank you. And as we did so, the full summer moon broke free of the mountains and raised her huge royal form, red and magnificent. We sat among the olive trees, breathing the fragrant night air, tangibly in the Presence of the One who sustains all things.

BIBLIOGRAPHY

Adams, Edward. 'Paul's Story of God and Creation: The Story of How God Fulfils His Purposes in Creation'. In *Narrative Dynamics in Paul: A Critical Assessment*, edited by Bruce W. Longenecker, 19–43. Louisville, KY: Westminster/John Knox Press, 2002.

Anderson, Janice Capel. *Colossians: An Introduction and Study Guide: Authorship, Rhetoric, and Code*. T & T Clark's Study Guides to the New Testament. London: T & T Clark, 2018.

Arnim, Hans von. 'Stoicorum Veterum Fragmenta (SVF)'. Vol. 1: *Zeno et Zenonis discipuli*, 1905; Vol. 2: *Chrysippi fragmenta logica et physica*, 1903; Vol. 3: *Chrysippi fragmenta moralia, fragmenta successorum Chrysippi*, 1903; Vol. 4: *Indices*, conscripsit Maximilianus Adler, 1924. All reprinted Stuttgart: Teubner, 1964.

Arnold, C. E. *The Colossian Syncretism: The Interface Between Christianity and Folk Belief at Colossae*. WUNT 2/77; Tübingen: Mohr Siebeck, 1995.

Bagshaw, Eryk. '"I Support the Law of the Country": Debate over Sexuality and Religion Creeps into Election Campaign'. In *The Sydney Morning Herald*, 13 May 2019. Available online: https://www.smh.com.au/federal-election-2019/i-support-the-law-of-the-country-debate-over-sexuality-and-religion-creeps-into-election-campaign-20190513-p51mxm.html (accessed 21 February 2019).

Baird, Julia and Hayley Gleeson. '"Submit to Your Husbands": Women Told to Endure Domestic Violence in the Name of God'. Available online: http://www.abc.net.au/news/2017-07-18/domestic-violence-church-submit-to-husbands/8652028 (accessed 20 May 2019).

Balabanski, Vicky. 'Colossians 1:23: A case for translating ἐπιμένετε (continue) as imperative, not indicative'. *TynBul* 70/1 (2019): 85–94.

Balabanski, Vicky. 'Critiquing Anthropocentric Cosmology: Retrieving a Stoic "Permeation Cosmology" in Colossians 1:15–20'. In *Ecological Hermeneutics*, edited by Norman C. Habel and Peter Trudinger, 151–9. SBL Symposium Series 46; Atlanta, GA: SBL, 2008.

Balabanski, Vicky. *Eschatology in the Making: Mark, Matthew, and the Didache*. SNTSMS 97; Cambridge: Cambridge University Press, 1997.

Balabanski, Vicky. 'Hellenistic Cosmology and the Letter to the Colossians: Towards an Ecological Hermeneutic'. In *Ecological Hermeneutics: Biblical, Historical and Theological Perspectives*, edited by David G. Horrell, Cherryl Hunt, Christopher Southgate and Francesca Stavrakopoulou, 94–107. London & New York: T & T Clark/Continuum, 2010.

Balabanski, Vicky. '"Neither Greek nor Jew…for Christ Is All and in All" (Col 3:11-17), A Bible Study'. In *Receptive Ecumenism: Listening, Learning and Loving in the Way of Christ*, edited by Vicky Balabanski and Geraldine Hawkes, 5–14. Hindmarsh, South Australia: ATF Press, 2018.

Balabanski, Vicky. 'Pauline Letters: Paul's Vision of Cosmic Liberation and Renewal'. In *The Oxford Handbook on Bible and Ecology*. Forthcoming.

Balabanski, Vicky. 'Stoic Echoes in Non-Stoic Sources: Exploring Stoic Influence in the First and Second Centuries CE'. In *Living in a Cultural Wilderness, Journal of Modern Greek Studies (Australia and New Zealand) – Special Issue*, edited by George Couvalis, Michael Tsianikas and Maria Palaktsoglou, 11–26. *Modern Greek Studies (Australia and New Zealand)* Supplementary Volume. Adelaide, 2017.

Balabanski, Vicky. 'The Holy Spirit and the Cosmic Christ: A Comparison of Their Roles in Colossians and Ephesians, or, Where Has the Holy Spirit Gone?' *Colloquium* 42/2 (2010): 173–87.

Balabanski, Vicky. 'Where Is Philemon? The Case for a Logical Fallacy in the Correlation of the Data in Philemon and Colossians 1.1-2; 4.7-18'. *JSNT* 38/2 (2015): 131–50.

Balabanski, Vicky and Geraldine Hawkes, editors. *Receptive Ecumenism: Listening, Learning and Loving the Way of Christ*. Hindmarsh, South Australia: ATF Press, 2018.

Baltzly, Dirk. 'Stoic Pantheism'. *Sophia* 42/2 (2003): 3–33.

Barrett, C. K. *The First Epistle to the Corinthians*. 2nd edn. London: A & C Black, 1971.

Barth, Markus. *Ephesians*. AB 34–34A; New York: Doubleday, 1974.

Barth, Markus and Helmut Blanke. *Colossians: A New Translation with Introduction and Commentary*. AB 34B; New York: Doubleday, 1994.

Bauckham, Richard. *God Crucified: Monotheism & Christology in the New Testament*. Grand Rapids, MI: William B. Eerdmans, 1998.

Bauckham, Richard. 'Where Is Wisdom to Be Found? Colossians 1.15–20 (2)'. In *Reading Texts, Seeking Wisdom*, edited by David Ford and Graham Stanton, 129–38. London: SCM, 2003.

Bauckham, Richard. 'The Incarnation and the Cosmic Christ'. In *Incarnation: On the Scope and Depth of Christology*, edited by Niels Henrik Gregersen, 25–56. Minneapolis, MN: Fortress Press, 2015.

Bauer, Walter, F. W. Danker, W. F. Arndt, F. W. Gingrich, K. Aland, B. Aland and V. Reichman, *A Greek-English Lexicon of the New Testament and Other Early Christian Literature*. 3rd edn. Chicago IL: University of Chicago Press, 2000.

Bird, Michael F. *Colossians and Philemon: A New Covenant Commentary*. NCCS 12; Eugene, OR: Cascade, 2009.

Blinzler, Josef. 'Lexikalisches zu dem Terminus τὰ στοιχεῖα τοῦ κόσμου bei Paulus'. In *Studiorum Paulinorum Congressus Internationalis Catholicus 1961*, Vol. 2, 429–43. AnBib 18; Rome: Pontifical Biblical Institute, 1963.

Bockmuehl, Markus N. A. *Revelation and Mystery in Ancient Judaism and Pauline Christianity*. WUNT 2/36; Tübingen: Mohr and Siebeck, 1990.

Bruce, F. F. *The Epistles to the Colossians, to Philemon, and to the Ephesians*. NICNT; Grand Rapids, MI: Eerdmans, 1984.

Bujard, Walter. *Stilanalytische Untersuchungen zum Kolosserbrief*. SUNT 11; Göttingen: Vandenhoeck & Ruprecht, 1973.

Burgess, Stanley M. *The Holy Spirit: Ancient Christian Traditions*. Peabody, MA: Hendrickson, 1984.

Burke, Trevor J. 'Paul's New Family in Thessalonica'. *NovT* 54/3 (2012): 269–87.

Burrell, Barbara. 'False Fronts: Separating the Aedicular Façade from the Imperial Cult in Roman Asia Minor'. *American Journal of Archaeology*, 110/3 (2006): 437–69.

Buscemi, Alfio Marcello. *Lettera Ai Colossesi: Commentario Esegetico*. SBFA 82; Milano: Edizioni Terra Santa, 2015.

Cadwallader, Alan H. *Fragments of Colossae: Sifting through the Traces*. Hindmarsh, South Australia: ATF Press, 2015.

Cadwallader, Alan H. 'Refuting an Axiom of Scholarship on Colossae: Fresh Insights from New and Old Inscriptions'. In *Colossae in Space and Time: Linking to an Ancient City*, edited by Alan H. Cadwallader and Michael Trainor, 151–79. NTOA – SUNT 94; Göttingen: Vandenhoeck & Ruprecht, 2011.

Cadwallader, Alan H. 'The Historical Sweep of the Life of Kolossai'. In *Epigraphical Evidence Illustrating Paul's Letter to the Colossians*, edited by Joseph Verheyden, Markus Öhler and Thomas Corsten, 25–67. WUNT 1/411; Tübingen: Mohr Siebeck, 2018.

Cadwallader, Alan H. and Michael F. Trainor, editors. *Colossae in Space and Time: Linking to an Ancient City*. NTOA – SUNT 94; Göttingen: Vandenhoeck & Ruprecht, 2011.

Canavan, Rosemary. *Clothing the Body of Christ at Colossae: A Visual Construction of Identity*. WUNT 2/334; Tübingen: Mohr Siebeck, 2012.

Casadesús, Francesc. 'The Transformation of the Initiation Language of Mystery Religions'. In *Greek Philosophy and Mystery Cults*, edited by María José Martín-Velasco and María José García Blanco, 1–26. Newcastle upon Tyne: Cambridge Scholars Publishing, 2016.

Chapron, Guillaume, Yaffa Epstein and José Vicente López-Bao, 'A Rights Revolution for Nature'. *Science*, 363/6434 (29 March 2019): 1392–3. Available online: https://science.sciencemag.org/content/363/6434/1392?rss=1 (accessed 21 May 2019).

Charles, R. H. *The Apocrypha and Pseudepigrapha of the Old Testament*, Vol. 2, Oxford: Clarendon Press, 1913.

Charlesworth James H., editor. *The Old Testament Pseudepigrapha*, Vol. 2. London: Darton, Longman & Todd, 1985.

Chion. *Chion of Heraclea: A Novel in Letters*. Translated and edited by Ingemar Düring. 1951. Reprint, New York: Arno Press, 1979.

Clark, Bruce T. *Completing Christ's Afflictions: Christ, Paul, and the Reconciliation of All Things*, WUNT 2/383; Tübingen: Mohr Siebeck, 2015.

Clark, Elizabeth A. 'Antifamilial Tendencies in Ancient Christianity'. *Journal of the History of Sexuality* 3 (1995): 356–80.

Conradie, Ernst M, editor. *Creation and Salvation, Volume 1, A Mosaic of Selected Classic Christian Theologies*. Zurich: LIT, 2012.

Conradie, Ernst M, editor. *Creation and Salvation, Volume 2, A Companion on Recent Theological Movements*. Zurich: LIT, 2012.

Cooper, John W. *Panentheism. The Other God of the Philosophers. From Plato to the Present*. Nottingham: Apollos, Intervarsity Press, 2007.

Coxe, A. Cleveland, editor. *Ante-Nicene Fathers. Volume 7: Lactantius, Venantius, Asterius, Victorinus, Dionysius, Apostolic Teaching and Constitutions, 2 Clement, Early Liturgies*. New York: Christian Literature Publishing Co., 1886.

Cross, F. L. and E. A. Livingstone, editors. *The Oxford Dictionary of the Christian Church*. 2nd edn. Oxford: Oxford University Press, 1983.

Davison, Andrew. *The Love of Wisdom: An Introduction to Philosophy for Theologians*. London: SCM Press, 2013.

Deane-Drummond, Celia. *A Primer in Ecotheology: Theology for a Fragile Earth*. Eugene, OR: Cascade Books, 2017.

Deane-Drummond, Celia. *Christ and Evolution: Wonder and Wisdom*. Minneapolis, MN: Fortress, 2009.

Deane-Drummond, Celia. 'Deep Incarnation and Eco-justice as Theodrama'. In *Ecological Awareness: Exploring Religion, Ethics and Aesthetics*, edited by Sigurd Bergmann and Heather Eaton, 193–206. Berlin: LIT, 2011.

Deane-Drummond, Celia. 'The Wisdom of Fools? A Theo-Dramatic Interpretation of Deep Incarnation'. In *Incarnation: On the Scope and Depth of Christology*, edited by Niels Henrik Gregersen, 177–202. Minneapolis, MN: Fortress Press, 2015.

Deane-Drummond, Celia. 'Who on Earth Is Jesus Christ? Plumbing the Depths of Deep Incarnation'. In *Christian Faith and the Earth: Current Paths and Emerging Horizons in Ecotheology*, edited by Ernst M. Conradie, Sigurd Bergmann, Celia Deane-Drummond and Denis Edwards, 31–50. London: Bloomsbury/T & T Clark, 2014.

Deming, Will. *Paul on Marriage and Celibacy: The Hellenistic Background of 1 Corinthians 7*. 2nd edn, Grand Rapids, MI: Eerdmans, 2004.

Dettwiler, Andreas. 'La lettre aux Colossiens: une théologie de la mémoire'. *NTS* 59/1 (2013): 109–28.

Devall, Bill. 'The Ecological Self'. In *The Deep Ecology Movement: An Introductory Anthology*, edited by Alan Drengson and Yuichi Inoue, 101–23. Berkeley CA: North Atlantic Publishers, 1995.

Dillon, John. 'The Pleasures and Perils of Soul-Gardening'. In *Wisdom and Logos: Studies in Jewish Thought in Honor of David Winston*, edited by David T. Runia and Gregory E. Sterling, 190–7. SPhiloA, Studies in Hellenistic Judaism 9, BJS 312; Atlanta GA: Scholars Press, 1997.

Dindorf, Wilhelm, editor. *Aristides*, Vol. 1, Leipzig: Reimer, 1829.

Drengson, Alan and Yuichi Inoue, editors. *The Deep Ecology Movement: An Introductory Anthology*. Berkeley CA: North Atlantic Publishers, 1995.

Dübbers, Michael. *Christologie und Existenz im Kolosserbrief: exegetische und semantische Untersuchungen zur Intention des Kolosserbriefes*. WUNT 2/191; Tübingen: Mohr Siebeck, 2005.

Dunn, J. *The Epistles to the Colossians and Philemon: A Commentary on the Greek Text*. Carlisle: Paternoster, 1996.

Edwards, Denis. *Ecology at the Heart of Faith*. Maryknoll, NY: Orbis Books, 2006.

Edwards, Denis. '"Every Sparrow that Falls to the Ground": The Cost of Evolution and the Christ-Event'. *Ecotheology* 11/1 (2007):103–23.

Edwards, Denis. 'Incarnation and the Natural World: Explorations in the Tradition of Athanasius'. In *Incarnation: On the Scope and Depth of Christology*, edited by Niels Henrik Gregersen, 157–76. Minneapolis, MN: Fortress Press, 2015.

Edwards, Denis. 'Key Issues in Ecological Theology: Incarnation, Evolution, Communion'. In *Theology and Ecology Across the Disciplines: On Care for Our Common Home*, edited by Celia Deane-Drummond and Rebecca Artinian-Kaiser, 65–78. London: Bloomsbury, 2018.

Edwards, Denis. *Partaking of God: Trinity, Evolution and Ecology*. Collegeville, MN: Liturgical Press, 2014.

Edwards, Denis. 'Sublime Communion: The Theology of the Natural World in Laudato Si'. *Theological Studies* 77 (2016): 377–91.

Elvey, Anne F., Keith Dyer and Deborah Guess, editors. *Ecological Aspects of War: Engagements with Biblical Texts*. London: Bloomsbury/T & T Clark, 2017.

Engberg-Pedersen, Troels. *Cosmology & Self in the Apostle Paul: The Material Spirit*. Oxford: Oxford University Press, 2010.

Engberg-Pedersen, Troels. *Paul and the Stoics: An Essay in Interpretation*. Edinburgh: T & T Clark, 2000.

Engberg-Pedersen, Troels. 'Response to reviews of Troels Engberg-Pedersen, *Paul and the Stoics*'. RBL, 2002. Available online: http://www.bookreviews.org (accessed 18 May 2018).

Engberg-Pedersen, Troels. *The Stoic Theory of Oikeiosis: Moral Development and Social Interaction in Early Stoic Philosophy*. Studies in Hellenistic Civilization 2; Aarhus: Aarhus University Press, 1990.

Epictetus. *Discourses, Fragments, Handbook*. A new translation by Robin Hard, with an introduction and notes by Christopher Gill. Oxford World's Classics; Oxford: Oxford University Press, 2014.

Eusebius. *Die Praeparatio Evangelica*. Edited by Karl Mras and Édouard des Places; Eusebius Werke 8/1, introduction and books 1–8; Berlin: Akademie, 1982.

Ferguson, Everett. *Backgrounds of Early Christianity*. 3rd edn. Grand Rapids, MI: Eerdmans, 2003.

Francis. *Encyclical Letter Laudato si' of the Holy Father Francis on Care for Our Common Home*. Vatican City: Libreria Editrice Vaticana, 2015.

Friberg, Timothy, Barbara Friberg and Neva F. Miller. *Analytical Lexicon of the Greek New Testament*. Baker's Greek New Testament Library 4; Grand Rapids, MI: Baker, 2000.

Fee, Gordon D. *The First Epistle to the Corinthians*. Grand Rapids, MI: Eerdmans, 1987.

Foster, Paul. *Colossians*. BNTC; London: Bloomsbury/T & T Clark, 2016.

Fox, Warwick. 'Deep Ecology: A New Philosophy of our Time?' In *Environmental Ethics*, edited by Andrea Light and Holmes Rolston III. Malden: Blackwell, 2003.

Gaca, Kathy L. 'Review of Troels Engberg-Pedersen, *Paul and the Stoics*'. RBL, 2002. Available online: http://www.bookreviews.org (accessed 18 May 2018).

Geddert, Timothy. *Watchwords: Mark 13 in Markan Eschatology*. JSNTSup 26; Sheffield: JSOT Press, 1989.

Gordley, M. E. *The Colossian Hymn in Context: An Exegesis in Light of Jewish and Greco-Roman Hymnic and Epistolary Conventions*. WUNT 2/228; Tübingen: Mohr Siebeck, 2007.

Gordley, Matthew E. *Teaching through Song in Antiquity*. WUNT 2/302; Tübingen: Mohr Siebeck, 2011.

Gorman, Michael J. *Becoming the Gospel: Paul, Participation and Mission*. Grand Rapids, MI: Eerdmans, 2015.

Gourinat, Jean-Baptiste. 'The Stoics on Matter and Prime Matter: "Corporealism" and the Imprint of Plato's *Timaeus*'. In *God and Cosmos in Stoicism*, edited by Ricardo Salles, 46–70. Oxford: Oxford University Press, 2009.

Green, Peter. *Alexander to Actium: The Hellenistic Age*. London: Thames and Hudson, 1993.

Gregersen, Niels Henrik. '*Cur deus caro*: Jesus and the Cosmic Story'. *Theology and Science* 11/4 (2013): 370–93.

Gregersen, Niels Henrik. 'The Cross of Christ in an Evolutionary World'. *Dialog: A Journal of Theology* 40/3 (2001): 192–207.

Gregersen, Niels Henrik. 'The Extended Body of Christ: Three Dimensions of Deep Incarnation'. In *Incarnation: On the Scope and Depth of Christology*, edited by Niels Henrik Gregersen, 225–6. Minneapolis, MN: Fortress Press, 2015.

Griffin, Miriam T. *Seneca: A Philosopher in Politics*. Oxford: Clarendon Press, 1976.

Grindheim, Sigurd. 'A Deutero-Pauline Mystery? Ecclesiology in Colossians and Ephesians'. In *Paul and Pseudepigraphy*, edited by S. E. Porter and G. P. Fewster, 173–95. Pauline Studies 8; Leiden/Boston: Brill, 2013.

Gupta, Nijay K. *Colossians*. SHBC 27c; Macon, GA: Smyth & Helwys, 2013.

Gupta, Nijay K. 'What Is in a Name? The Hermeneutics of Authorship Analysis Concerning Colossians'. *Currents in Biblical Research* 11/2 (2013): 196–217.

Habel, Norman C. *Finding Wisdom in Nature: An Eco-Wisdom Reading of the Book of Job*. Sheffield: Sheffield Phoenix Press, 2014.

Habel, Norman C. and Geraldine Avent. 'Rescuing Earth from a Storm God: Psalms 29 and 96–97'. In *The Earth Story in the Psalms and the Prophets*, edited by Norman C. Habel, 42–50. Sheffield: Sheffield Academic Press, 2001.

Hahm, David E. *The Origins of Stoic Cosmology*. Columbus, OH: Ohio State University Press, 1977.

Halliday, M.A.K. and C.M.I.M. Matthiessen. *An Introduction to Functional Grammar*. 4th edn. London: Routledge, 2014.

Harrer, G. A. 'Senatorial Speeches and Letters in Tacitus' Annals', *Studies in Philology* 15/4 (1918): 333–43.

Harris, M. J. *Colossians & Philemon, Exegetical Guide to the Greek New Testament*. Grand Rapids, MI: Eerdmans, 1991.

Hays, Richard B. 'A Hermeneutic of Trust'. In *The Conversion of the Imagination: Paul as Interpreter of Israel's Scripture*, 190–201. Grand Rapids MI: Eerdmans, 2005.

Hays, Richard B. *The Conversion of the Imagination: Paul as Interpreter of Israel's Scripture*. Grand Rapids MI: Eerdmans, 2005.

Hays, Richard B. *The Faith of Jesus Christ: The Narrative Substructure of Galatians 3:1–4:11*. 2nd edn. Grand Rapids, MI: Eerdmans, 2002.

Head, Peter M. 'Tychicus and the Colossian Christians: A Reconsideration of the Text of Colossians 4:8'. In *Texts and Traditions: Essays in Honour of J. Keith Elliott*, edited by Peter Doble and Jeffrey Kloha, 303–15. NTTSD 47; Leiden/Boston: Brill, 2014.

Heil, John Paul. *Colossians: Encouragement to Walk in All Wisdom as Holy Ones in Christ*. ECL 4; Atlanta, GA: SBL, 2010.

Heininger, Bernhard. 'Soziale und politische Metaphorik im Kolosserbrief'. In *Kolosser-Studien* edited by Peter Müller, 55–82. Biblisch-Theologische Studien 103; Neukirchen-Vluyn: Neukirchener Verlag, 2009.

Henderson, Suzanne Watts. 'God's Fullness in Bodily Form: Christ and Church in Colossians'. *Expository Times* 118/4 (2007): 169–73.

Hermitage museum – The Pazyryk carpet dated to the fifth century BCE. Available online: https://hermitagemuseum.org/wps/portal/hermitage/digital-collection/25.+Archaeol ogical+Artifacts/879870/?lng=en (accessed 30 July 2018).

Holladay, Carl R. *A Critical Introduction to the New Testament: Interpreting the Message and Meaning of Jesus Christ*. Abingdon: Abingdon Press, 2005.

Holtmann, Catherine. 'Women Seeking Safety: Nonviolent Responses to Intimate Partner Violence'. In *Advancing Nonviolence and Social Transformation: New Perspectives on Nonviolent Theories*, edited by Heather Eaton and Lauren Michelle Levesque, 188–200. Sheffield: Equinox, 2016.

Hooker, Morna D. 'Were There False Teachers in Colossae?' In Morna D. Hooker, *From Adam to Christ: Essays on Paul*, 121–36. Cambridge: Cambridge University Press, 1990.

Horrell, David G., Cheryl Hunt and Christopher Southgate. *Greening Paul: Rereading the Apostle in a Time of Ecological Crisis*. Waco TX: Baylor University Press, 2010.

Hrynkow, Christopher. 'No to War and Yes to So Much More: Pope Francis, Principled Nonviolence, and Positive Peace'. In *Advancing Nonviolence and Social Transformation: New Perspectives on Nonviolent Theories*, edited by Heather Eaton and Lauren Michelle Levesque, 135–52. Sheffield: Equinox, 2016.

Hunter, Archibald M. *Paul and His Predecessors*. 2nd edn. London: SCM, 1961.

Irenaeus. *Against Heresies* 4.20.2. Available online: http://www.newadvent.org/fathers/01 03420.htm (accessed 20 May 2019).

Jewett, Robert. *Romans: A Commentary on the Book of Romans*. Hermeneia; Minneapolis, MN: Fortress Press, 2007.

Johnson, Elizabeth A. 'An Earthy Christology'. *America: The National Catholic Review* 200/12 (2009): 27–30.

Johnson, Elizabeth A. *Ask the Beasts: Darwin and the God of Love*. New York: Bloomsbury, 2014.

Johnson, Elizabeth A. 'Deep Christology'. In *From Logos to Christos: Essays in Christology in Honour of Joanne McWilliam*, edited by Ellen M. Leonard and Kate Merriman, 163–80. Waterloo, ON: Wilfrid Laurier University Press, 2009.

Johnson, Elizabeth A. *Creation and the Cross: The Mercy of God for a Planet in Peril*. Maryknoll, NY: Orbis Books, 2018.

Johnson, Elizabeth A. 'Jesus and the Cosmos: Soundings in Deep Ecology'. In *Incarnation: On the Scope and Depth of Christology*, edited by Niels Henrik Gregersen, 133–56. Minneapolis, MN: Fortress Press, 2015.

Käsemann, Ernst. 'A Primitive Christian Baptismal Liturgy'. In *Essays on New Testament Themes*, translated by W. S. Montague, 149–68. SBT 41; London: SCM, 1964.

Keener, Craig S. *Acts: An Exegetical Commentary*, Vol. 3. Grand Rapids, MI: Baker Academic, 2014.

Kelhoffer, James A. *Conceptions of 'Gospel' and Legitimacy in Early Christianity*, WUNT 1/324; Tübingen: Mohr Siebeck, 2014.

Kidson, Lyn. '1 Timothy: An Administrative Letter'. *Early Christianity* 1/5 (2014): 97–116

Kooten, George H. van. *Cosmic Christology in Paul and the Pauline School*. WUNT 2/171; Tübingen: Mohr Siebeck, 2003.

Lambert, Nathaniel M., Frank D. Fincham, Tyler F. Stillman and Lukas R. Dean. 'More Gratitude, Less Materialism: The Mediating Role of Life Satisfaction'. *The Journal of Positive Psychology* 4/1 (2009): 32–42.

Lampe, Peter. *From Paul to Valentinus: Christians at Rome in the First Two Centuries*. Minneapolis, MN: Fortress Press, 2003. A translation of the second edition of *Die stadtrömischen Christen in den ersten beiden Jahrhunderten*. WUNT 2/18; Tübingen: Mohr Siebeck, 1989.

Lewis, Nicola Denzey. *Cosmology and Fate in Gnosticism and Graeco-Roman Antiquity: Under Pitiless Skies*. Nag Hammadi and Manichaean Studies 81; Leiden: Brill, 2013.

Lincoln, Andrew. *Ephesians*. WBC 42; Dallas, TX: Word Books, 1990.

Loader, William. *Sexuality in the New Testament: Understanding the Key Texts*. Louisville, KY: Westminster/John Knox, 2010.

Loader, William. *The New Testament on Sexuality*. Grand Rapids, MI: Eerdmans, 2012.

Lohse, Eduard. *Colossians and Philemon*. Hermeneia; Philadelphia, PA: Fortress Press, 1971.

Loisy, Alfred. 'The Christian Mystery'. *Hibbert Journal* 10 (1911–12): 45–64.

Long, Anthony A. and David N. Sedley. *The Hellenistic Philosophers. Vol. 1: Translations of the Principal Sources with Philosophical Commentary*. Cambridge: Cambridge University Press, 1987.

Long, Anthony A. and David N. Sedley. *The Hellenistic Philosophers. Vol. 2: Greek and Latin Texts with Notes and Bibliography*. Cambridge: Cambridge University Press, 1987.

Longenecker, Bruce W. *Remember the Poor: Paul, Poverty and the Greco-Roman World*. Grand Rapids, MI: Eerdmans, 2010.

Longenecker, Richard N. *Galatians*. WBC 41; Dallas, TX: Word Books, 1990.

Louw, J. P. and Eugene Nida, *Greek-English Lexicon of the New Testament: Based on Semantic Domains*. New York: United Bible Societies, 1988.

Luz, Ulrich. 'Der Brief an die Kolosser'. In *Die Briefe an die Galater, Epheser und Kolosser*. Jürgen Becker and Ulrich Luz, translators and commentators. NTD 8/1; Göttingen: Vandenhoeck & Ruprecht, 1998.

MacDonald, Margaret Y. 'Can Nympha Rule This House? The Rhetoric of Domesticity in Colossians'. In *Rhetoric and Realities in Early Christianities*, edited by Willi Braun, 99–120. Studies in Christianity and Judaism / Études sur le christianisme et le judaïsme 16; Waterloo, ON: Wilfrid Laurier University Press, 2005.

MacDonald, Margaret Y. *Colossians and Ephesians*. SP 17; Collegeville, MN: Michael Glazier/Liturgical Press, 2000.

Marchand, Stéphane. 'Sextus Empiricus' Style of Writing'. In *New Essays on Ancient Pyronnism*, edited by Diego E. Machuca, 113–41. PhA 126; Leiden/Boston: Brill, 2011.

Marcus Aurelius. *The Meditations of Marcus Aurelius*. Translated by George Long. London: Blackie & Son Ltd., 1910.

Martin, Neil. 'Returning to the *stoicheia tou kosmou*: Enslavement to the Physical Elements in Galatians 4.3 and 9?' *JSNT* 40/4 (2018): 434–52.

Meier, Harry O. 'There's a New World Coming! Reading the Apocalypse in the Shadow of the Canadian Rockies'. In *The Earth Story in the New Testament*, edited by Norman C. Habel and Vicky Balabanski, 166–79. The Earth Bible 5; London, New York: Sheffield, 2002.

Meijer, P. A. *Stoic Theology: Proofs for the Existence of the Cosmic God and of the Traditional Gods*. Delft: Eburon, 2007.

Metzger, Bruce. *A Textual Commentary on the Greek New Testament: A Companion Volume to the United Bible Societies' Greek New Testament (Fourth Edn, Revised)*. 2nd edn. Stuttgart: Deutsche Bibelgesellschaft, 1994.

Middleton, J. Richard. *A New Heaven and a New Earth: Reclaiming Biblical Eschatology*. Grand Rapids, MI: Baker Academic, 2014.

Moo, Douglas J. *The Letters to the Colossians and to Philemon*. Pillar New Testament Commentary; Grand Rapids, MI: Eerdmans/Nottingham: Apollos, 2008.

Mosley, A. W. 'Historical Reporting in the Ancient World'. *NTS* 12/1 (1965): 10–26.

Müller, Peter. 'Gegner im Kolosserbrief: Methodische Überlegungen zu einem schwierigen Kapitel'. In *Beiträge zur urchristlichen Theologiegeschichte*, edited by Wolfgang Kraus and Ulrich Müller, 365–94. BZNW 163; Berlin/New York, 2009.

Naess, Arne. 'The Shallow and the Deep, Long-Range Ecology Movement: A Summary'. *Inquiry* 16/1–4 (1973): 95–100.

Noreña, Carlos, 'The Social Economy of Pliny's Correspondence with Trajan'. *AJP* 128 (2007): 239–77.

Nuffelen, Peter van. *Rethinking the Gods: Philosophical Readings of Religion in the Post-Hellenistic Period*. Greek Culture in the Roman World series; Cambridge: Cambridge University Press, 2011.

Protopapadakis, Evangelos D. 'The Stoic Notion of "Cosmic Sympathy" in Contemporary Environmental Ethics'. In *Antiquity, Modern World and Reception of Ancient Culture*, Антика и савремени свет (Antiquity and Modern World) Series 6, edited by Ksenija Maricki-Gadanski, 290–305. Belgrade: Scientific Publications of the Serbian Society for Ancient Studies, 2012.

Putzger, F. W. 'Wirtschaft des Römischen Weltreichs'. In F. W. Putzger, *Historisches Weltatlas*. Berlin & Bielefeld: Velhagen & Klasing, 1965.

Ramelli, Ilaria. 'The Stoic Doctrine of Oikeiosis and Its Translation in Christian Platonism'. *Apeiron* 47/1 (2014): 116–40.

Riley, Joan. 'Beyond the Mainstream: The Cultural Environment of Asia Minor as a Matrix for Expressions of a Highest God'. PhD diss., Flinders University of South Australia, 2017.

Robinson, J. A. T. *The Human Face of God*. London: SCM Press, 1973.

Rosenmeyer, Patricia A. *Ancient Epistolary Fictions: The Letter in Greek Literature*. Cambridge: Cambridge University Press, 2001.

Rosenmeyer, Thomas G. *Senecan Drama and Stoic Cosmology*. Berkeley CA: University of California Press, 1989.

Rowe, C. Kavin. *One True Life: The Stoics and Early Christians as Rival Traditions*. New Haven & London: Yale University, 2016.

Saller, Richard P. 'Symbols of Gender and Status Hierarchies in the Roman Household'. In *Women and Slaves in Greco-Roman Culture*, edited by Sandra R. Joshel and Sheila Murnaghan, 85–91. London/New York: Routledge, 1998.

Sanders, E. P. 'Literary Dependence in Colossians'. *JBL* 85 (1966): 28–45.

Schweizer, Eduard. *The Letter to the Colossians: A Commentary*. London: SPCK, 1982.

Southgate, Christopher. 'Does God's Care Make Any Difference? Theological Reflections on the Suffering of God's Creatures'. In *Christian Faith and the Earth: Current Paths and Emerging Horizons in Ecotheology*, edited by Ernst M. Conradie, Sigurd Bergmann, Celia Deane-Drummond and Denis Edwards, 97–114. London: Bloomsbury/T & T Clark, 2014.

Southgate, Christopher. *The Groaning of Creation: God, Evolution and the Problem of Evil*. Louisville, KY: Westminster/John Knox Press, 2008.

Spjut, Petter. 'The Protestant Historiographic Myth and the Discourse of Differentiation in Scholarly Studies of Colossians'. In *Svensk Exegetisk Årsbok 80*, edited by Göran Eidevall, 169–85. Uppsala: Svenska exegetiska sällskapet, 2015.

Standhartinger, Angela. 'Colossians and the Pauline School'. *NTS* 50/4 (2004): 572–93.

Stepp, Perry L. *Leadership Succession in the World of the Pauline Circle*. New Testament Monographs 5; Sheffield: Sheffield Phoenix Press, 2005.

Sterling, Gregory E. 'Prepositional Metaphysics in Jewish Wisdom Speculation and Early Christian Liturgical Texts'. In *Wisdom and Logos: Studies in Jewish Thought in Honor of David Winston*, edited by David T. Runia and Gregory E. Sterling, 219–38. The Studia Philonica Annual 28: Studies in Hellenistic Judaism 9, BJS 312; Atlanta GA: Scholars Press, 1997.

Stettler, Christian. *Der Kolosserhymnus: Untersuchungen zu Form, traditionsgeschichtlichem Hintergrund und Aussage von Kol.1*, 15–20. WUNT 2/131; Tübingen: Mohr Siebeck, 2000.

Stettler, Christian. 'The Opponents at Colossae'. In *Paul and His Opponents*, edited by Stanley E. Porter, 169–200. Pauline Studies, 2; Leiden; Boston: Brill, 2005.

Still, Todd D. 'Eschatology in Colossians: How Realized Is It?' *NTS* 50/1 (2004):125–38.

Stowers, Stanley K. 'Review of Troels Engberg-Pedersen, *Paul and the Stoics*', *RBL*, 2002. Available online: http://www.bookreviews.org (Accessed 18 May 2018).

Sumney Jerry L. '"I Fill Up What Is lacking in the Afflictions of Christ": Paul's Vicarious Suffering in Colossians'. *CBQ* 68/4 (2006), 664–80.

Swancutt, Diana M. 'Paraenesis in the Light of Protrepsis'. In *Early Christian Paraenesis in Context*, edited by James Starr and Troels Engberg-Pedersen. BZNW 125; Berlin/New York: Walter de Gruyter, 2004.

Tabb, Brian J. *Suffering in Ancient Worldview: Luke, Seneca and 4 Maccabees in Dialogue*. London: Bloomsbury/T & T Clark, 2017.

Tertullian. *Prescription against Heresies 7*. Available online: http://www.newadvent.org/fathers/0311.htm (accessed 26 May 2019).

Theobald, Michael. 'Der Epheserbrief'. In *Einleitung in das Neue Testament*, edited by Martin Ebner and Stefan Schreiber, 408–24. Stuttgart: Kohlhammer, 2008.

Thompson, Marianne M. *Colossians and Philemon*. Two Horizons New Testament Commentary Series; Grand Rapids, MI: Eerdmans, 2005.

Thorsteinsson, Runar M. *Roman Christianity and Roman Stoicism: A Comparative Study of Ancient Morality*. Oxford: Oxford University Press, 2010.

Tidball, Derek J. *In Christ, in Colossae: sociological perspectives on Colossians*. Milton Keynes: Paternoster, 2011.

Tonstad, Sigve K. 'Creation Groaning in Labor Pains'. In *Exploring Ecological Hermeneutics*, edited by Norman C. Habel and Peter Trudinger, 141–9. Atlanta, GA: Society of Biblical Literature, 2008.

Tonstad, Sigve K. *The Letter to the Romans: Paul among the Ecologists*. Sheffield: Phoenix Press, 2016.

Trainor, Michael F. *Epaphras: Paul's Educator at Colossae. Paul's Social Network: Brothers and Sisters in Faith*. Collegeville, MN: Liturgical Press, 2008.

Trebilco, Paul. 'Christians in the Lycus Valley'. In *Colossae in Time and Space: Linking to an Ancient City*, edited by Alan H. Cadwallader and Michael Trainor, 184–5. NTOA – SUNT 94; Göttingen: Vandenhoeck & Ruprecht, 2011.

United Nations' IPBES Global Assessment Report on Biodiversity and Ecosystem Services. Available online: https://www.un.org/sustainabledevelopment/blog/2019/05/natur e-decline-unprecedented-report/ (accessed 22 May 2109).

Uniting Church in Australia Standing Committee Report on Marriage and Same Gender Relationships. Available online: https://uniting.church/b23-standing-committee-repo rt-on-marriage-and-same-gender-relationships/ (accessed 22 May 2019).

Vegge, Tor. 'Baptismal Phrases in the Deuteropauline Epistles'. In *Ablution, Initiation, and Baptism: Late Antiquity, early Judaism, and early Christianity*, Vol. 1, edited by David Hellholm, Tor Vegge, Øyvind Norderval and Christer Hellholm, 497–556. BZNW 176/1; Berlin/New York: W. de Gruyter, 2011.

Vegge, Tor. 'Polemic in the Epistle to the Colossians'. In *Polemik in der frühchristlichen Literatur: Texte und Kontexte*, edited by O. Wischmeyer und L. Scornaienchi, 255–93. BZNW 170; Berlin/New York: W. de Gruyter, 2011.

Vollenweider, Samuel. 'Hymnus, Enkomion oder Psalm? Schattengefechte in der neutestamentlichen Wissenschaft', *NTS* 56/2 (2010): 208–31.

Walsh, Brian J. and Sylvia C. Keesmaat. *Colossians Remixed: Subverting the Empire*. Downers Grove IL: Intervarsity Press, 2004.

Whitaker, E. C. *Documents of the Baptismal Liturgy*. London: SPCK, 1960.

White, Joel. 'Paul Completes the Servant's Sufferings (Colossians 1:24)'. *Journal for the Study of Paul and His Letters* 6/2 (2016): 181–98.

Whitehead, Alfred North. *Process and Reality*. New York: Free Press, 1979.

Wiedemann, T. E. J. 'Tiberius to Nero'. In *The Cambridge Ancient History*. Vol. 10, 2nd edn, edited by A. K. Bowman, E. Champlin and A. Lintott, 198–255. Cambridge: Cambridge University Press, 1996.

Witherington, Ben III. *The Letters to Philemon, the Colossians, and the Ephesians: A Socio-Rhetorical Commentary on the Captivity Epistles*. Grand Rapids, MI: Eerdmans, 2007.

Wright, Brian J. 'Ancient Rome's Daily News with some Likely Implications for Early Christian Studies'. *TynBul* 67/1 (2016): 145–60.

Wright, N. T. *Colossians and Philemon*. Grand Rapids, MI: Eerdmans, 1986.

Yazici, Erdal. *Hierapolis (Pamukkale), Laodicea and Surrounding Area*. Translated by Uğur Ahmet Toprak. The Ancient Cities 3; Istanbul: Uranus, 2014.

Loeb Classical Library volumes cited

LCL 25 *The Apostolic Fathers, Volume II: Epistle of Barnabas. Papias and Quadratus. Epistle to Diognetus. The Shepherd of Hermas.* Edited and translated by Bart D. Ehrman. Cambridge, MA: Harvard University Press, 2003.

LCL 40 Cicero. *On Ends.* Translated by H. Rackham. Cambridge, MA: Harvard University Press, 1914.

LCL 47 Plutarch. *Lives, Volume II: Themistocles and Camillus. Aristides and Cato Major. Cimon and Lucullus.* Translated by Bernadotte Perrin. Cambridge, MA: Harvard University Press, 1914.

LCL 58 Marcus Aurelius. *Marcus Aurelius.* Edited and translated by C. R. Haines. Cambridge, MA: Harvard University Press, 1916.

LCL 75 Seneca. *Epistles, Volume I: Epistles 1–65.* Translated by Richard M. Gummere. Cambridge, MA: Harvard University Press, 1917.

LCL 76 Seneca. *Epistles, Volume II: Epistles 66–92.* Translated by Richard M. Gummere. Cambridge, MA: Harvard University Press, 1920.

LCL 77 Seneca. *Epistles, Volume III: Epistles 93–124.* Translated by Richard M. Gummere. Cambridge, MA: Harvard University Press, 1925.

LCL 87 Plutarch. *Lives, Volume V: Agesilaus and Pompey. Pelopidas and Marcellus.* Translated by Bernadotte Perrin. Cambridge, MA: Harvard University Press, 1917.

LCL 125 Quintilian. *Institutio Oratoria, Volume 2: Books 4–6*, Edited and translated by H. E. Butler. Cambridge, MA: Harvard University Press, 1921.

LCL 129 Callimachus, Lycophron, Aratus. Hymns and Epigrams. Lycophron: Alexandra. *Aratus: Phaenomena.* Translated by A. W. Mair, G. R. Mair. Cambridge, MA: Harvard University Press, 1921.

LCL 131 Epictetus. *Discourses, Books 1–2.* Translated by W. A. Oldfather. Cambridge, MA: Harvard University Press, 1925.

LCL 141 Cicero. *Tusculan Disputations.* Translated by J. E. King. Cambridge, MA: Harvard University Press, 1927.

LCL 170 Homer. *Iliad, Volume I: Books 1–12.* Translated by A. T. Murray. Revised by William F. Wyatt. Cambridge, MA: Harvard University Press, 1924.

LCL 181 Lucretius. *On the Nature of Things.* Translated by W. H. D. Rouse. Revised by Martin F. Smith. Cambridge, MA: Harvard University Press, 1924.

LCL 184 Diogenes Laertius. *Lives of Eminent Philosophers, Volume I: Books 1–5.* Translated by R. D. Hicks. Cambridge, MA: Harvard University Press, 1925.

LCL 185 Diogenes Laertius. *Lives of Eminent Philosophers, Volume II: Books 6–10.* Translated by R. D. Hicks. Cambridge, MA: Harvard University Press, 1925.

LCL 192 Plato. *Laws, Volume II: Books 7–12.* Translated by R. G. Bury. Cambridge, MA: Harvard University Press, 1926.

LCL 211 Strabo. *Geography, Volume V: Books 10–12.* Translated by Horace Leonard Jones. Cambridge, MA: Harvard University Press, 1928.

LCL 214 Seneca. Moral Essays, *Volume I: De Providentia. De Constantia. De Ira. De Clementia.* Translated by John W. Basore. Cambridge, MA: Harvard University Press, 1928.

LCL 218 Epictetus. *Discourses, Books 3–4. Fragments. The Encheiridion.* Translated by W. A. Oldfather. Cambridge, MA: Harvard University Press, 1928.

LCL 224 Athenaeus. *The Learned Banqueters, Volume III: Books 6–7.* Edited and translated by S. Douglas Olson. Cambridge, MA: Harvard University Press, 2008.

LCL 234 Plato. *Timaeus. Critias. Cleitophon. Menexenus. Epistles.* Translated by R. G. Bury. Cambridge, MA: Harvard University Press, 1929.

LCL 226 Philo. *On the Creation. Allegorical Interpretation of Genesis 2 and 3.* Translated by F. H. Colson, G. H. Whitaker. Cambridge, MA: Harvard University Press, 1929.

LCL 227 Philo. *On the Cherubim. The Sacrifices of Abel and Cain. The Worse Attacks the Better. On the Posterity and Exile of Cain. On the Giants.* Translated by F. H. Colson, G. H. Whitaker. Cambridge, MA: Harvard University Press, 1929.

LCL 247 Philo. *On the Unchangeableness of God. On Husbandry. Concerning Noah's Work as a Planter. On Drunkenness. On Sobriety.* Translated by F. H. Colson, G. H. Whitaker. Cambridge, MA: Harvard University Press, 1930.

LCL 266 Philo. *On the Creation. Allegorical Interpretation of Genesis 2 and 3.* Translated by F. H. Colson, G. H. Whitaker. Cambridge, MA: Harvard University Press, 1929.

LCL 268 Cicero. *On the Nature of the Gods. Academics.* Translated by H. Rackham. Cambridge, MA: Harvard University Press, 1933.

LCL 291 Sextus Empiricus. *Against Logicians.* Translated by R. G. Bury. Cambridge, MA: Harvard University Press, 1935.

LCL 310 Seneca. Moral Essays, *Volume III: De Beneficiis.* Translated by John W. Basore. Cambridge, MA: Harvard University Press, 1935.

LCL 320 Philo. *On the Decalogue. On the Special Laws, Books 1–3.* Translated by F. H. Colson. Cambridge, MA: Harvard University Press, 1937.

LCL 322 Tacitus. *Annals: Books 13–16.* Translated by John Jackson. Cambridge, MA: Harvard University Press, 1937.

LCL 337 Plutarch. *Moralia, Volume VI: Can Virtue Be Taught? On Moral Virtue. On the Control of Anger. On Tranquility of Mind. On Brotherly Love. On Affection for Offspring. Whether Vice Be Sufficient to Cause Unhappiness. Whether the Affections of the Soul are Worse Than Those of the Body. Concerning Talkativeness. On Being a Busybody.* Translated by W. C. Helmbold. Cambridge, MA: Harvard University Press, 1939.

LCL 352 Pliny. *Natural History, Volume II: Books 3–7.* Translated by H. Rackham. Cambridge, MA: Harvard University Press, 1942.

LCL 358 Dio Chrysostom. *Discourses 31–36.* Translated by J. W. Cohoon, H. Lamar Crosby. Cambridge, MA: Harvard University Press, 1940.

LCL 363 Philo. *Every Good Man Is Free. On the Contemplative Life. On the Eternity of the World. Against Flaccus. Apology for the Jews. On Providence.* Translated by F. H. Colson. Cambridge, MA: Harvard University Press, 1941.

LCL 376 Dio Chrysostom. *Discourses 37–60.* Translated by H. Lamar Crosby. Cambridge, MA: Harvard University Press, 1946.

LCL 450 Seneca. *Natural Questions, Volume I: Books 1–3.* Translated by Thomas H. Corcoran. Cambridge, MA: Harvard University Press, 1971.

LCL 470 Plutarch. *Moralia, Volume XIII: Part 2: Stoic Essays.* Translated by Harold Cherniss. Cambridge, MA: Harvard University Press, 1976.

INDEX OF AUTHORS

Other Ancient Authors

SUBJECT INDEX

holy/holiness 5, 6, 85, 86, 90, 94, 114–15, 133, 137–8
Holy Spirit 52, 137, 176
hope 2, 9, 11–12, 20, 39, 43–55, 63, 86, 87, 90, 91, 96, 99–104, 116, 123, 124, 136–7, 149–51, 158, 166, 171
household 16, 17, 38, 46, 65, 85, 105, 125, 130–2, 145–6, 148–53, 156, 162, 165, 167, 171, 177
Household Code/s 11, 16, 131, 132, 146–9, 169
hymn, hymns 9, 38, 40–2, 47–8, 54, 72–7, 79, 81, 87, 89, 129, 130, 133, 140, 142, 144, 151, 170

kithara 124–5
Klaros 81–2

Laodicea 9, 11–13, 16–17, 37, 38, 46, 96–7, 117, 150, 153, 155–6, 160, 161–5, 167
Laudato si' 2, 80, 174
Logos 6, 21, 24, 26, 30, 38–48, 52–3, 57, 60, 69–72, 74, 87, 96, 103, 104, 124, 128, 133–4, 139, 142–4, 146, 150, 154, 157, 164, 167, 170, 174, 176–7
Lycus Valley 8–9, 11, 17, 53, 63, 65, 95, 109, 111, 112, 114, 116, 122, 140, 149, 153–4, 160–2, 165, 167, 171
lyre 92, 125

Most High God 37–8, 42, 56, 61, 82, 106
mystery/mysteries 6, 11, 22, 31–2, 38, 48–50, 80–1, 95–101, 103–5, 111–12, 116, 120, 124, 154, 157–8, 167, 171

Nympha 4, 11, 15–17, 37–8, 56, 65, 81–2, 92, 105–6, 124–5, 149–50, 155, 156, 162, 165, 166–7, 171, 177–8

panentheism 40, 70, 77, 118, 171–3
pantheism 40, 77
Platonism/Platonic xii, 3, 5, 19, 25, 32, 47, 54, 85, 88, 89, 109, 132, 133, 173
plerophory/plerophoric 7, 60–2, 71, 76, 90, 171

porneia 137–8
providence/providential 24, 27, 29, 35, 36, 39, 40, 42, 47, 73–4, 91–2, 130, 144

reconciliation/reconcile 1, 34, 54, 71, 72, 75–6, 79–80, 82, 84–90, 101–3, 116–17, 121–2, 135, 139, 142, 144, 170, 177
rhinoceros 2, 177

salvation 43, 49, 53, 63, 72, 77, 86–8, 91, 98, 100, 102, 113, 140, 143, 158
self-limit/self-limitation 6, 64, 92, 105, 138
sheep/ewes/lambs 17, 56, 106, 167
slave(s), slavery/slavish 8, 16, 19, 34, 38, 39, 45–6, 60, 63, 81, 102, 117, 131–5, 140–1, 144, 146–9, 153–5, 160–1, 167, 173
Stoic concepts
  body/embodiment/corporeal 25, 27, 34, 41, 58, 69, 70, 124, 131, 136, 172
  cognition 83–4, 86–7, 171
  concord/*homonoia* 25, 151–4, 158, 160, 162, 164, 170–1
  consistency/*homologia* 21, 30, 32, 44, 58, 59, 64, 128–9, 140
  cosmic sympathy 83–5, 88–92, 154, 171, 176
  elements/*stoicheia* 70, 75, 109, 110–14
  exist/subsist, existence 25, 29, 67–70, 74, 78, 87–8, 121–4, 138, 142, 169, 171, 173–4
  happiness/*eudaimonia* 27, 28, 32, 39–40, 42, 44, 47, 52, 143, 149, 171
  indifferents/*adiaphora* 27, 39, 46, 47, 93–5, 101, 108, 153, 160, 171
  restoring kinship/*oikeiōsis*/affiliation 31, 85, 89, 130, 131, 132, 144, 147, 148, 171, 176
  'something'/*ti* 67–9
  spirits/*daimonia* 39
suffering/suffer 6, 11, 12, 14, 27, 30, 34–6, 38–9, 43, 44, 47, 59, 85, 93–8, 101, 105, 116–17, 120, 157, 166, 167, 170–1, 175